Estevan Valdez

Matanzas

Cuba.

FLASHES OF LIGHT

FROM

THE SPIRIT-LAND,

THROUGH THE MEDIUMSHIP

OF

MRS. J. H. CONANT.

COMPILED BY

ALLEN PUTNAM,

AUTHOR OF "SPIRIT WORKS;" "NATTY, A SPIRIT;" "MESMERISM, SPIRITUALISM, WITCHCRAFT, AND MIRACLE;" ETC., ETC.

BOSTON:
WILLIAM WHITE AND COMPANY,
"BANNER OF LIGHT" OFFICE,
158 WASHINGTON STREET.
1872.

Electrotyped at the Boston Stereotype Foundry,
No. 19 Spring Lane.

PREFACE.

MANY a reader of the following work may welcome a brief account of its source and history. The origin, object and influence of the

BANNER OF LIGHT

were set forth at a public séance, September 4, 1871, by Spirit THEODORE PARKER, in the following

ADDRESS.

I have been requested to make a statement concerning the result of our labors as ministering spirits through the Banner of Light. In preface I would say, that we are entering upon the fifteenth year of our ministerial labor through that journal; but it is nearly nineteen years since a band of far-seeing, energetic spirits resolved that they would be heard on earth through the press; and as all the journals then extant were conservative, creed-bound, and, what is worse, money-bound, it became necessary for these spirits, if their theory or project was to be put in operation, to start a journal of their own.

This being determined upon in convention, agents were sent out to see who among the children of earth could be selected and adapted to the work. After months of searching they were found; but they were in the rough. It then became necessary to employ artists to chisel them, and hammer and polish them. This was done by sickness, by losses, by sorrow, by various trials which were imposed upon those persons, until, at last these artists announced to the assembly that the subjects were ready to be vitalized. They were then separately visited by a committee selected for the purpose, and were baptized with a holy ghost of aspiration, of spiritual desire, and were made ready to stand in front of the opposition incident to the introduction of a truth to the world.

It was well known by this band of spirits what dangers their mortal coadjutors would be obliged to meet if led in the path marked out; well known that they would be assailed by pulpit and press, and that shots would be fired at them from every avenue in life; but they also knew that they should be able to sustain them; for they understood of what elements they were composed, and knew that when once these mortal coadjutors put their hands to the spiritual plough, they would not turn back, for they were so largely inspired with faith in those who were leading them that they could not. And to-day the result of our labors is this: Our spiritual statistics show that we have brought seventy-two thousand seven hundred and forty-six into the spiritual fold here in this earth-life. We have enumerated only those who are sound, honest Spiritualists, leaving out all the nondescripts. And the number which has been added to the ranks of freedom — been liberated from the darkness of creeds, and from the various conditions of darkness that the spirit often carries with it from this world to the higher life — that number has been quadrupled, leaving out all those who are not firm and sound in the way of spiritual right.

This much, then, by the grace of Almighty God, we have been enabled to do; and to-day our glorious Banner floats in every clime: it has been read by every race of human beings; we have found it in the Esquimaux hut, and upon the throne; it has gone forth with the God-speed of the angel world, and to-day it is stronger than it ever was before. It proposes to gather under its folds a larger multitude than are already there; and although this band of spirits may not be able to reward their mortal coadjutors as they might wish, their reward in the hereafter is sure, and they have nothing to fear, for they are so firmly grounded in truth and justice that the gates of hell cannot prevail against them.

PENALTIES OF MEDIUMSHIP.

Do kind spirits ever subject certain selected, sensitive mortals to prolonged, harsh and agonizing experiences, for the special purpose of making them obedient subordinates and facile instruments in beneficent philanthropic labors? The foregoing address implies that they do. Read the autobiography of the prophet Ezekiel, noting carefully the discipline to which he was subjected by "the spirit that entered into him," and so "took him away" that "he went in bitterness," and one will notice that humiliating and agonizing trials are *not new* instrumentalities for developing and supplizing mediumistic susceptibilities and subduing the powers of human self-determination. The world's most venerated seers and prophets, almost without exception, were men of sorrows, acquainted with grief, hardships and privations.

The common judgment of men often assumes that pure, kind and wise spirits can use no persons as mediums who are devoid of eminent moral worth. But no exceptional moral merit or demerit is apparent to the external observer of modern mediums, or to the reader of history, as belonging to those who have been, in every age, chiselled, polished and baptized to make them satisfactory instruments and coadjutors of spirits for disclosing marvels and truths to mortals. To show that the common assumption is unwarranted, and that mediumship is mainly the offspring of *physical peculiarities*, we quote part of a definition of mediumship by Parker, December 16, 1867. See page 106.

"A medium is simply a body that is sensitive to the od forces in the universe — forces which you do not thoroughly understand; those that have not come within the sphere of human science; those with which human science has not yet dealt. A medium possesses a peculiar quality of magnetism and electricity."

A New Testament writer (Heb. xi.) defined *Faith* as "the evidence of things not seen," and used the word Faith to express precisely such trust in higher powers as our facile mediums often manifest, and, many centuries after the fall of Jericho, catalogued the *harlot* Rahab with Abel, Enoch, Noah, Abraham, Isaac, Jacob and Joseph, as worthy of remembrance for what they achieved by *Faith* — by "the evidence" they had "of things not seen." The principles on which mediums are selected are the same now as in the days of Joshua; they involve chiefly *physical* fitness.

The Visible Banner-Bearers.

Selected, induced and aided by spirits, certain mortals, in 1857, unfurled the Banner of Light, started on a march, crept along the verge of bankruptcy for years, once toppled over the brink, and threw off a load of thirty thousand dollars' indebtedness, and yet have never failed on any subsequent week to give the Banner an airing. Loaded with the very heavy extraordinary expenses of the *Message Department*, the paper to-day, apart from the book publishing business of the proprietors, is not self-sustaining, and through every former year failed to reimburse its cost. Unflagging toil and financial anxieties have been constant experiences with these Banner-Bearers. Faith in the wisdom, power and justice of their invisible co-laborers has given them hope, strength and perseverance. Whether one credits the account above given of the establishment and supervision of the Banner or not, that paper has long outlived every kindred companion of its infancy, and is now in vigorous and efficient manhood.

The extreme sensitiveness and physical frailties of the chief medium have required daily visits by a paid physician, quiet, neat and airy apartments, and an invalid's many delicacies; the cost of these, supplemented by the general needs of herself and her dependent husband, calls for more than three thousand dollars per annum; and when we add to that sum the rent and care of the Circle Room, and fair compensation to a reporter magnetically, sympathetically, and in all other respects, fitted for the place and its duties, it will be obvious that the cost of the message department is very onerous.

The original band of visible workers, all consciously susceptible to spirit promptings, were William Berry, William White, Luther Colby and Mrs. Conant, the latter being the trusted channel of oracles. Isaac B. Rich and Charles H. Crowell, brother of Mrs. Conant, subsequently joined the Banner firm. Berry and Crowell have joined the pioneers in spirit-land, and are there helping to open pathways for and increase the efficiency of their associates and successors.

Luther Colby, now and from its commencement chief editor of the Banner, has long been making his mark and recording his own biography in its columns. Fretting resolutely, now and then, under the harrowings of conflicting influences from both around and above him; suffering sorely, and almost frenzied by the tearings of the harrows, he yet perseveringly manifests his faith in and obedience to spirit instructions and impressions, blended with no small amount of personal independence and self-reliance in the management of his paper, and in his judgments as to the wisest and most efficient methods for advancing the cause of Spiritualism. In these labors he has long been efficiently aided by his calm and worthy assistant editor, L. B. Wilson. A future day will be early enough for an extended account of Colby's inspirations, labors and sufferings.

The public may expect an extended and authentic biography of Mrs. Conant some time in the present year; therefore our notice of her may be very brief. She has been a medium from infancy. "Angels spoke through" her "lips," as they did through Swedenborg's, in early childhood, and have continued the use of them with uncommon persistency and method. It is said by those who know her well that she possesses no intellectual or literary abilities above or aside from the common average of females; that her education is quite limited, and that in her normal state she is manifestly incompetent to such utterances as her organs put forth when used by spirits. This is much more than credible; for, during several sessions of service in the legislature, beginning almost forty years ago and ending in 1852, covering a period when Massachusetts halls were daily familiar with the speeches of very eloquent and cultured men, we can recall but one or two of them who would not in extemporaneous debate frequently forget the grammar lessons of their youth, and utter sentences which would shame them if seen in print. But in this work are more than two hundred pages of impromptu answers, through Mrs. Conant, verbatim as they fell from her lips. And as such they are a prolonged miracle of correct grammar, of perspicuity and relevancy.

Occasionally very good versification, bordering at times upon good poetry, flows forth from her lips; yet in her normal state nothing of the kind ever came from her tongue or pen.

Throughout many years she has endured much physical debility and suffering, enhanced by solicitude for and support of a husband in whom the light of reason is unsteady and waning, who must pass his years in seclusion from general society, away from his home. Rarely can any mortal say more truthfully than she, "My burden is greater than I can bear." Seemingly her spirit is held to the body mostly by the sympathy and aid of other spirits on the two sides of the separating veil. Thus frail, burdened and saddened is the instrument for clear, strong, forcible, and correct enunciations. Who wields the instrument? Frail Mrs. Conant alone? Let common sense make answer.

Origin of Questions and Answers.

The compiler, finding no department headed Questions and Answers in the earlier volumes of the Banner, and it being from under that heading alone that he was permitted to select, privately asked the editor when and why that department was introduced; when and why the controlling spirits arranged to make themselves simply responders to inquiries put by inquisitive man.

At the public séance, April 1, 1872, Spirit Parker said, I

may as well answer at this place as anywhere else a request that has been made. It is this: —

Give us the *origin* of the questions and answers making up a portion of the message department of the Banner of Light.

The inauguration of this special department originated with a public need — with a demand made upon the spirits controlling at this place by audiences here convened. This demand at last became so urgent that it could no longer be resisted by the spirit-world; and so, in answer to this prayer or demand, this special department was inaugurated, and it was determined that whatever spirit presided on any occasion should be the spirit who would receive and answer the questions propounded, and that that spirit, and that one alone, should be accountable for the answers. If it was a Theodore Parker and he told a lie, he should be accountable for it. If it was a Swedenborg and he told a lie, he should be accountable for it. If it was a Jesus Christ and he told a lie, he should be accountable for it. If it was a prostitute from North Street and she told a lie, she should be accountable for it.

The spirit-world was in ignorance for a long time as to the best methods of imparting what they knew to those who were in need of such knowledge here. For years information from the spirit-world came at random shots; but, thanks be to the overruling Providence, these shots did their work. By and by bands were organized all throughout the various spirit-realms — some for one purpose and some another — to disseminate truth upon the earth, to sweep away those old conditions of darkness that had so long dragged the soul down, and made it drink the bitter waters of error.

The band organized to control at this place consisted of a President, Vice-President, Secretary, Chairman, and General Committee. Under their supervision have come all things that were given at this place. And so far as they were able, these presiding spirits were to learn concerning the truthfulness or falsity of each returning spirit. They did so, and having satisfied themselves of the truthfulness of each one desiring to return, it then became their duty to assist them over this rainbow bridge of life that they might meet their loved ones here, whose hearts were unconsciously aching for the same truth which they could bring them.

THE SÉANCES.

Tri-weekly for many years a band of spirits have given impromptu answers to the world's promiscuous questions, through Mrs. J. H. Conant, at the Banner of Light Circle Room, 158 Washington Street, Boston, Mass. The doors of that room, the walls of which are adorned with likenesses of many spirits and prominent Spiritualists, and with spirit-drawings, are gratuitously opened to all comers. Not less than a hundred to a hundred and twenty-five persons are usually present at a séance.

Promptly at the designated hour for meeting Mrs. Conant takes her seat upon a platform raised about two feet above the floor. The doors are then locked; the medium soon passes under control, and the controlling spirit enunciates impressively and fervently a brief invocation to the supreme Intelligence. That ended, he or she calls for any questions the chairman may have. A question, if any have been sent or handed in, is read in the hearing of the whole assembly, and is forthwith replied to, — sometimes in a brief monosyllable, but generally by a discussion more or less extended. This course is followed till all the questions in the chairman's keeping have been answered. That point reached, permission is given to any person in the audience to make verbal inquiries relating either to what has been said or to any other subject, and questions thus propounded are promptly responded to. The dialogue over, the controlling spirit yields possession of the medium to some other invisible. Usually at each séance three, four or more spirits successively are allowed to enunciate their wishes or sentiments at this public resort, whence the words will be sent on their way to those for whom they are specially intended.

Enveloped letters addressed to particular spirits may be laid upon the medium's table by any persons as they enter the room. From fifteen to thirty visitors usually avail themselves of this privilege, and after the speaking is over, the medium, in the presence of the whole company, fingers these letters one after another, and rapidly writes a few words upon the unopened envelope of most of them. That work finished, the medium's hand is used to write the name of the spirit who has conducted that séance, and of the one who answered the letters. This slip the chairman (who is usually Mr. William White, one of the publishers of the Banner) reads to the whole assembly, and then announces that the exercises of the occasion are ended. While the assembly is passing out from the room, the letters, which are private property, are reclaimed and taken away by those severally who placed them upon the table. Such is a brief account of the circumstances amid which the questions and answers have their birth.

The Compiler's Work.

The compiler's connection with the Banner is solely that of temporary employee. When invited to assume his task he was informed that Theodore Parker desired that a compilation from the Banner questions and answers should be published in book form, and favored the employment of himself as the compiler.

Shortly after that he called upon Mrs. Conant at her lodgings, and had, through her, an interview with Parker. The main inquiry put to that spirit was whether the selections should be so arranged as to present in consecutive paragraphs the scattered and sometimes discrepant statements relative to particular topics, — such as atonement, forgiveness, immortality, &c., — or whether chronological order, as in the Banner, should be preserved.

The reply called for retention of the chronological sequence, — for selections from none but utterances subsequent to the commencement of verbatim reports (summer of 1867), and for preservation of the exact language of each communicator. The purport of the information then gained was, that the spirit controllers of the Banner circles desired that the compilation should be a fair and ample compendium of their teachings upon every subject of general interest which they had discussed at the séances within a given time.

The act of compilation, therefore, was not to impose any responsibility for the truth, wisdom or moral influences of the contents of the work; discretionary power was limited to judgment as to what parts contained more and what less that would be novel, interesting or instructive to the reading world, and to the exclusion of the less important.

Personal approval or disapproval of the doctrines or sentiments communicated must be allowed no influence upon the compiling judgment; and wherever diversity of opinion should be found among the spirit teachers, it would be duty to let the diversity reappear in the epitome. Even the most absolute incredibility and seeming absurdity of statements must favor their reappearance rather than their suppression. The reader's astronomical and geographical knowledge and science may stand aghast when he comes to what spirits say they *know* about the size of our globe, and its yet undiscovered continents and peoples; but the compiler is not privileged to suppress any distinct utterances because they surpass the comprehension of us moles. He must comply with the instructions and restrictions of his engagement.

The files of the Banner from the autumn of 1867 down to January 1, 1872, contained "Questions and Answers" enough to constitute a volume of twelve hundred pages, while the book must be limited to about four hundred. The compiler's work required neither skill nor taste in literary composition and arrangement, but very much reading and re-reading, and great care to select in such ways that each controlling speaker, each topic of general interest, and each significant difference of statement or opinion, might appear in the Compendium, and that without any abridgment or change of language. But repeated and re-repeated clippings failed to bring the mass down to the desired compression, and a portion of the approved matter is held in reserve for constituting a part of another volume, to be issued in some future year.

Persons of all grades of intellect and culture, of various creeds, and from different motives, gather in the Circle Room, and promiscuously propound questions varying from the most profound to the most frivolous, from the most liberal to the most bigoted, from the most philanthropic to the most selfish, from the most spiritual to the most temporal, all of which are kindly answered — are reported and printed in chronological order. Also, essentially the same questions occur over and over again, and there is no concordant conception of the meaning, or systematic application of the words *soul*, *spirit*, *mind*, *intellect*, &c., on the part of either the questioners or of those who give the responses. All these things conspire to make the repetition and re-repetition of many replies that are *almost* identical, necessary to a fair presentation of all that has been taught. The work is a medley — necessarily so; and it is a truncated medley, cut squarely to date at each end. A satisfactory condensation was attempted, but has not been accomplished. The compiler's success falls far below his aim.

The Compiler's Reflections.

Many scores of bright intelligences, who carried with them some one and some another of the various and conflicting creeds of earth as talisman or panoply when they passed through the portals of death, are coming back, clad with the authority of personal observation and experience in spirit life, and unitedly teaching that all faiths in special creeds are now hinderances instead of helps to their happiness and progress, and that man's only useful and his all-sufficient religion is simply the keeping himself unspotted from the world, and doing justly by others, in the most plain and common sense way possible. They are teaching that all punishments and all rewards are natural results from universal and ever-acting forces. Protestants of various sects, Roman Catholics, Jews, Turks, Arabs, Chinamen, Indians, and many others, dwelling in the life beyond, transiently reincarnate themselves, and, from amid the light of their experiences, respond to man's inquiries. And they all teach, substantially, that each man can read his own future destiny, his retribution beyond the grave, in the single fact, dissevered from all qualifying or smothering interpretations, that "whatsoever a man soweth, that shall he also reap." They teach that the reign of law is co-extensive with eternity and infinity. Such is the gospel revealed by these Flashes of Light from the Spirit Land, — an inspired gospel of plain, liberal common sense, come to grapple for victory or death with the mystical and cramping dogmas of Christendom, not with the essence, but with the perversions of Christianity.

When and where in the world's past history did man receive so methodical, prolonged and copious an efflux of illumination from beyond the veil, as this which is still streaming forth at the Banner circles? At what other spot have so many different disrobed intelligences promulgated here, knowledge gained by personal experiences, and unfoldments in the hereafter? What other set of human vocal organs than Mrs. Conant's ever felt the touch, responded to the call, and subserved the will of near ten thousand different spirits in their distinct utterance of messages back to man? Where else have the names and former residences of so many travellers backward bound, ever been registered as at the Banner Circle Room?

This age does not see, need not see, probably *cannot* see the power and beneficence of the Banner band of spirits. The Banner is now a prophet in its own age and country. Both the legitimate action and the enchantments of distance and time are essential to just admeasurements of the importance and influence of truths. Future generations may trace the origin of momentous reformations in the creeds, ceremonials, habits, customs, moralities and governments of mankind to the doctrines, advice and aid which ascended spirits are now furnishing. The time will come — and it is not in the very far future — when the world will have learned that the inspirations and "mighty works" now transpiring in our midst are as divine, as miraculous, as immediately the productions of the infinite Power, as those of any former age. Modern Spiritualism will make and mark a brilliant epoch in human history, and the Banner of Light will be one of the most extended and authentic records of its early evolvements.

Has the compiler been standing on holy ground, and culling flashes of light from a "burning bush"? Be that as it may, while his pen was recording the above meditations and prophetic gleams, a solemn sense of the possibility that many in the distant future may regard these cullings as oracles from above, use them as lights to illumine the darkness of earth, and disclose the paths of virtues whose fruits will be heavenly peace, — a solemn sense of such a possibility seemed to give him, through these pages, a possible connection with generations to come, and caused him to invoke from the Father of Light such illumination of the minds of his present and future children on the earth that they may at once discern and eschew whatever may be false or baneful, and discover and appropriate whatever may be true and healthful in these Flashes.

ALLEN PUTNAM.

April 13, 1872.

NAMES OF THE SPEAKERS.

THE Banner circles are under the charge of Theodore Parker, who is the most frequent speaker, yet often is relieved by some substitute. During the period within which the contents of the present volume were spoken, he was aided by the twenty-five spirits whose names, when in the earth life, were these, viz.: —

Ballou, Rev. Hosea,
Beri, Rabbi Joshual,
Channing, Rev. W. E.,
Cheverus, Cardinal,
Davy, Sir Humphrey,
Dayton, Prof. Edgar C.,
Dow, Rev. Lorenzo,
Fairchild, Rev. Joy H.,
Fenwick, Bishop,
Fitzjames, Father Henry,
Fitzpatrick, Bishop,
Fuller, Rev. Arthur,
Ka-da Ab-dal,
Hare, Prof. Robert,
Howard, Lewis,
Hubbard, Prof. John,
King, Rev. T. Starr,
Kneeland, Abner,
Lowenthal, Rabbi Joseph,
Murray, Rev. John,
Parker, Rev. Theodore,
Paine, Thomas,
Pierpont, Rev. John,
Redman, Geo. A., medium,
Stowe, Rev. Phineas,
Ware, Rev. Henry.

APPENDIX TO PREFACE.

Request was made that a few Invocations in verse, uttered at the public circles, and some poetical effusions, through the same organism, at other places, should be included in this volume. They could have no fitting place among Questions and Answers, and are made an Appendix here.

INVOCATION.

Holy angels, guide these mortals
  O'er the mystic waves of time;
Open wide the shining portals
  Leading unto heights sublime;
Lift, O lift the veil that hides them
  From their loved ones, gone before!
Show them but their shining faces,
  Waiting on the other shore.

CHRISTMAS INVOCATION.

O Thou, whose mysterious presence
  Fills the earth, the air and sea,
We would chant undying praises,
  We would worship only thee.

From the earth's unnumbered altars
  Human sighs and tears are born,
Praying for a glad hereafter —
  Weary watchers in the storm.

Let them hear the chime of voices —
  Voices from the spirit-land —
Waking all the slumbering echoes,
  Strengthening heart and strengthening hand.

Let them see the star of promise
  That shall lead to brighter days,
Over all the plains of error,
  Where the babe of Bethlehem lays.

Let them sing that holy anthem,
  Sung by angels long ago, —
"Peace on earth, good will from Heaven,"
  Golden side of human woe.

Then the night shall grow to morning,
  Then the angels join the song,
For the day of peace is dawning;
  Lo! the Son of Truth is born!

INVOCATION.

O THOU source of endless wisdom,
Lord of earth and land Elysian,
We would bathe our weary spirits
In the fullness of thy love.

We would drink the healing waters
Flowing from unnumbered altars, —
Altars where no blood-stained offerings
Fill the earth with woe.

We would rise redeemed, redeeming,
Losing all our earthly seeming,
In the holy words, forgiveness
Of all earthly sin.

We would dwell with saints and sages,
Whose great thoughts have thrilled past ages,
Calling all men to adore thee,
Lord of heaven and earth.

Hear our prayer, ye guardian angels;
Be to us as bright evangels,
Bearing our poor sin-stained message
To the throne of love.

INVOCATION.

O God of all nations! O light of our souls!
Whose loving hand guides us, whose wisdom controls,
Through the weakness, and darkness, and sorrows of time,
O lead these thy children to soul-heights sublime.
Let us teach them to love thee and serve thee aright,
Never fearing the darkness, yet loving the light;
Never doubting thy presence, ever trusting thy grace,
To give to each soul its true portion and place.

And unto thee, O God of our life, be the homage and honor of nations and individuals, forever. Amen.

INVOCATION.

O Thou, whose love prevaileth
  Over all the ills of life,
Whose mercy never faileth
  When we are weary of the strife
That comes of human weakness, —
  By some called human sin, —
Whose wisdom opens heaven's gates,
  That all may enter in;
We would sing thee glad hosannas,
  We would join the earth and air
In their everlasting chorus,
  And their one eternal prayer.
For all that life can give us,
  For all that hath been given,
For every tear of sorrow,
  And every hope of heaven,
We thank thee, O, our God.

INVOCATION.

O Spirit of mercy, of justice, and love,
O'ershadow thy children with peace from above;
Let the phantoms of fear, of doubt and despair,
Be lost in the radiance of spiritual air;

Let the songs of the angels be heard in the skies,
Proclaiming the truth that the soul never dies;
That all things are carefully guarded by thee,
But the soul in its beauty at death is set free.

CHRISTMAS INVOCATION.

O God, our God!
Faint and weary are thy children,
Toiling up the steep of time,
Seeking for the Eastern token,
Listening for the morning chime;
Waiting, waiting, ever waiting
For the voice of long ago,
With its soft, melodious accents,
Soothing every human woe.
Know they not the star has risen,
And its glory gilds the earth?
Hear they not the song of angels
O'er this glorious second birth?
"Peace on earth! good will from Heaven!"
Sing that white-robed angel band;
"Peace on earth! good will from Heaven!"
Echoes over all the land.
O thou God of past and present!
O thou light of every soul!
We will chant thee deathless praises
While eternity shall roll.

The following poem, portraying a singular Indian custom, was given through Mrs. J. H. Conant, in the Melodeon, in this city, Sunday evening, March 11, 1866.

The poem was composed in spirit-life, and delivered by Metoka, mother of Winona, the subject of the poem, and wife of the sachem Wänandago, whose hunting-grounds, over two hundred years ago, included the territory on which the city of Boston is built, and his wigwam was at the brow of the hill where the State House now stands.

The chairman read a brief legend, furnished by an Indian spirit, which explains the custom that often doomed the fairest daughters of the red man to a cruel fate, as follows: —

"The white man has customs; so has the Indian. What the Indian thinks right, the white man thinks wrong. What the white man thinks right, the Indian thinks wrong. Many moons ago, where the white man now hunts his game, the Indian hunted his. Your big books will tell you that. When any two or more tribes were at war, the weaker, after two suns' fasting, would come together in council, led by a sachem, to see what the Great Spirit would tell them to do with their young squaws (for it was the custom of the conquering tribe to make slaves of all the young squaws, killing the old, who should fall into their hands). At the rising of the sun, after the council had been held all night, it was the custom to call the fairest squaw of the tribe and give her the right to choose between *death* at the hands of her nearest kin, or the *risk of being captured and enslaved by the conquering tribe.* Her decision was believed to be the voice of the Great Spirit, from which there was no appeal.

"Winona, the subject of the simple poem which follows this introductory, was the first-born of the house of Wänandago, who was at the time sachem * of the tribe. The hunting-grounds of this tribe were *here*, where your many wigwams now stand; and the wigwam of the sachem was at the brow of the hill where your great wigwam of council now stands. When the white man came from over the water, he hunted the Indian's game, and gave him no return. He planted his corn on the sacred mounds of the Indian, and shed no tears — *but he gave him his fire-water!* And so the Indian grew hot against the white man, and he determined to make war with him. It was then the Great Spirit spoke to Winona, and the arrow of Wänandago sent her to the land of sunshine and clear water, where Metoka, the fair squaw of Wänandago had gone at the coming of Winona."

* The word *sachem*, with the Indian, means *prophet*, or spiritual leader.

Then Metoka, in clear tones, poured forth, in sweet, musical cadences, the story of

THE INDIAN MAIDEN WINONA.

In the sunlight, in the starlight,
  In the moons of long ago —
Ere the virgin soil of Shawmut
  Quivered 'neath the white man's plow;

Ere the great lakes and the rivers
  Listened to the white man's song;
Ere the Father of all Waters
  Bore them in his strong arms on;

On from distant lands and wigwams,
  Where the sun from slumber comes,
Where the warriors hear the warwhoop
  In the voices of the drums,

Lived Winona — child of Nature!
  First-born, beauteous, dark-browed maid,
At whose coming fair Metoka,
  Where the flowers bloom, was laid.

Grew Winona, strong and beauteous,
  Fairer than the flowers of spring;
And the echo of her sweet voice
  Made the hills and valleys ring.

Did the red deer pass her wigwam,
  Soon it quivered on the plain —
For the arrow of Winona
  Never left its bow in vain!

Sixteen times the snow had fallen,
  Sixteen times the sun grew dim,
Since the warriors and the maidens
  Sung Metoka's funeral hymn.

Then the strange voice of the white man
  Rang through all our hunting-grounds;
And their swift feet never faltered
  When they neared our sacred mounds!

All our game their long guns hunted,
  Quickly making it their own;
Heeding not the maiden's sighing,
  Fearing not the warrior's frown!

Then the voice of Wänandago
  Fell in accents soft and low,
Asking, would the fair Winona
  To the land of sunlight go?

Quick the answer came, like shadows
  Filling all his soul with night—
"I will go, O mighty sachem,
  Where the sky is always bright;

"Where our hunting-grounds are greater;
  Where the water's always clear;
Where the spirits of our fathers
  Chant the red man's hymn of cheer!"

Soon the warriors and the maidens
  Sing again their funeral song!
For the spirit of Winona
  To the land of light was borne!

But to-night she comes to greet you,
  Comes in meekness, comes in love;
And with gentle hands would lead you
  To that land of light above;

Where no white man robs the Indian;
  Where no more the sun grows dim;
Where the warriors and the maidens
  Chant no more their funeral hymn;

In that land where stars are brighter,
  Where the moonbeams softly fall,
And the great Manito's blessing
  Like the sunlight's over all;

There the Indian holds his council,
  And his thoughts grow great and strong—
As the angels teach forgiveness
  For the white man's fearful wrong.

Here his tomahawk and arrows
Rest beneath your wigwams grand;
There his soul drinks in the wisdom
Of the glorious spirit-land.

Fare you well, ye pale-faced mortals,
Till in council you shall stand
Face to face with fair Winona
In the Indian's Morning-Land.

INDIAN SPIRITS' LEVEE.

A PLEASANT affair took place, a few evenings since, in Watertown, at the residence of Mr. Charles H. Crowell (Kanagawah Lodge — so named by Indian spirit-friends), at present the home of Mrs. J. H. Conant. Shortly after Mrs. Conant located there, her Indian spirit-friends, who have enjoyed the privilege for years of communicating to mortals through her organism, expressed a desire to give some of their "pale-faced" friends a reception at the lodge. Consent being given, the time assigned for the gathering was Friday, August 17, 1866; and a select company of between 50 and 60 ladies and gentlemen responded to the invitation. Shortly after the friends had assembled in the drawing-room, Mrs. Conant was entranced by

Winona, a young Indian girl (subject of the poem given by *Metoka*, through Mrs. Conant, at the Melodeon last March), who greeted each one of the party in her peculiar manner, and then quietly retired, to give

Starlight, another Indian girl, an opportunity to greet the "pale-faces" present. She was very modest and retiring in her manners, winning the hearts of all. She was known in earth-life as Naonta, and was educated at an English school in Canada. She is said to have been very beautiful. To this spirit was granted the privilege of welcoming the guests, which was gracefully done in the following characteristic Indian style: —

"Pale-faces, Naonta, in behalf of her people, welcomes you to the lodge of the Indians. Their hearts are warm towards you, and their hands are full of blessings. May yours be so towards them. They meet you from the mountains and the valleys, from the lakes and the rivers, and they ask to learn of you, and in turn will teach you much of the great hunting-ground, where you must come when you sleep as they have. When Naonta has gone, Metoka will come, greeting you with her *singing* talk."

All hearts seemed touched with the simplicity and beauty of this brief address, and evidently wished to hear more from her; but she gave way to the sprightly and loquacious

Springflower, who chatted in the liveliest manner with "the squaws and braves" for some time. Then bidding them "good moon," she retired, when the calm and dignified

Metoka, mother of Winona, assumed control, and gave utterance to the following

POEM.

Like the music of the waters,
 Like the sighing of the trees,
Like some soft and gentle whisper
 Floating on the evening breeze,

Come the dead, the long departed,
 To the island of the blest,
Breathing forth unnumbered blessings,
 Telling of a land of rest.

Not the rest that knows no action,
 Like the silence of the tomb,
But the rest that comes from toiling,
 Toiling for the yet to come.

Come they when your fires are lighted,
 Lighted on your wigwam walls,
And their dew of inspiration
 Over every spirit falls, —

Falls like moonlight on the waters,
  With a soft and silvery light,
Or like starlight through the shadows,
  Robbing of its gloom the night.

From the lakes and from the rivers,
  Over plains and mountains tall,
Many braves and many maidens
  Come in answer to your call.

Are they welcome to your wigwam?
  Will your kindly greeting fall,
Like your winter's spotless blanket,
  Over black, and red, and all?

When the Lodge of Kanagawah
  Breathes its blessings far and wide, —
Over mountains, over valleys,
  Over death's resistless tide, —

Then the great Manitou's blessing
  Enters at the open door,
And your dead, the long departed,
  Fold you in their arms once more.

August, 1866.

THE STAR OF HOPE.

[DEDICATED TO TELULAR,* THE STAR OF KANAGAWAH LODGE, BY MRS. HEMANS.]

BRIGHT star of hope! still let your beams
  Of radiant beauty, shine
Upon the enfranchised souls who dwell
  Beyond the stream of time.

* "Telular" is the name Mrs. Conant received from her Indian spirit-friends. With the Indian it means a something to see by or through. "Kanagawah Lodge" is the name the Indians have given Mrs. Conant's present home at Watertown. "Kanagawah" signifies *teacher;* and as Mrs. Conant has done much towards enlightening and elevating the Indians, it will be readily perceived that the name is not inappropriate.

O, give to them your hand of love
  Across the rolling flood,
And lead them back, through Nature's bowers,
  To wisdom and to God.

Fling back the shadows by your light,
  As Moses smote the rock,
Till every soul within your sphere
  Shall feel the mighty shock.

Enter within the cypress shade,
  And rob it of its gloom,
Gilding with radiance all divine
  The portals of the tomb.

Stand close beside the parting soul,
  Who fears to cross the tide,
Leading beyond all earthly pain,
  Where loving friends abide.

Strengthen the weak and wounded souls
  Who falter in the way,
And lead them back to wisdom's path
  By truth's unerring ray.

Be thou a guide, a beacon light,
  To wanderers on the shore;
And be contented with thy lot
  Forever — evermore.

So shall your heaven on earth begin
  By every deed of love,
While angels sing your song of praise
  In worlds of light above.

BANNER, August 18, 1866.

ANNA CORA WILSON.

"BIRDIE," the lovely spirit-daughter of Mr. and Mrs. L. B. Wilson, who has manifested several times on previous occasions, after obtaining control of the medium, took up a bouquet of delicate flowers that lay upon the table, and turning to her mother, who sat near by, placed her hand on her head, stooped down, and kissing her fervently, said, "Dear mother, I thank you for these beautiful flowers." She then proceeded to address her in the following touchingly significant lines: —

"BIRDIE'S" POEM.

I SLEEP not, dear mother, where daisies bloom,
And wild birds warble their hymns of praise;
Where the stars look down through the silent gloom,
And the cypress nods to the passing breeze.

No, no; I am living beyond the tomb,
Where the shadows of time no longer fall,
Where the angel Death has never come,
For eternal life is the gift to all.

Yet I have not left you; I am not dead,
Though a voice is missed from the trio band, —
Though tenantless stands my little bed,
And you miss the clasp of "Birdie's" hand.

I am living, and loving, and waiting for you
In my beautiful home on the other side,
Where legions of angels, with fond hearts and true,
Are waiting for loved ones to cross the tide.

Through the long, dreary hours of sadness and pain,
When your brow with the tempest of fever was tossed,
Your "Birdie" was with you; yes, with you again;
Though the world in its blindness says "Birdie" is lost.

The following lines were addressed to Mrs. L. B. Wilson (Cora's mother), in tones of endearing affection, accompanied with such tender caresses as to give living evidence that the spirit, after leaving its mortal form, retains all its love for those it left on earth: —

A POEM BY "BIRDIE" (ANNA CORA WILSON).

MOTHER, dear mother! from the land of the blest,
Where the earth-weary spirit finds comfort and rest,
I have come with my buds and blossoms so sweet,
And I lay them, as soul-gifts, at your tired feet.

Be joyous, dear mother, and banish the clouds,
And linger no longer 'mid cypress and shrouds;
But lift up your eyes to that fair land of rest,
Where Cora, your "Birdie," has builded your nest.

The four following effusions were from "Birdie," through Mrs. Conant: —

SONG OF THE AUTUMN WIND.

I COME, I come, my watch to keep
   On the cold New England shore —
To diamonds sow where the flowers grew,
   And the summer winds sing no more.

I wail and I weep where the daisies sleep,
   On the graves of your early dead;
And I sing a low song through the tall pine trees,
   O'er the soldier's nameless bed.

I chant a sad strain, or a wild refrain,
   Through every city and town;
And I chase the green leaves from all the trees,
   Or I change their greenness to brown.

I roar on the mountains, I bind all the fountains,
   And enter the poor man's home;
While the babe lies sleeping, and the mother sits
      weeping,
   I join in her cry of alone — all alone!

Then I speed away o'er the ocean's spray,
   Where the loved and lost are sleeping;
Where Neptune's band, with relentless hand,
   Their watch of death are keeping.

I kiss the pale cheek, in that lone retreat,
  While the sea-birds are loudly screaming;
Where life and death have together met,
  And the sleeper knows no dreaming.

I scatter the snows, as every one knows,
  Like a carpet of silver sheen,
And I bind all the streams with glittering chains,
  Where once the lilies have been.

Farewell! farewell! I go — I go
  From the cold New England shore;
For the Winter winds have begun to blow,
  And the Autumn leaves fall no more!

For, far away, over river and bay,
  In my home beyond the sea,
The mild-eyed seal and swift gazelle
  Are keeping their watch for me.

BIRDIE'S LAST OF EARTH.

HUSHED were the voices and muffled the tread
Of kind friends who lingered near "Birdie's" death-bed;
But they saw not the angels who entered unheard,
And dipped in heaven's chalice the wings of their bird.

And they whispered so soft that you heard not a sound —
"Come, Birdie, your wings shall no longer be bound!"
Then, quick as the eagle's eye drinks in the light,
Your Birdie was free from mortality's night.

And now from the heights of Eternity's plains,
From the land where Death comes not, and Night never reigns,
Your Birdie returns, on swift pinions of love,
With fresh-gathered buds from her bright home above.

When the world, in its coldness, says, "Birdie's dead,"
O tell them, dear mother, I've only been led,
By the hands of the angels, away from the night,
Away from earth's darkness to heaven's clear light.

BIRDIE'S NEST.

IN the bowers of love supernal
  There your Birdie's built her nest,
For the Father's hand eternal
  Led her from the earth's unrest.

Hear you not my song of gladness,
  Swelling o'er life's troubled sea?
Surely then it were but madness,
  E'er to mourn my loss to thee.

I have gained a deathless morning —
  All my mortal woes are o'er,
And the angels now are crowning
  Me with gems from heaven's store.

Cease your mourning, dearest mother,
  Let tears no more for Birdie fall;
God is love — there is no other —
  And His mercy's over all.

When the shades of Death are falling,
  And your mortal day is o'er,
And you hear the angels calling
  You from earth to our bright shore —

Then your Birdie's song of welcome
  All your fears shall chase away,
And the bitter buds of morning
  Blossom into endless day.

November 9, 1863.

BIRDIE'S VIGIL.

I AM here, dearest mother, though the summer has flown,
  And the roses their beauty have shed;
For the world in its blindness determines alone,
  That the soul in its freedom, is dead!

I am here to watch over and keep you from harm,
  To guide you from darkness to light;
I am here, and I'll wait till the morning bells chime,
  Proclaiming the end of the night.

And then through the bright shining way of the stars,
  Where the saints and the angels have trod,
I will lead you away from the earth and its cares,
  To the spiritual temple of God.

FLASHES OF LIGHT

FROM THE SPIRIT-LAND.

QUESTIONS ANSWERED.

By Joseph Lowenthal, of Jewish Faith, Sept. 3, 1867.

Question. Do children who leave this earth-plane in infancy progress in stature the same as if they had continued to live on earth?

Answer. The law of physical life determines concerning the stature or external form that is given to every soul; and as souls generally remain very near the earth and its laws, until they have gained a certain amount of experience, which can be gained from no other plane than the earth-plane, they are under this law, and do grow in stature precisely the same as they would had they remained on earth to mature age.

By John Pierpont, Sept. 5, 1867.

Q. On earth, to a great, if not absolute extent, we are bound in the channels of phrenological or hereditary bias, often of a very unfortunate character. Does death remove these restrictions, and confer the freedom to expand in *all* directions, not continuing man, as here, an exile from many beautiful arts and accomplishments, because the power of gift for their acquisition was not in the germ at birth?

A. Man slowly acquires a state of perfect freedom. If he were suddenly ushered into a state of perfect freedom in the spirit-land, he would not know how to use it; therefore the Universal Disposer of all events has taken care of this. All the steps in life are gradual and well proportioned. You must press every round in the ladder of progress in order to be fully rounded in the physical, in the mental, and in the spiritual.

Q. Are all souls in spirit-life satisfied with the prospect of a boundless, eternal existence, or do some desire oblivion there, as misery makes some seek it here?

A. As happiness and unhappiness belong strictly to the spirit — to the thinking power of the individual, so this condition of happiness or unhappiness it carries with it to the spirit-land; it is part of its possessions there. Therefore there must be some souls who would desire oblivion, if it were possible to be bestowed upon them. There are some who are so miserable in the spirit-land that they would fain curse God and die. But even these unhappy souls are not outside the law of progress; and by and by, when they shall be made able to perceive that there is a better way, and that the way is open for them to ascend from their hell and enter heaven, as for all others — if they can perceive the truth of this, they will embrace it, and rapidly ascend out of darkness into light.

Q. Can the pure and sinless, as infants, appreciate and enjoy heaven as highly as those who have known life's conflicts and trials?

A. Well, the infant's heaven is just as perfect a heaven as the heaven of mature age. The infant can enjoy just as large an amount of heaven, according to its own life, as mature age. It is only a different condition of the same element — happiness.

By Theodore Parker, Sept. 9, 1867.

Q. Will the intelligence give his opinion of the following text?

"And Jesus, when he was baptized, went up straightway out of the water, and lo! the heavens were opened unto him, and he saw the spirit of God descending like a dove and lighting upon him, and lo! a voice from heaven, saying, This is my beloved son, in whom I am well pleased."

A. There can be but one rational opinion concerning that text, it seems to us. It is a well-known fact, or it is generally believed by those who claim to have a knowledge of the manifestations of spirits disembodied, that Jesus was a medium for such manifestations; that his entire life was but a series of spirit manifestations. He seemed to stand with one foot upon the spirit-shores and the other here, and there was a perfect distribution of spiritual power through his organization. The record tells us that the heavens were opened, and he saw the spirit of God, like a dove, descending upon him, and he heard a voice, saying, "This is my beloved son." Well, why not? The spirit of God performs like so-called miracles even to-day, and has performed them in every age, for in every age there have been ears attuned to spirit-voices; there have been eyes that could perceive spirit-forms; there have been those, in their physical senses, who could take cognizance of the conditions of spirit-life. Now, as Jesus possessed a highly developed physical and spiritual organization, or, in other words, as he was perfectly rounded in spiritual and in physical form, so then he would be well able to receive perfect manifestations from the world of mind. We believe it to be but a spirit manifestation precisely similar to the manifestations that have occurred in every age, and that are occurring on a very large scale in this age.

Q. Will the controlling intelligence please to tell us why spirits do not give their whole names when asked so to do while communicating through test mediums? They will give their first name, but seldom give the surname, when, if the whole name were given, it would give much better satisfaction to sceptical people.

A. All spirit is obliged to use the medium of matter in communicating upon the plane of matter. You use the body which you call your own. It is your medium, and by long assimilation you have become thoroughly used to its control. You know how to use it. It has become in the external a part of your spirit, because all the manifestations of your spirit have been to a certain extent done with the medium, the body; therefore, through this medium you can more perfectly manifest as a spirit, than through any other. By and by death comes. It cuts the cord that bound you to the medium, the body. The golden bowl is broken, the cord is destroyed, or cut asunder, but the fountain of life remains. Now, then, if the fountain would manifest again upon the earthly plane, it must seek out a medium; and your own good sense will tell you that unless the medium could be used for many times by the spirit, and become perfectly assimilated with it, the manifestations must be more or less imperfect. If the spirit can but manifest imperfectly through the medium that Nature has furnished it, — your own bodies, namely, — then surely you should not expect perfect manifestations through a medium that is simply taken up for the occasion. Spirits labor under a great many more disadvantages in returning to manifest here after death than you have any idea of. When they return, they are suddenly ushered back again to the world they had been taken from, and a thousand — perhaps ten thousand times ten thousand — things, thoughts, forms, conditions, press upon them, and their medium is imperfect; consequently they find their work very hard, and they struggle, O, how earnestly and laboriously sometimes, to give even one word. Names are hard to give; first, for this reason: When the sitter comes into *rapport* with the medium and the spirit who has a desire to possess the medium and to manifest through it, the first, most intense, and most positive thought of the sitter is the name of the party that is to control. It is perfectly natural that this should be first; that it should occupy the most prominent seat in the realm of thought, but its naturalness does not prevent it from being the greatest barrier to the giving of the name that could possibly be interposed. If it were possible for the sitter to render his mind entirely passive to what might come, the manifestations would be far more reliable, and names would come much easier. Why is it that there is scarcely any difficulty in giving names at this place? Now ask yourself the question as I have asked it. Is it not because you do not know who is coming? Because you have no expectation of what name is to be given? Surely it is. If you expected Edward Everett to speak to you on a certain occasion, all your minds would be possessed with the name of Edward Everett, and it would be almost impossible for him to give the name. He might identify himself in a thousand other ways, but to give the name would be hard. All persons who are in the habit of visiting mediums, should remember there is a great law governing all spirit manifestations. It governs you in the control of your own body. That is your medium while you are here. The great law holds good after you have left that body. If you desire to return through some other body, there is the law meeting you face to face. You cannot infringe upon it, cannot put it under your feet. It is there greater than you are, and you must obey it. And the nearer you come to an understanding of the law governing spirit manifestations, the better will be the manifestations, and the more perfect and satisfactory. But the further you are from an understanding of the law, the more vague will be the manifestations, and the more unsatisfactory. Therefore become students, every one of you. Enter the school of spiritual science, and there study day after day, year after year, if need be, till you shall be able to grapple with the law understandingly. Even then you cannot control it, but you will know how to take advantage of it, or, in other words, to act in harmony with it. The law is constantly by you. You cannot separate yourself from it, not in any one thought or act. Therefore, whether living here, or living as your speaker lives after death, it matters not; the law is clear, and obey it you must. And if the law says it is hard to give a name that is registered upon the mind of the sitter, then the law must be obeyed. There is no going around it nor through it. You must bow down before it.

By Joseph Lowenthal a Jew, and George A. Redman, Sept. 10, 1867.

Q. We often see through personating mediums the death scene, as we call it, so faithfully enacted, that it seems but a repetition of the same thing. Now, what I wish to know is this: How is it so faithfully reproduced? Is the departing spirit conscious all the time enough to remember so definitely all those motions of the physical? I have always thought there was a time when most, if not all, were unconscious — at the time of change, or immediately after. Is it so?

A. The soul never for one instant loses its consciousness — that which belongs to it as an immortal soul. But it is sometimes shut out from the experiences of human life by the circumstances that surround itself, and attend human life. Therefore it is that it is sometimes unconscious to external circumstances, but never in the absolute unconscious of its own soul realities. These repetitions of scenes, called scenes of death, are easily produced, because they make a very vivid and very clear impression upon the mind of every spirit. Though in the external there is no consciousness, in the internal the spirit is conscious and active, and the recording angel never fails to take down the most minute circumstances. Everything is faithfully transcribed, and therefore can be, under proper circumstances, reproduced. These mediums are mirrors that seem to be hung between the two states of being, and if the surface is clear, the reflection will be correspondingly clear; but if it is spotted, the reflection will be correspondingly deformed.

Q. from one of the audience. I would ask what is the recording angel?

A. It is sometimes called *memory.* That name or term may answer as well as any other. You have often been told that the attribute of memory was eternal; that whatever condition the soul passed through, that condition it retained by virtue of the power of memory, and under certain circumstances it was able to call it up again into active life. The circumstances through which every soul is called to pass, become the external characteristics of that soul, and no one thing, even the most minute, is ever lost.

By Theodore Parker, Sept. 12, 1867.

Q. Do all spirits who have left the human form, after they arrive in the world of spirits, have the power to communicate through mediums here, or do only those who were the most mediumistic while here in the form have the power to communicate?

A. Those who were the most mediumistic while here, have the most power in making these mundane manifestations. However, it is a gift that all may avail themselves of, if they seek so to do.

Q. by one of the audience. The saying is, that like attracts like. Still we do find the opposite sometimes. What are the causes that attract spirits to persons of an entirely opposite character?

A. The causes are legion. It would be impossible to enumerate them. Sometimes a disembodied intelligence or spirit is attracted to a subject or medium in consequence of the external surroundings — surroundings that are in no way connected with the medium. Sometimes it is in consequence of some physical ailment, sometimes the contrary. Sometimes the quiet mind of the subject attracts them, sometimes the turbulent mind. Indeed, the causes that are in constant operation to attract all classes of spirits earthward are innumerable.

Spirit. A query has come to us, as emanating from the late National Convention at Cleveland, and it is this: " What do higher intelligences in the spirit-land believe concerning the manifestations of the Davenports and other mediums through whom similar manifestations are given? Are they genuine spirit-manifestations, or are they jugglery?" Well, whatever your speaker might assert, would be simply an assertion. Whatever belief belongs to him, as a spirit, belongs exclusively to him. Therefore whatever opinion is offered belongs also to him, and he alone is responsible for it. The manifestations given through the Davenports, and other so-called physical mediums, are, in the majority, genuine and of spiritual origin. And whoso desire to understand this thing for themselves, have only to put the manifestations in one scale and their reason in the other, and the solution will come as a natural sequence.

These or analogous manifestations have had existence throughout every condition of intelligent being. There has never been a time in the history of the world when these so-called physical manifestations have not been in existence in some form or some peculiar phase. It is absolute folly, and betrays the sheerest ignorance on the part of those who deny their genuineness, or assume that they are entirely dependent upon trickery, jugglery, or whatever like term you may see fit to employ. I say it betrays ignorance, and still more, it betrays a certain something which is akin to church bigotry; for there are other bigots than theological bigots, and quite as many bigots in Spiritualism as in any other ism. We are sorry to be obliged to affirm this so forcibly, but it is absolutely true. We will go still further, and declare that there are more bigots among those who have come out from the churches, and declared themselves free from all kinds of bigotry, than there are to be found in the churches. The Presbyterian is bound hand and foot by a certain kind of belief, and he sticks to it, in most cases, very rigidly. Spiritualists are bound in the self-same way, for we find them here, there, and everywhere setting up certain very rigid standards of their own, and declaring that they are absolutely right, and there is no appeal from their standard. They have got the highest, the best, and the only genuine Spiritualism, when the truth is, the churches have had experience in it, and those who have no belief in any kind of God have had it. It is as free as the air. It is extensive as life. Spiritualism means something more than what is bound up in the simple name. It means the science of life. It means that life God manifests through every kind of form, through every possible degree of thought. It means that God can rap upon a table to convince you that you will live after death, and not degrade himself, as he can speak through the highest angel in the courts of heaven. Spiritualism of itself is humble. It takes upon itself no crowns. It is exceedingly simple. A child may understand it. But they who prate so loudly against these lower manifestations, as they are pleased to term them, simply betray their ignorance — ignorance of God and his laws, ignorance of the alphabet of life. They would fain destroy the ladder over which they have ascended, because, forsooth, they need it no longer, or because they have entered the temple by some other way, though thousands and tens of thousands have need to enter it this way. They, in their foolishness, determine that God doesn't understand his business, and because he doesn't, they are going to guide the car of progress for themselves. But poor, puny humanity will find by and by that God is God, despite all forms and ceremonies, and he descends to the simplest manifestations of life without losing his Godship. He blooms in the violet, is heard in the tiny rappings. His voice is in the thunder, and his wisdom with the angels. He is everywhere.

Yes, these manifestations are, in the majority, genuine, absolutely genuine, and whoso says they are not, says what is false.

By William E. Channing, Sept. 16, 1867.

Q. Has the spirit-body corresponding organs, anatomically considered, which pertained to the mortal body? And when the spirit enters the spirit-world, has it the same desires, inclinations, and tastes that governed it here? And further, is the spirit-body an exact likeness or counterpart of the mortal body, of a well developed mortal body at the ultimate of its mundane life?

A. Externally, the spirit-body corresponds to the natural body; but there is a constant internal change going on. As the spirit, mentally, becomes larger, more advanced in wisdom, the external takes on the changes of the internal; becomes more beautiful, more perfectly formed, more in accordance with the needs of the indwelling intelligence. The characteristics of the soul are the agencies intrusted with the formation of the spirit-body, and they were never known to forget, never known to make false representations; on the contrary, they are very precise, and they always give a delineation in the external from the internal. Whatever a man or woman *is* in the spirit-land, the representation appears upon the external. They cannot seem to be what they are not. There is no such thing as disguising one's soul characteristics after death. All things are governed by stern, immutable law, and the soul is not exempt from law; form is not exempt from law, but all move by virtue of law, and law that is adapted to their unfoldment. Every form in being changes its external characteristics according to its own internal law. These human forms that exist upon this continent to-day are not exactly what they were many, many years ago. No; there are certain marked characteristics remaining, but a close observer, a critical analyzer can behold a very great change. Yes, the spirit-body does retain the external organic life so far as form is concerned, if you speak of it as belonging to human life. All the various organs are represented in the spirit-body. And if they are represented in the spirit-body, they are for use. Yes; and the soul has need of them. But the necessities of the soul are not exactly the necessities of the physical body. One may need the grains and fruits and animal life of the sphere to which it has been born, and the other also needs the fruits and grains and animal life of the sphere to which it belongs. There is a difference. One is the crude, the other is the refined, the ethereal. One is the outside life, the other is the inside life. The mechanic in the spirit-land deals with the thoughts of the mechanic; the fruit-grower in the spirit-land deals with the thoughts of the fruit; The artist deals with the thoughts of the beautiful representations that you have here in mortal life. And yet thought is present in tangible form in the spirit-land, clearly and brightly and lawfully defined. It is not a world of imagination. It is not a vague, unsubstantial, unreal world. No. It is a world substantial and real. It is a step beyond this mundane physical world. It is the beautiful perfection of this world. If the rose is beautiful here, it is far more beautiful there. All forms that are represented on the earth — and these physical forms are no exception — find also a representation in the spirit-land. You will all learn the truth of my statements sooner or later. To-day they may seem to be vagaries, founded upon nothing, but by and by you will realize their truth, their soundness, and know by experience what you can never know by theory.

Q. Would it not be better for the world, and for the mediums who possess such bad health or bad dispositions as to attract only evil spirits, to give up their mediumship? Ought not mediums to be a pure and holy class to do much good?

A. Your correspondent talks of giving up mediumship, as if it were a thing easily done, when the real truth is, it cannot be given up, any more than it can be taken on. Mediumship — genuine mediumship — is the gift of God. He gave it, and he alone can take it. When we hear mediums, or those who call themselves such, declaring that unless the people and the spirits do thus and so they will give up their mediumship, we know that such are not what they purport to be; for as mediumship is of God, it is God who guards it, and God alone who can take it from the subject. The spirit world is peopled with a vast variety of intelligences, from the highest to the lowest, and it is a law of divine life that every soul shall unfold or perfect itself through the agencies of being as best it can. Now, then, if some depraved souls find that they can unfold more readily by returning to earth and manifesting through media, who shall say they shall not come? Who has the right to determine concerning their coming? It is vain for you to declare that no undeveloped or depraved spirit can return unless there is some attraction within the medium's life. Jesus, the purest of all mediums, either ancient or modern, attracted to himself a legion of undeveloped spirits; and he taught them — he preached unto them — he liberated *them* from their dark surroundings — he led them by his own light up the mount of Transfiguration. He was their Saviour. But if he had banished them, could he have been? Never. Go ye, and learn of him; and if darkness comes to you praying for light, even if its manifestations are of the most diabolical kind, turn not a deaf ear, but listen, and perchance you may catch the notes of an angel even there. Extend the hand. Though thy brother or thy sister be in the very depths of hell, if you are all right they cannot harm you. Be sure that your own garments are spotless, be sure of your own internal holiness, then no filth can attach itself to your external lives. Though you may walk through all the darkness that ever closed around the depraved spirit, it cannot harm you.

By John Pierpont, Sept. 24, 1867.

Q. Where does the spirit of Mrs. Conant remain while another spirit takes possession of her organism?

A. Sometimes she remains in a dormant state within her own physical life. But oftener her conscious part retires, goes out sometimes among her friends here in earth life, and sometimes is attracted off to different lands here on earth, and is able to observe, in her spirit, the different conditions of being where she is at the present time. As spirit is superior to matter, it can break the bonds of matter, and go forth from matter at will; therefore, if there is any attracting power to those points, if the spirit desires to follow that attraction, it can do so.

Q. And does it retain its identity?

A. And at the same time retains its identity. The body is but the medium of the spirit; and although it is better adapted to the spirit that has dwelt with it from its natural birth, yet it can be used also by any spirit who understands the laws governing in such cases. There are several instances recorded where the spirit of the medium has given distinct and positive and unmistakable evidence of its identity in places besides where the form was located during the manifestation of some foreign spirit. She has manifested in England, in Germany, in Roxbury, — localities apart from the place where the body was at the time. And when questioned concerning answers that were given to questions put to her while she was apart from the body — when questioned of them, after returning to the body, her answer was, I should have said so if I had been questioned while in conscious relation with the body, — thus proving that the spirit was the same outside of the body that it was within it, and acting through it.

By Theodore Parker, Sept. 26, 1867.

Q. Please to distinguish between the phenomena that characterized the seers or prophets of the Old and New Testament, and the phenomena now witnessed through our mediums.

A. There is a difference, but it is not in principle. It is simply in outward life, outward expression. The occult manifestations that were said to have had life in the past, were dependent upon the forms through which they were called to manifest. The stream receives its shape from the channel through which it flows. The rays of light receive their colors from the channel through which they flow, and the mediumistic atmosphere by which they are surrounded. So it is of spirit-manifestations. The manifestations of every age partake of the intellectual, the moral, and the religious standard of the age. The manifestations of ancient times corresponded to the development of those times, — the development of mind, the development of matter; and the manifestations of to-day correspond with the development of to-day. They answer the requirements of the time in which they exist. The manifestations of ancient times would *be hardly* thoroughly digested by you of to-day. And yet their inner life is absolutely the same. When resolved to their primaries, they are one, and you cannot separate them. The condition exists only in another form of manifestation.

Q. Was Jesus any other than a brother of our humanity — a gifted and distinguished medium?

A. No — none other — absolutely none other. He was the child of our great Father, God, and our brother, gifted as all God's children are gifted, according to their own capacities of reception. Whoever can receive largely, becomes largely gifted, and is able to give much unto those by whom they are surrounded. Jesus could receive largely from the fountain of wisdom and truth, and he became thus a shining light, not only to the age in which he lived, but that light that continued to shine down the ages, until to-day it is radiant as ever to us.

By Father Henry Fitz James, Sept. 30, 1867.

Q. Can a spirit, after leaving the form, take cognizance of material forms any farther than what is seen by the medium?

A. A spirit that has passed through the chemical change called *death*, perceives the external of all forms that are upon the face of the earth, through the electro-magnetic aura that emanates from mediumistic physical bodies. It is not necessary that the spirit should have absolute control of such a body at the time it perceives these objects, but it is absolutely necessary that it should come within that magnetic atmosphere; for by so doing they come into *rapport* with the external forms that have an existence upon the face of the earth. For instance, when I am apart from this physical body, — this medium, — should I wish to behold any object in this room, I should first seek to come within the atmosphere or magnetic sphere of this medium, or some other that might be in this locality. When the scientific man desires to gain a clear understanding of the heavens, he takes his glass, that he may come into *rapport* with the heavenly bodies through the peculiar power of the glass. Upon precisely the same conditions the spirit uses the medium, or the magnetic life that passes from these mediums, by which they may come into *rapport* with these external forms. There are heavenly bodies so far distant from your external vision that you cannot, without some extra aid, behold them; but if you can obtain the necessary extra aid, you can behold them. So with regard to these objects. We can see them; we can feel them. We can smell the aroma of your flowers by coming into *rapport* with them. But in our proper spiritual state we behold only the spiritual part of these flowers. (Referring to a vase of flowers upon the table.)

By William E. Channing, Oct. 1, 1867.

Q. If I believe the administration of the laws cruel and wrong, is it not a sin for me to support the government by vote or by paying taxes?

A. All individual opinion should, under all circumstances, be sacrificed for general good. Whenever and wherever the good of the masses is involved, individual opinion should be sacrificed. Though this government is not the highest form of government that the soul is capable of conceiving, yet it is the very best kind of government that the times can give birth to. It belongs to this age. It is the result of the growth of mind, — mind in the present and mind in the past, — and it holds, also, a divine relationship to mind in the future. As it is fitted to the wants of the present, as it answers the requirements of the masses, then surely individual opinion concerning it should have little weight.

By T. Starr King, Oct. 3, 1867.

Q. Are there any persons that are more mediumistic when under the influence of liquor than at any other time?

A. We are informed by those intelligences who have made the science of mediumship a study, that there are some mediums who are more readily brought under the influence of a certain class of spirits, disembodied, when under the influence of liquor.

Q. How does the use of liquor make one more mediumistic?

A. Under certain circumstances it reduces the power of the body over the spirit, or, in other words, it lessens the control of the indwelling spirit upon the external body, and therefore renders the body an easy prey to some other spirit who is more positive.

Q. Can you tell us why sometimes a medium who visits another cannot get any communication?

A. Because two negatives have met, and, therefore, the law cannot act. Two positives, when meeting, are apt to gain no response one from the other. Spirit-manifestations are governed by electric and magnetic laws — subtle forces underlying the external. Physical forces are very powerful. They are, indeed, the law, and whoso would receive their aid, must come into communion and assimilation with them. It is very rare that one medium can gain satisfactory communication from the departed through any other, except in such instances as where the medium used by the communicating spirit is, of the two, the most powerful; but where they both stand upon the same mediumistic plane of mind and body, it is very hard for the spirit to commune with the one who desires communion.

Q. Do spirits measure time as we do?

A. No, they do not. There is no time nor place in the spirit-world proper. If they measure time at all, it is according to your understanding of time. It is in accordance with the rules of earth, the rules of these external forms — not with the internal, the spirit.

Q. Is spirit the product of matter, or matter of spirit, or are both eternal?

A. Your speaker believes they are both eternal. There are certain intelligences who contend that matter is the result of spirit, and certain others who contend that spirit is the result of matter. I believe that you cannot well separate spirit from matter. I believe that spirit acts upon matter: matter changes its forms to satisfy the requirements of spirit. The mechanic must first have the idea, or the thought of the article he wishes to construct, ere it comes into the objective world. Here you see spirit behind the form; and so I believe it ever is. But as spirit is dependent, for its mode of manifestation, upon matter, so matter is dependent for its existence upon spirit. The two act in concert together. One would be a nonentity without the other. This world and the world of mind are wedded together. These forms and their indwelling life are wedded together. Mind and matter go hand in hand throughout eternity, I believe.

Q. Matter is transmuted from one form of being to another. Is it equally true of spirit? Is animal life transmuted into human, human into angelic, and thus back again into human?

A. The spirit or essence of life, we believe, is the same yesterday, to-day, and forever. In essence it never changes. It always was perfect, is, and always will be perfect. It is only the external that changes. I may influence the dog or the horse; he may obey my will, and to that extent he may become my medium or subject through which my spirit manifests, precisely similar to that which is seen through the physical form. Indeed, the spirit has all forms by which it manifests itself to the external world. The mechanic manifests his life in constructing these objects (table, &c.). The artist, when he pictures his thoughts, places his life there. The astronomer, when he searches out worlds, throws his life there. The geologist, when he enters in thought down deep into the heart of the earth, throws his life there. Soul goes everywhere. Soul has dominion over the fish of the sea and the fowls of the air; over all things that ever have been, are, or ever will be. All things become mediums through which the soul manifests. You mistake when you suppose that these physical forms are the only machines through which the soul, the intelligent part, manifests itself. Look abroad throughout the universe, and you will see that you are mistaken. Mind is exerted everywhere, and you cannot exert your mind upon any one object, or in any one direction, without throwing your life there, and that life has become incorporated into the object. The artist manifests through his glorious landscape; the sculptor through the grand form of marble, which seems as though it would speak. His life is there; though the marble utters no sound, though it gives back not even a sigh to your admiration, still the artist's life is there. If you will only search into this glorious science of life, you will behold for a certainty that mind is acting everywhere; not only through these forms, but through every conceivable form that has an existence.

By Hosea Ballou, Oct. 8, 1867.

Q. As human souls unfold in spirit-life, will they also pass farther away from our earth? If so, will the memory of having lived upon the earth finally become obliterated from their minds?

A. The soul is not bound to any special locality. It exists independent of locality. It is not at all necessary that the soul should pass away from the earth and its conditions after it rises from a state of ignorance to a state of wisdom, or from unhappiness to happiness, for there are quite as many souls in the kingdom of wisdom on the earth as anywhere else; and quite as many souls in the kingdom of heaven even, here upon earth, as in the farthest condition of human existence that you are able to conceive of. The soul is not governed by localities, or by the conditions of time. It is of itself a thing eternal. It belongs to eternity, and progresses according to the laws of eternal life.

Q. Was there ever a period in the history of man when his soul was not an immortal entity?

A. The soul we believe to be co-existent with God, and therefore eternal. We believe it ever had an existence as a distinct entity, and we believe it will ever continue to have an existence; but that it will perpetually change its form of manifestations, so that while you recognize it by its external expressions, you will be apt to consider that it has changed states, has lost its priority; but it is not so. It is the same yesterday, to-day, and forever.

By William E. Channing, Oct. 10, 1867.

Q. If astrology and prophecy be true, so that future events can be foretold, does it not teach foreordination, and that we are not wholly responsible for our acts?

A. There are different kinds of responsibility: as many different kinds as there are souls to be responsible. That a great eternal law runs through all the events of life, I believe. I believe, also, that it determines concerning all the events of life; and that, whether we will or no, it will shape our destiny; whether we will or no, we are carried on by this great tide of being, which we cannot successfully go against. I believe that every human soul, as an intelligence, possesses each its distinctive quality of responsibility. Just so far as that soul understands what right is, just so far that soul is responsible to that law of right. And whoso sins against it, sins against what may properly be termed the Holy Ghost; for I know of nothing holier than the divine law which makes us conscious of right.

Q. One says, in the "Banner of Light," that the spirit, the intelligent part, the motive power, does not dwell within the body. Now I had supposed that the spiritual body dwelt within the material body, and separated from it at death, and became the immortal form of the inner spirit. Will you explain this point?

A. No, it does not dwell within the body, any more

than the performer on the musical instrument dwells within the instrument. It is outside of the body, but adapted to it so far as it is in *rapport* with the body. So far as there is disease, the spirit is not present in full action — has lost its control precisely upon the same principle that a musical performer would lose control of the instrument when one of the keys was out of order. People who believe that the spirit dwells within the body, will have to unlearn their mistake sooner or later.

Q. When you control the medium, do you enter her form, or come in *rapport* with the physical aura of her system?

A. No, I surround it; I enclose it within my spiritual embrace. I act upon it precisely as she, in her normal condition, acts upon it.

THE DIVINITY OF CHRIST.

Our attention has been called to an article which appeared in your last issue.* It seems to be in part a criticism upon an article which appeared some time since concerning the birth of Jesus the Christ, and, in part, it seems to be the opinion of the writer, founded upon certain mythological and theological researches. In his opinion Jesus the Christ did have a miraculous birth and conception. In his opinion, the Virgin Mary was overshadowed by the Holy Spirit, the great God-principle, and as a result of the overshadowing, Jesus the Christ was born. He believes also that his birth was foretold long before the event took place; and he cites, as one of his greatest reasons for

* Referring to an article signed "Justice" (printed in the "Banner of Light" the second week in October), in which the writer criticises the answer given by the spirit of Rev. Dr. Channing to a "Minister of the Gospel" on the same subject.

believing in the miraculous conception of Jesus Christ, the appearing of the star of Bethlehem; and he informs us that the star disappeared when Jesus disappeared in form from earth; that it appeared only for the short space of his lifetime, and then went away, having performed its princely mission. It is impossible to give an elaborate answer to the article in the short space of time allotted to us on this occasion. But we can throw out a few hints, which, if they do not serve him well, may serve somebody else.

Standing, then, upon what he deems to be the most conclusive evidence of the miraculous conception of Jesus the Christ, we have only to look the world through, to scan the history of all nations, all the different tribes that have existed on the face of the earth since intelligence had a being, and we shall learn that every nation under heaven, every distinct tribe that had any idea of religion, has a similar tradition. Let us look, for instance, at the Chinese records, the oldest upon the earth. There we find a passage, when translated, running thus: "And a star appeared in the East, showing to the magi where the king reposed, and its beams did lead his earthly life, and enter his celestial life, showing to us that he was born of the star, and destined to be king over the people of the celestial empire."

Now this tradition dates far, far back in the past, and this is only one account of the many which we have in mind; indeed, as we have before affirmed, every tribe that lays claim to religious intelligence has the same tradition. How then has the Christian world any more right to it than any other? We cannot see that they have. We look upon it as simply a tradition that belongs to all ages, and we believe that it has its origin in the worship of the heavenly bodies. It could have originated nowhere else. The writer of the article seems to be impressed with the idea that modern Spiritualism is the exhibition of Anti-christ, and that it is to the second coming of Christ what John the Baptist was to his first appearing. He seems to believe, if we have rightly understood him, that Jesus the Christ at his second appearing is to set apart his kingdom on the earth, and is to reign supreme over all the nations of the earth. He believes that he will be acknowledged, that he will assert his power; and he seems to believe that he will be attended by all the paraphernalia of Heathen mythology, by the glory of life, or, as he says, by a glory so far exceeding human sense that human senses cannot understand it. Now to us there is clear evidence that he has mixed up within his reasoning faculties certain portions of Heathen mythology and Christian theology, and has so woven the two together that he himself cannot distinguish between them. He has erected an altar, partly real and substantial, or spiritual and substantial, and partly from a belief in the ignorance of past ages. He goes on to prove that Christ was an exception to all other forms on the earth, by citing what the record tells us the angel said to Mary. Well, there are as many different constructions put upon these words which the record gives us as there are minds to think upon them. No two, even in theology, determine exactly alike concerning them.

Again, the writer says, if he was not unlike all other forms, if he was not wholly different in a special sense, why is it that he could control the winds and the waves? Why could he perform such healing works, when no one else has been able to do the same?

Here we shall take exception. So far as the healing is

concerned, there are persons north and south, east and west, who, under proper conditions, are able to do the same that he did, and even more, for he says himself, "I cannot work wonders here, because of your unbelief. I cannot cure your sick here, because you do not believe in me or my works." Modern healers go farther than that: they set aside your unbelief, and in many instances cure you, whether you believe or no. Now, as regards the walking upon the water, which he cites as evidence of his divinity: You may as well call the Davenport Brothers especially divine because their guardian spirits took them over the water and they were not drowned. There is positive evidence that this was done. You may as well declare that Shadrach, Meshech, and Abednego were specially divine because they came out of the furnace heated seven times hotter than it was wont to be heated, without the smell of fire upon them. It is well to look religion fairly in the face, as well as everything else. It is not well to stand too far from it, because if you do you are apt to lose its reality. It is not well to stand apart from our God and endeavor to analyze him. If we would know him, we must come into distinctive *rapport* with him. The position which we held in the article which has been so severely criticised, we still hold, because we know it is absolutely of good foundation.

We do not believe in a God outside and apart from Nature. We believe in a God that is in humanity. We believe in a God that makes all things divine. We believe in a God that hallows the flowers as he hallows our souls; and we most fervently pray that we may never so far forget ourselves as to believe in a God who would bestow special favors upon any one of his children more than upon the whole.

In conclusion, we would say, if the writer of the article has any more thoughts to throw out upon the ocean of intelligence, if we are able to cope with them we shall gladly do so.

By Theodore Parker, Oct. 13, 1867.

Q. Can you give us an idea of the language in use in spirit-land? We have an impression that you have neither speech nor laughter, as known to us; that all thought, "from grave to gay, from lively to severe," is understood rather than expressed.

A. If there were no expression there would be no external; there would be no individualization; there would be no form; but everywhere one vast void, which to the soul would be meaningless. But, thanks be to the great, wise Master Mechanic, form is carried into the spirit-world. Outward expressions are seen and felt and heard even there. There is music in the land of souls, so far beyond the music of earth's spheres, that were you this hour to be translated there, you would scarcely comprehend it. And if you had any devotion within your inner life, you would be very likely to fall down and worship the God of Music. O, yes, there is sound, sight, and feeling in the land of souls. It is not a mere world of imagination, a something devoid of beauty, a great chaos, with neither form nor fashion. No. It is more beautiful than this earthly sphere of action, having forms and various conditions of being.

Q. If there is no disease in spirit-land, and all are physically perfect, why is a medical science there? what the motive for its pursuit where there is no object for its exercise?

A. There is disease in the spirit-land, for there are

quite as many mental ailments as there are physical ailments. Every kind of sorrow is a disease, and souls experience the keenest sorrow in spirit-land. It is far more acute than that you take cognizance of here in this world. There is quite as much need of soul-physicians as of physicians to take charge of the human body. And it would be well for those medical men whose business it is to restore diseased physical forms to health, to carry their science a little farther, and seek to become physicians of the soul, that they may carry their practice into the spirit-land, and be of use when they shall enter there.

Q. If our spirit-friends are with us in earth-life, and are acquainted with our surroundings, why is it that they do not control those surroundings for our good? and why is it that we are not conscious of their presence? Your inquirer has long prayed for some manifestation of their presence, but without success.

A. It does not follow that because they may understand the surroundings of those with whom they come in contact in the earth-life, that they should be always able to control those surroundings, nor does it follow that they would always wish to. It should be understood that each soul has duties of its own to perform. You may as well ask why a certain merchant on Washington Street, or any of them, do not leave their own business to interest themselves in the business of some other merchant, because, forsooth, they know of the business affairs of that merchant, and know, perhaps, that he is in trouble? Simply because duty to self is not only the first law of earth, but of heaven; and, because it is, every spirit should depend upon its own internal and external sources for happiness — for what it desires. That that comes from the external, from another, is rarely appreciated by the spirit; but that which is outwrought from its own life, or gathered from the external by the earnest workings of its own inner life, is always best adapted to the needs of the spirit. Therefore it is that those millions of sympathizing spirits who have passed through death, though they may be in the fulness of sympathy with their suffering friends, yet you may hear no sound from them. They may be, as it were, shut out from their consciousness, having no interference with your earthly affairs, because it is better that it is so. It is better, perhaps, that they let you work out your own salvation, though it be with fear and trembling.

Q. The followers of Ann Lee believe she was inspired, and uttered many things which they say were communicated to her from the spirit-world. Were those influences from the spirit-world, or was she under the influence of liquor at the time, as many suppose? They believe, too, that their peculiar manner of life and mode of worship came from the spirit-land, through the mediumship of some of her followers. Is that so? And, if the system is what they believe it to be, why do they not increase as other sects do?

A. I believe that the founder of Shakerism was a very superior medium, and under the special direction of a class of disembodied spirits, — not ardent spirits, but souls, who once lived in forms of flesh. There are not many who desire to leave the pleasures of the world to enter a society which eschews many of the so-called evils of the world. Therefore it is that there is not a large increase among them; nor would it be well for them to increase largely. They are acted upon, I believe, by a spirit-band in the land of souls, and are acted upon to this end: that they may throw out a certain magnetic influence that the world's people have need of. They are what they are, more for the benefit of the world's people than for their own benefit, though they know it not. They are laboring magnetically, or the spirits through them, for the world entire, not for themselves.

By Joseph Lowenthal, Oct. 15, 1867.

Q. Do the spirit-intelligences who control at this circle approve of the Massachusetts prohibitory liquor law, or otherwise?

A. Restraint, when guided by wisdom and love, is of good; but when it is guided by ignorance, and love is wanting, then it is apt to lead to destruction, and the very end that is sought for is never reached. I believe that there are many spirits who visit this place who are in favor of the Massachusetts prohibitory liquor law. There are also many others who are against it, and who seem to use all the power of which they are possessed to throw obstacles in the way of its success. For be it understood, the inhabitants of the world that is unseen do very often come into close, very close, *rapport* with those who are still clothed with the flesh, and exercise a very large amount of power over those who are in the flesh, and over the conditions of time. That class of spirits who favor the so-called license law, are those who believe that this generation, and particularly the class of mind that finds expression upon this continent, — this republican people, — they believe will be better governed by moral suasion; better governed by erecting for them a certain standard which they themselves subscribe to; rear for them an altar which they are willing to recognize and worship at. "Then," say these intelligences beyond the grave, "the end sought for by both parties will at last be reached." Your speaker has no opinion to offer, save that he believes that as God is walking through the nations, he himself will finally purge you from all the so-called evils that float in social life.

Q. I would like to ask if a large number of those who are among us addicted to the inordinate use of alcohol, are not, to a great extent, influenced by those in the other world who have not yet been able to rid themselves of the habits and appetites they possessed here; and if so, whether it is not possible to reach the parties suffering, rather by calling back the spirit of one in the spirit-body and treating him through a medium or otherwise, so as to deliver him from the condition from which he has been suffering? We wish to ascertain your opinion as to the possibility of ridding ourselves and others of those habits, which are diseases; and equally of other physical diseases in that way.

A. A certain amount, I may say a very large amount, of all diseases, either physical, or mental, or moral, are augmented by the interference of foreign spirits; therefore, if you would gather in their causes entire, so far as you are able to, you must gather such in also. If you would rid the little branches of disease, you must commence at the root. Then you will commence right. But generally it is the habit of mortals to deal heavy blows at all evil effects, failing to touch the cause, so the effect is fought against and fought against, and it continually rears its head like a monster in your midst, over which you seem to have no control. Sometimes mental, physical, and moral diseases have their source entirely within the human physique, and no outside interference can be traced. But those are the exceptions, not the rule. When you understand the laws governing through all the minutiæ of life, you will know how to live in health. Disease will depart from you, and a heaven upon earth will have begun.

By William E. Channing, Oct. 17, 1867.

Q. Does the fact of one's having committed suicide impede his progress in the spirit-world more than if another had killed him, or render him more unhappy?

A. Yes, because the soul that has committed suicide, as you term it, is very apt to learn that that is not the better way; very apt to learn that it must, through severe experience, learn of the better way, and very apt to learn that it would have been far easier to have gained the experience that was necessary for the soul in and through its own body, than in any other way; therefore it must, of necessity, drink more or less deeply of the cup of remorse. But, like all other mistakes in life, it always carries its own antidote. When a sufficient quantity has been ministered unto the spirit, it comes forth washed clean, regenerated and rejuvenated, and ready for the march of life.

Q. How do we reconcile the existence of evil in this world with the goodness and wisdom of God?

A. We reconcile it in this way. As God is everywhere, and as there is no place without him, no condition without him, so then God is in what you call evil, and, being stronger than the evil, is amply able to take care of it. I believe that all the experiences of life, all the conditions of life, however low they may seem to be, are of a necessity, — a necessity growing out of the condition of the earth upon which you exist, a necessity growing out of the condition of the planets by which you are surrounded, and a necessity growing out of your own internal and external condition. Therefore, if this position be a correct one, the goodness of God is displayed in the exhibition of the so-called evil, as it is displayed in any other condition in life.

By William E. Channing, Oct. 24, 1867.

Q. After a long separation, how are we to recognize our friends in the spirit-land? — the body we have seen and known, but not the soul.

A. Surely you are not to recognize them by their outward characteristics alone. It is not alone by form that you are to know those who have gone on before you, when you shall meet them in the land of the hereafter. But there is a certain power by which the soul can recognize those with whom it has been familiar; it matters not whether ages have passed between them since they have met in the external or not. There is no such thing as forgetfulness for the soul. Memory is eternal. It is an attribute of the soul, and therefore is eternal. You need not fear that you will not be recognized by your friends, or that you will fail to recognize them, for by that law that binds you together as friends, you cannot fail to recognize them. The law is ever active, and all may make use of it whenever they desire so to do.

Q. Are the surroundings and influences for good and evil the same in the spirit-land as in earth-life? If so, what do we gain by the change?

A. They are proportionately the same, but you are just one step, and one only, in advance of the earth-life.

Q. Is there night and day there? In other words, are light and darkness the same there as here?

A. There is what is equivalent to night and day,

light and darkness, but it is not the same as you have here. That you have here is adapted to your earthly needs; that we have is adapted to spiritual needs.

If there are no more questions, we will proceed to answer in brief a question which we have received from an individual who is radically opposed, as he informs us, to King Alcohol. And because he is, he asks that those spirits who declare that they have power, or can exert power over the conditions of time, will return exercising their power towards the destruction of King Alcohol. He says, "I am told that the law of chemistry is well understood in the spirit-world. Now if it is, cannot the spirits, by taking advantage of the law, destroy King Alcohol? drive him out of the domain of Nature, so that there shall be no more tears shed on his account? so that much of the misery that now fills the earth may disappear?"

Well, allowing that any class of disembodied spirits had that power to change the conditions by which you mortals are surrounded, — allowing that they are permitted to exercise their power upon you, — would it be well for them to carry out the wishes of him who has called upon us? Would it be well to even seek to drive King Alcohol out of the domain of Nature? We argue it would not be well. Let us briefly consider from what King Alcohol has come. Let us analyze him. Scientific men inform us that he has been born of carbon, hydrogen, and oxygen. These are the causes that have produced him. They are in existence everywhere. There is no place devoid of them. Life would cease to be life without them. Rob the vegetable kingdom of them, and it becomes extinct, and the same is true of every other department in Nature. Now, since it is always well to strike at the cause of every so-called evil effect, if we expect to destroy effectually the effect we must begin at the cause. Now supposing for a moment we had the power to drive these elements out of Nature, what would be the result? Why, destruction, certainly. Nothing short of it. It would be as possible to destroy the universe, to blot it out of existence, as to blot out the essential cause of King Alcohol. It cannot be done. God himself cannot do it, and at the same time sustain his laws.

We are not arguing in favor of alcohol. We argue against its abuse. But its uses are many — too many for us to attempt to enumerate them here. Now, would it be wise for us to seek to destroy even this effect of these great principles in Nature, since it can be put to so many good and proper uses? Would it be wise to seek to destroy it because, forsooth, one half of creation sees fit to abuse it? No, it would not. Rather seek to enlighten men and women. Rather seek to bring them upon a higher level, and then they will use and not abuse it. First, begin back — away back. Turn the leaves over, leaf by leaf, and you will perceive that nine tenths of all those people who bow down as servants to King Alcohol, are absolutely forced into that condition by ante-natal forces over which they have no control. Seek, then, to regulate your affairs in this direction. Seek to bring men up beyond the abuse of it, and beyond the abuse of everything God has given you. Use all, but abuse none, remembering that the great All-Father has given you all these things by which you are surrounded — and alcohol is no exception — for your good. Instead of seeking to destroy these evils, — evils you call them, — seek to get yourselves a plane beyond them, so that you can rule them, and they cannot rule you. Bring the nations up to a standard beyond the abuse of anything God has given, and then all these evils will cease, and earth will become indeed a heaven.

By Lewis Howard, Oct. 28, 1867.

Q. Has our late war so far settled the disturbing element of slavery and its party entanglements and entailments, North and South, that we may avoid another conflict? And, furthermore, does the negro possess the characteristics that will enable him to live successfully and happily with the white at the South, or would it not be better for him to remove to some other country and live by himself, and this without derogating from his rights, which we see God has determined he shall have?

A. The dark scenes of war through which this nation has but just passed are still fresh in your minds, and every scene is peculiar to itself and possesses its own life. Every son and daughter claiming a home on this American continent, that has come to years of understanding, need not be told that there is still a spirit of discord alive. The hoarse mouth of the cannon and the sharp edge of the sword have failed to destroy it. It lives still, and has its own law outside the law of active life. Therefore, if it is in action, you may know that it will culminate in some peculiar form or other, at some time or other; it may be in the far distant future, and it may be very near at hand. I believe that the present scene of strife — it *is* present, for it is with you even now — will be followed by one upon a mental plane. It may be called a mental war. And, as the pen is said to be more terrible than the sword, so thought is more terrible than deed, though you may not so understand it. And I believe that war that is to come will do more towards liberating the slaves upon this continent than that through which you have just passed. The physical war has brought the North to a better understanding with the South, and *vice versa*. And, therefore, it has conditioned both so that this mental war, when it shall be opened, will result in good. The North will say to the South, "You have a right to expect this much of me;" and the South will say to the North, "You have a right to expect this much of me." The negro claims his home here, and he has the right so to do. The soil is as much his as yours, and should you attempt to remove him — it matters not whether your motive be good or bad — you will find that the policy will not work as well with him as it has worked with the red man. He knows you too well, and, knowing you, will exercise his God-given power in consonance with his knowledge. He will not be driven from hence without warfare. He knows his rights, and will fight for them, and the great army of freedmen who have gone yonder will fight for him too. The lesson that the great All-Father has sought to impress upon your minds, namely, the right of freedom for all, and justice — as it means with God — you have failed to learn. Notwithstanding your homes have been desolated, and your hearts have been wrung by the loss of near and dear friends, still your lesson is not half learned. Now that the negro is in part a freedman, now that you cannot buy or sell him bodily, you determine — many of you — to do so mentally and socially. Now that it has been determined that he has a right to his freedom, many of you determine that he must exercise that right in some foreign land. But, I tell you, inasmuch as he knows his rights, he will fight for them. The last few years have educated him in warfare, and, if need be, he will throw his knowledge into the scale against your injustice, and who, think you, will come off victorious? The voice of God has been sounding for years over your land, "Let my people go!" but you have held them in body, and when you can do so no longer, you desire that they shall depart out of your coast. No, no, it cannot be. It never will be.

Q. Is the doctrine of pre-existence, or the idea that man always existed as a conscious individual being, true?

A. I believe it is true. If I doubted that I had existed as a conscious, individualized intelligence throughout all past eternity, I should have no hope for the future.

Q. Does the controlling influence have any knowledge of a life previous to that which he experienced while in the body here?

A. Absolute, perfect, and clear.

Q. Does not the theory of progression believed in by Spiritualists, and so often found in communications from spirits, carry with it, as a natural sequence, the idea of a starting-point or a beginning?

A. No, by no means. Because you live under a law of infinite progress, you are not to suppose that there was a time when you were beyond the limits of that law. No, I do not believe that the soul ever had any starting-point. I believe it always has existed, else I could have no hope that it always would exist.

By Arthur Fuller and G. A. Redman, Oct. 29, 1867.

Q. Can departed friends sever the silver cord that binds us to our material body, if the spirit inhabiting that body desires it, and the spirit-friends are anxious or willing to grant that desire? We believe they can. Are we right or wrong?

A. You certainly are right in your belief; for if the spirit was possessed of that power while in the body, it certainly is possessed of it after leaving the body.

Q. In the Banner of the 22d of September, 1866, the controlling spirit, in answer to certain questions, uses the following language: "This is a truth — a great and mighty truth — that you are all changing places. That you die, is proof of it; that you live again beyond the tomb, is another proof of it; that as ages shall again roll on you will again inhabit human forms, is still further proof of it." Does the controlling spirit mean that spirits, after being separated from their earthly tenement, will again occupy a human body as they did before the dissolution? And if so, will those bodies be subject to decay as were the former ones? The above message of the intelligence is not clear, and a little explanation and further information is solicited.

A. The theory of the resurrectionists is by no means without foundation. But they have arrived at a wrong conclusion. One of our most able speakers once said that the air was full of truth, and whoso was most susceptible would receive it first. Now these resurrectionists have perceived the truth and grasped it, but they have applied it in the wrong place. They believe that the spirit is to return after the lapse of years and inhabit this old body again, living on a new earth and under new circumstances, but having the old body. Well, that the spirit will return to earth again and become re-incarnated in a human body, there is much evidence. Indeed, all that we have been able to gain is very largely in its favor. But our experience does not determine that we shall come again and inhabit the old bodies that we have lain off. The soul, the thinking, the intellectual part of man, finds expression alone through organized form, and if it expresses itself upon earth, it must express itself according to the laws of earth; and as the human form is the highest in existence, and the form through which the soul can best express itself, we believe that the souls of those who have gone beyond this world of man, full of shadows and sunbeams, will return again at some far-off future period, to live again through human life, and that human life, we believe, will be in a different condition from the life of to-day, yet it will be organized life in human form. The ancients, who believed in this theory to a certain extent, had more correct ideas than the world has to-day. We do not wonder that many souls in contemplation of this theory shudder at it, since they have, many of them, tasted very largely of the sorrows of time; but if they would pause and consider that they are in the hands of an infinite law that will guide them whithersoever it will, whether they will or no, they would cease to mourn, methinks, over what is best for them — over what all their mourning will not change. All life, we are told, moves on by distinct degrees, and it moves in cycles. It is rounded into being by passing through the various experiences of human and intellectual life. If this be true, have we any guarantee against returning again to earth? Able minds contend that we have none; and your speaker himself believes that there is much soundness in the theory.

By Prof. Edgar C. Dayton, Oct. 31, 1867.

TRIBUTE TO JOHN A. ANDREW.

We are told that Massachusetts this day mourns the loss of a favorite son — an honored child. Though a sister State claims him by right of birth, yet Massachusetts claims him by right of love and public duties. But is he lost? Will no echo answer the question? Is the power that prompted him to kindly deeds and kindly words forever silenced in death? Will he linger no longer in the midst of the family circle? Will he bless no longer the Commonwealth of Massachusetts? Is he dead? These are questions that Massachusetts should answer. The spirit of the age can answer them to the entire satisfaction of Massachusetts whenever she shall call upon her for an answer. Are all those leading minds that made glorious the page of her history dead? Those who have passed beyond mortal state; those whose forms you have mourned over; those whose voices you hear no longer, are they lost? If they are, then Massachusetts is poor indeed. But thanks be to the overruling power and the Great Spirit of infinite love, they are not lost; nor are they removed to some far-off clime, to some distant star, to pursue a course of action entirely different from that they pursued while here. No; the power of love, though earthly, is infinite and grand. Death cannot touch it. Change has no power over it. It outlives all change. It bids defiance to death; for the Great Father of life has been pleased to crown it with his own being, and seal it with his own seal. It cannot die.

Even while we are speaking, the honored dead, — or he who is dead to you, — even while we are speaking, his happy spirit — happy in the consciousness of having done right so far as he understood it when here — is being welcomed to the land where the soul understands itself far better than amid the clogs of mortality. Every soul desires to hear those sublime and cheering words: "Well done, good and faithful servant; thou hast been faithful over a few things, now I will make thee ruler over many." And the spirit of these words is being shed this hour upon him who has just left you. And he knows that his earthly labor is not done. Though the golden bowl is broken at the fountain, though the silver cord is loosed, yet life remains the same, and all those sublime traits of character that go to make up an honest man still live, and will be called into action in the world of mind whither it has flown.

Massachusetts, who could afford to execute those persons who fain would have brought tidings from the great hereafter many years ago, should afford to-day to answer the question concerning her dead. Are they lost? or are they found in the Summer Land of action? Have they been removed to satisfy vindictive vengeance? No. All Nature answers no. But in strict accordance with the great immutable law of universal life, they have changed states — have laid off the mortal, and are now standing up in the dignity and royalty of immortality. Will they weep over your sorrows and mistakes? Ay, they will. Will they rejoice over your honest victories? over your best endeavors? Ay, they will. Will they enter with all their soul-power into the high and holy objects which absorbed their mortal lives? They will. Will they be satisfied with the enjoyment of a far-off heaven? No, they cannot. For the attracting power earthward is too strong, and earth has still longer need of them. And because she does need them, here they will remain, working for the enfranchisement of humanity everywhere; praying to the great God of universal mind that you may speedily be free from the shadows that close around you, as nations and as individuals.

When the shadow of the wing of the Angel of Death falls across the way of human hearts, then it is, if ever, that those hearts are turned away from the scenes of earth; turned away, far, far beyond these material scenes, to those that are more real and more sublime — to those that belong to the spirit. Then out of the shadow the crushed heart lifts its prayer to the great God of all, asking to know "Where, O, where are the loved ones who have been removed from our sight? We see the cold, silent form before us, but where, O, where is the spark that made glad its being? Where, O, where is that that recognized and answered to our love?"

In answer to such prayers as these, modern Spiritualism has come. She has flung back the shadows, and has invited every soul to come straightway to the throne of almighty truth, there to receive whatever may be necessary for their unfoldment. Spiritualism leads you to a recognition of the life after death. It shows you something more than the shadow of death. It shows you the sunbeam beyond. It tells you where your loved ones have found their home. It answers all their questions with regard to life after death. O, then, ye who mourn the loss of loved ones, turn to this modern and ancient angel combined in one, asking for light. And Massachusetts, you whose love is far greater than your injustice, O, turn by the torch of that love the leaves of life's Book, and as you turn them, you will read the answer to the question, Where, where are our honored dead?

Q. Will parents and children who are unavoidably separated long years upon the earth, be united in that relation in the spirit-world? or will the children outgrow all recollection of, and affection for, their parents, and not know they ever belonged to them?

A. The attraction or law that binds soul to soul, is not in any way dependent upon the body or its experience. If a parent and child are bound together by a spiritual law of attraction, there is nothing that can sever it, no power that can separate them, and they as naturally gravitate together as an apple will fall to the ground if some interposing power does not break its fall. The law of spiritual affinity is supposed by many to be dependent, to a certain extent, upon human conditions, human experience. But it is not so. It stands above and apart from human life. There are many parents who have no spiritual love for their children, and *vice versa*. Such cannot hope to enjoy each other's society in the spirit-land, nor will they wish to.

Q. Is the theory of the spirit's home, or "zones of spirit-land," as described by Hudson Tuttle in his "Arcana of Nature," correct in its main features? If so, what becomes of them in the far distant future, when this earth shall have grown old and passed away, — as an earth, — as I understand it will, by almost all writers on the Harmonial Philosophy?

A. Everything, spirit as well as matter, is subject to the law of progress. Everything is constantly passing through an unending series of changes; therefore if the spirit-land is a distinct locality, as many writers affirm, you are to believe, if it holds connection with the earth, that as the earth passes out of its material orbit into a spiritual orbit, the spirit-land or zone will change to correspond to the earth. But your speaker does not believe that the spirit-land is confined to any particular locality. The brief experience that has been his in the spirit-land, has taught him that the spirit-world is everywhere: on the earth, under the earth, above the earth; wherever there is life, there is the spirit-land.

By Prof. John Hubbard, Nov. 4, 1867.

Q. If it is true that the soul has had a previous existence in some other form before its connection with the body, why is it that it has no distinctive recollection of that existence?

A. The soul existed in embryo before it was projected into the external world, before it was made apparent as an individual according to the laws of time. And yet the soul, through its human organism, has no memory of that prior existence. It can remember back to the days of childhood, but it can go no farther. There seems to be a power governing the attribute of memory that is, to a very great extent, dependent upon form and the conditions of form. Memory expresses itself through form. It turns to the past through form, and it stretches its clairvoyant vision from the past to the future through form; it is dependent upon the laws of form to a very great extent. Therefore it is that you do not remember having had a prior existence to the one which is now your own, so-called, as an individual. I have no recollection of an existence prior to the existence of my earthly life, yet I have listened to many who declared that they have a distinct recollection of scenes far, far back in the past, dating long before their earth-lives.

Q. Memory is eternal, and the soul's remembrance of such a state of life before the present would be as indelibly impressed on the future of its existence as its connection with the body is.

A. That part of the subject has been answered, we think. Memory is, indeed, eternal, and, as we before remarked, it is dependent for expression upon form, and for its peculiar mode of expression it is dependent upon form. What is memory to one individual is not exactly memory to another. The attribute of memory differs according to the characteristics of the form through which it is expressed.

Q. Some people believe in the transmigration of souls. Do we take some other form, and so go on in a constant round of progression? Does the soul enter other bodies sometimes better and sometimes worse than its own?

A. In one sense it does enter other bodies, and acts through other bodies than the human; and, in another sense, it does not. For instance: The mechanic may, to all intents and purposes, act through his mechanical skill, and express his life in some outward form, a table, it may be, a chair, a dwelling-place. Who shall determine that the life of the mechanic is not there? Certainly no one can. The soul expresses itself, I believe, through all that is beneath it. Everything becomes a medium for the soul. The granite rocks are the soul's mediums, the skies, the air, the water, the flowers, the beasts, the birds, the fishes — everything that is beneath the soul becomes the agent of the soul; and so far as the soul is able to find expression through these forms, or by the agency of these forms, so far it becomes incorporated in the form allied to it. The ancients grappled with a very great truth in their theory of the transmigration of souls. They intuitively perceived the power of the soul over all matter, and, perceiving its power, they very naturally were led to conclude that it would use the power, and, therefore, become incarnated in other forms than the human.

By Thomas Paine, Nov, 5, 1867.

Q. If spirits do, as they say, visit other planets, I would ask if they are inhabited? and if so, do you learn anything of them — of their history, character, and condition, as compared with the inhabitants of the earth?

A. Very many of the planets are inhabited by animal and intellectual life, while very many of them are not inhabited, they not having arrived at the stage where they can sustain animal and intellectual life combined. It is impossible to visit any such locality and not learn something in consequence of the visit. We find that all the planets that we have been made in any degree conversant with, possess essentially, and to a great extent objectively, the same life as the earth. The atoms are aggregated differently, to be sure, but the essence of the atoms is precisely the same, and the same general law seems to govern them. The products of those planets that seem to be unfolded in nearly the same plane of the earth, are nearly the same as those of the earth. There is, to be sure, a difference; but it is in the external more than the internal. The great power that governs this earth governs all other planets, and they all are subservient to this law; therefore the method of unfoldment must be similar.

By Theodore Parker, Nov. 7, 1867.

Q. Why is it that Spiritualists speak so disrespectfully of religion, and so malignantly towards any one that has done any harm, if he belonged to a church? Does belonging to a church make the person any worse?

A. There are many persons who claim to be Spiritualists who are only such in outward expression, while the inward life of Spiritualism they know nothing about. Spiritualism teaches large charity, and it also teaches you to be just. It does not teach you to array the peculiar condition of any individual before the world, that the world may censure and finally condemn. No, Spiritualism does no such thing. Spiritualism points you to yourself, and bids you to be exceedingly watchful over yourself, guarding your every act, and rendering all acceptable to even the highest angels in the sphere beyond time. Spiritualism does not propose to wage war against the churches, or against the members composing the churches, but it does propose to wage war against the darkness within the churches — that which belongs particularly to the churches, not the outside acts of individual members. Spiritualism does not tell you to blame the church because one of its members commits murder or any other crime. No, it advises to no such course. Now your querist asks why Spiritualists do thus and so? Well, they do so because they are ignorant of the better way — spiritually ignorant. They do not see that in this course they are following directly in the wake of theological darkness and bigotry. They fail to see that they are enacting over and over again what they condemn in others. If they did see it, they would be ashamed for themselves. They would turn from the course, knowing it was not the better way. Spiritualists, — those even who have only the outside of Spiritualism, who know nothing of its inner life, even that class who only make a profession of belief in the return of dead men, women, and children, — should be exceedingly careful how they send out words and thoughts that are so exceedingly bitter against any one, whether in or out of the church. For their opponents, north and south, east and west, are watching them, trying to determine concerning Spiritualism by the fruits those Spiritualists bear. If they bear slander, what sort of notion can your opponents have concerning you or the glorious cause you represent? If their fruits are bitter, who can be nourished by them?

No, no, ye Spiritualists! even ye who float only on the surface, beware! for this great cause that is, so far as its expression on earth is concerned, dependent on you for its growth, beware, I say, how you cause it to blush for you. The time may come when Spiritualism will receive a sifting; when all such as are not Spiritualists at heart, as well as at head, will be set aside; and by whom? Why, by the God of their own natures; for they will be ashamed of their course, because they will see it in its deformity, and they will set themselves aside, waiting till they shall be more worthy to enter the ranks of pure and undefiled Spiritualism.

We will answer a question in brief, which has been presented us from one of the liberal minds of the age, — liberal, in certain directions, in politics, in religion — Spiritualism excepted, — for he tells us at the outset that he has not made up his mind as to whether or not Spiritualism is true; he hopes it is true, thinks it is a glorious religion, hopes it may soon become exceedingly popular; and he might have added, When it does, I will openly embrace it. And then he asks what is our opinion, — ours, the presiding spirits at the Banner of Light rooms, — with regard to universal suffrage. "Tell us," he says, "ye who profess to be spirits that have once lived in forms of flesh, whether you believe it is right for women to vote; whether you believe it is right for them to stand side by side, politically, morally, socially, and intellectually, with man. I am but one of many, therefore can only answer for myself as a distinct individuality. I claim to be responsible for all that I utter, and for nothing more. Is it right for women to vote? Is it best? Do you think they are capable of voting, and doing justice to themselves and their country?"

These were questions that passed through his mind, but found no external utterance. Our answer may be given in a very few words. If woman is capable of being a mother to those who make the laws of nations; if she is capable of training the young mind up to mature age, and shaping its physical, social, and intellectual destiny, surely she is capable of taking a part in politics. In very many instances she is man's intellectual superior, and I know that, when taken as a whole, she is in no way his inferior. It is only the superstition of past ages that has placed her upon a level below man. God never placed her there. Then has man the right to? Certainly not. And the same power that hath said, with regard to the black man, "Let my people go," says the same with regard to woman. Give her her freedom, in its largest and divinest sense. First, the religion in woman is opposed to war. She intuitively feels that peace is better than war. Woman, by nature, is better fitted to receive impressions from the higher and diviner life. Hence it is surely very possible that she may be so guarded and guided by that life, that she will make no mistake, even in casting her vote. Yes, as an individual, I am in favor of universal suffrage. I am in favor of bursting every kind of bonds. I am in favor of lifting the race higher, and still higher.

But the great rushing tide of human progress is settling this question for you. I need not come to discuss it; whether I come or not, it will be discussed and settled. The same great power that determines concerning all things, also will determine concerning this; and since the dams that superstition has built against this great flood-tide of human progress are being swept away need we fear for the result? I certainly do not for one. I know that, as the race is bound to rise in all things, it will rise in this. And I know also that as the great congress of spirits are exerting now a wide-spread and deep-seated power on the earth, they will not overlook this most momentous question.

By Bishop Fitzpatrick, of Boston, Nov. 11, 1867.

Q. We are told that Christ was of poor parentage. He, of course, had no opportunities for education. Yet he was able to confound the greatest Jewish doctors of his day. How do you account for this, if he was not divinely inspired?

A. By the action of a natural law upon the physical body. I account for it as I would account for the same manifestation elsewhere. We are told, upon the very best of authority, that the lady subject — the medium through whom I am at present speaking to you — at seven years of age held converse with men and women who were versed in the sciences of the times, and utterly confounded them with her wisdom. It was said to be some strange mystery; the brain was affected; but how, they did not see. At all events, a far greater amount of wisdom was given through her when under the inspiration of her guardian spirits, or entranced by them, than she could by any possibility have attained during her seven years of earth-life. Now you pass by these things that are taking place in your day; you go back eighteen hundred years, to search for what was done through the man Jesus. You seek to worship the glory of the past, overlooking entirely the glory of the present. I do not censure any one who cannot understand the glory of this great truth, which has burst upon the world in such refulgence. I do not blame those who sit in the shadow; I sat there, but a few months ago, myself. But I do most earnestly pray, that the sun may soon shine, and the darkness of the past, that has forced its way into the present, may soon be forced out by the glory of the present hour. This is my prayer; and, as I have faith in God, I believe it will be answered.

By Thomas Paine, Nov. 12, 1867.

Q. Can we, after the spirit has left the body, appreciate and enjoy the beauties of nature and art with the same facility that we do now? And if so, then please say, Can you, as individual spirits, in and of yourself, independently of any extraneous aid from any other source, — a medium, for instance, — take full and complete cognizance of any and all the beautiful scenes you were accustomed to frequent and admire while you were on earth?

A. The soul is so constituted that it is able to take cognizance of whatever it is attracted unto under all circumstances. But, of necessity, there are a great variety of degrees. For instance, if when I was on earth observing through human senses the glory of a certain landscape, and having the power to remember that in my spiritual state, and the desire also to behold it again, I could not, without the aid of earthly senses, be able to take cognizance of the earthly part of the glorious picture; but I should be able to take cognizance of the more real, the more substantial, the more glorious part, which was the spirit. You have been taught by those who have returned, giving their views, their experience in the spirit-world, that every material form has its inner life, its spiritual life, its divine representation; and that that inner, that spiritual, that divine, corresponds to the external. God, I believe, would be very partial, exceedingly unjust, if he were to clothe the earth with so much grandeur and beauty, and deny the same blessing to the heavens. I have more faith in his wisdom. I believe his love extends beyond the boundaries of earth; ay, more, I know it. Therefore, all that finds expression on the earth in natural form, finds expression also in the spirit-land in spiritual form, which corresponds to the external, the natural.

By Thomas Paine, Nov. 14, 1867.

Q. I saw in the "Banner of Light," of September 14, an answer to the question pertaining to an intermediate state. The answer was, "I do not believe you will ever reach that condition of perfection, in the absolute, that so many souls are so earnestly seeking for. There will always be a haven of rest in the future — a something better than that you have reached." Now, I should like to ask, what process the soul, or spirit, has to undergo in making these several changes? and if the changes are as absolute and great as the change from the natural, or earth-life, to the spiritual, or invisible life, as it is sometimes termed? and if so, does it teach the immortality of the soul?

A. There are an infinite number, I believe, of very marked changes to be passed through in the spirit-life, similar to the chemical change which has been termed death. The speaker, on the occasion referred to, answered the query for himself, and for himself alone; but there are thousands and tens of thousands of spirits who have laid aside the notion of ever being able to reach a point of perfection, or even of rest, from which there is no appeal. Indeed, all those spirits with whom your speaker has had the privilege of coming into mental relations, who have made the science of life a deep and soul study, have come to this determination. They believe in the eternal progress of the soul, and, believing this, they cannot see or realize any time or state of being wherein the soul can say to itself, "I shall go no farther; I am content;" but, on the contrary, the soul can only be happy by virtue of its own internal and external being — by constantly reaching out for something better than it has already found. Yes, good friend, you will find that, as a spirit disembodied, you will constantly be called upon to pass through changes distinct and marked, and changes that you will not in the external realize.

By William E. Channing, Nov. 19, 1867.

Q. I saw in the "Banner," a few weeks since, this question: "What are the functions of the spleen?" Now, I would ask still further, what effect does a diseased spleen have upon the physical system generally?

A. Medical men, who have made that branch of medical science a study, tell us that the spleen may be called the magnetic stomach, the organ that receives all the magnetic force that is necessary to assist in running the machine, the body, from outside conditions. It receives them, and by certain processes adapts them to the use of the body. They tell us, further, that a diseased spleen produces most disastrous effects throughout the entire body, because it vitiates the entire magnetic currents, and as it is upon them that all the other organs are dependent for natural vital connections, if that is not what it should be, the connection of all the organs is correspondingly imperfect. This being true, it is of the utmost importance to life that the spleen be in good order.

Q. What connection is there between the phenomena, or prodigies of modern Spiritualism, and the truths of religion and Christianity?

A. Modern Spiritualism is a natural, well-established truth. That truth which runs through Christianity is the same. They are all referable to the science of life; these and all other spiritual phenomena, of whatever class or kind, are all referable to the science of life. All may be resolved back to life.

Q. Are not the words of a wise, honest, and good man, speaking from the fulness of a good and generous heart, superior to anything ever uttered by a medium, and far more trustworthy?

A. No. Why should they be? If both are uttered from wise, good, honest stand-points, why should you exclude the moral validity of the one while you embrace the other? Truth is truth, from whatever source it comes, or through whatever channel it is given. Ignorance is ignorance; wisdom is wisdom. I have seen just as great an exhibition of wisdom from the lips of childhood as I ever did from mature age. Sometimes the wisdom of a Solon may pale before the wisdom of childhood.

Q. What is the practical utility, either morally or religiously, arising from such communications as were revealed at the last two circles?

A. To *some* souls they demonstrate life after death.

This is of more importance than everything else combined. Christianity has never demonstrated the immortality of the soul. Modern Spiritualism has done it: therefore it stands, in that respect, pre-eminently above Christianity. I mean that Christianity that is floating throughout the length and breadth of the land in the present day. I do not mean that pure and undefiled Christ-spirit that is so entirely covered up with external observances and ceremonies that are called Christianity. I mean the *life* of all those vague ceremonies, which is entirely obscured by the external. I have faith that by and by this internal life, this pure principle of truth that has run through every religion, will finally work itself to the surface, will finally so clear itself from the clouds, from the superstition and darkness that surround it, as to be made apparent to the soul that seeks for pure, undefiled Christianity. The Christ-spirit teaches universal love. Do we find it with those who profess Christianity? No, we do not. On the contrary, they are very far removed from it. Christ taught his followers to love one another; the sacred law of love he sought to enforce upon all his followers. He constantly preached of love. It was the guiding star that led him on to glory. But, O, where shall we find it among the churches who have taken his name to-day. We look for it in vain.

By John Pierpont, Nov. 21, 1867.

Q. Is it true that thought takes form with spirits? In other words, if a spirit thinks, say, of a landscape, does that thought body forth to the spiritual sight a tangible presentation of the thing thought of?

A. No; I do not so understand it. I believe that thought, in concert with action, can produce many, and,

I may say, all the scenes of art. But I have no evidence that, by thinking of a beautiful flower, a beautiful landscape, or a beautiful face, in the spirit-land or anywhere else, that that beautiful landscape, or flower, or face will be projected into existence simply because I have thought of it, or desire that it might come to me. The earth and the spirit-land are filled with all that is essential to the soul's happiness. All the essential aids to spiritual progress are placed in the spirit-land and in earth-life, or wherever the spirit, as a spirit, can go. Now, as spirit is possessed of a very large degree, to say the least, of freedom when it casts off the mortal body, it is very reasonable to suppose, that if I think of a beautiful landscape, place, or thing, in my external life, I might commence action to reach that. I know in my soul-life that it exists in tangible reality somewhere, and I seek it out. If my desire is strong enough, I do not stop till I reach it — till the object is gained, and I am thereby satisfied. In this sense, and, I believe, in this sense only, does thought produce external objects, or bring them to us.

Q. If thought does not take form with the spirit, then is it true that the objectivities of the spirit-world appear fixed and permanent, as with us on earth? For instance, three persons, with us, look at the objects in a room, and we all see the same things. Is the correspondence of this true with spirits?

A. Yes, certainly. No two persons see or understand a thing exactly alike. You should remember that; and where you have that faculty of perception very poorly developed here, the spirit, in its enfranchised condition, has it very largely developed. For instance, I may say that is a very poor painting — a perfect daub. Somebody else may say, "It is perfectly beautiful; it is food for my soul." These soul-feelings, for they belong to the soul here, belong to it, to a very large degree, in the spirit-world. They have the largest room for the exercise of that freedom which belongs to the spirit after it has cast off the body; therefore, if I detest the picture here, and see no beauty in it, that feeling will be intensified in the spirit-world; consequently, two spirits returning from the same spiritual locality, will give you entirely different accounts of that locality. One will say it is beautiful, another that it is a barren waste. The capacity to understand is within, the variety is without; but the capacity to enjoy the variety is from within. So you see no two individuals can understand anything — not even any one thought — exactly alike. There will be a difference of opinion, because there is a difference in the internal constitution of the individual; for it is by the internal that the external is measured.

Q. Why do not the spirit-friends of those who may be present at a séance in the circle-room manifest, instead of those who have no personal friends present?

A. It is not thought best to allow such manifestation. First, because it would prove a great draft upon the medium — too great. Secondly, because the public, the sceptical public, would say, "O, it comes from the audience. The larger portion of those who manifest have friends in the audience. It is but the reflection of their mind." So it has been determined that the instances of spirit-manifestations to those who have friends in the audience shall be very few, — indeed, all will be debarred from coming, except such as can do so upon an entirely Platonic plane. If you could stand behind the scenes and watch all the *modus operandi* of this thing, you would not wonder that the guardians of these séances have considered it best to take such a course. And again, those who manifest are generally — the majority, at all events — those who cannot reach their friends by any other process; their friends are sceptical, and will not meet them at any other place where they can speak, and this is the only place from which they can give publicity to their manifestations and reach their friends.

By William E. Channing, Nov. 25, 1867.

Q. I understand from the controling spirit, that there is no forgiveness for sin; that an inevitable penalty follows every transgression of any law of our being. What becomes of the penalty when pains are removed and diseases healed?

A. Returning spirits always inform you — such as have been informed themselves upon this point — that there is no forgiveness for sins. Every sin begets its own judge, and the judge begets the punishment therefor. The three are so closely allied you cannot separate them. When you commit a sin against your physical nature, suffering is the consequence. When you commit a sin against your spiritual nature, spiritual suffering is the consequence — you produce punishment; a state of inharmony; and, as the spirit lives in heaven only by living in harmony, when it lives in the opposite it lives in hell, whether on the earth, under the earth, or in the skies. When it is in an inharmonious condition it is in hell. There are many degrees of inharmony, as of harmony. There are many degrees of heaven, as of hell. The child suffers a certain degree of hell by unconsciously outraging the laws of its physical being. The law does not excuse the little one because it does not understand the law. It acts precisely the same with the child as with the adult. It is no respecter of persons or of ages. The little one falls beneath its stroke as mature or old age falls beneath its stroke. It never fails to visit justice and judgment upon all who place themselves in antagonism to it. Your correspondent asks how it is in the case of cures performed by certain healing agents upon the earth. There is an end unto all conditions of existence. Conditions are changeable; they end that they may give place to others. Disease, inharmony, are but the conditions of life, subject to change. When the punishment has been severe enough the change comes. When the suffering one has suffered to an extent sufficient to induce him or her to seek the proper remedy, then there is a time to change. The spirit has received chastisement sufficient for the time, therefore salvation steps in in consequence of the exercise of reason. Now, when the criminal descends lower and still lower in crime, when his spirit has been deluged again and again with that which follows crime, — that mental suffering, that unrest, that dissatisfaction, — when, I say, it has been deluged again and again, by and by it begins to reason. The God without says to the God within, "Come, now, and let us reason together!" and the result is, the man or woman begins to feel that there is a better way, and that that way is for them as for others. They begin to seek to know of that way, to understand it, to walk in it, to pass out of the darkness of the present and enter the light of the future, and then begins a newer existence; then the fogs and mists and inharmonies that are the result of crime begin to pass away, and the soul begins to be resurrected from it. Is it by a direct interposition of the Great All-Father without in the universe? It may be; but we believe that the spirit rests, progresses, and leaves the world by virtue of that glorious germ of progression that the Infinite has implanted within it. The germ cannot always remain in darkness. It will eventually find its way to the light, and eventually disperse the shadows.

Q. I understand that the controling spirit has stated that sometimes people can be cleansed from immoralities in a somewhat corresponding manner as diseases are cured. How can such things be, without forgiveness?

A. Forgiveness is a term which your correspondent seems to have defined according to his own understanding. To us forgiveness is a something which avails without suffering. For instance, I place my hand in the fire. The fire does not burn. Forgiveness steps in between the action on my part and the action of the law. The fire does not burn. That is my idea of what forgiveness is. Now if I place my hand in the fire, and the fire burns, and I make use of the usual remedies to stay the progress of the burn, does it follow that I have been forgiven because the fire did not burn my hand up entirely? Surely not. You will learn, every one of you, sooner or later, that there is no forgiveness of sin, either in this world or the next. So sure as you place yourself in antagonism to the law, so sure it will smite you. There is no forgiveness. If you sin against the law of your own reason, there is no forgiveness therefor till you have paid the uttermost farthing for your wrong doing.

Q. Do clairvoyants and mediums retain and exercise the same or a corresponding power in the spirit-world as they have here?

A. They do, only the power is largely increased by the change.

Q. I desire to know if the following speculations, extracted from Sawyer's "Mental Philosophy," published in 1839, are true? "When divested of the organs of sense at death, the mind is thrown back upon the hands of God, to be provided with such other capacities as he sees fit to bestow. Its introduction to the other state, at death, will doubtless be analogous to its introduction to the present state at birth, so far as the bestowment of new capacities and powers is concerned. The powers and capacities requisite for the life to come will, no doubt, in like manner be conferred at death — the period of our being born into another world. Death divests us entirely of all the organs of sense, and, consequently, of all capacity for experiencing sensation of any kind. Our birth into another world will probably invest us with other capacities of a similar but higher nature."

A. The ground taken there is substantially correct. The spirit receives, at its second birth, new capacities. It casts off all that it has no further use for, and receives what it can use in the spirit-world. The change is distinct; so much so, that could you discern the spirit, in its true, spiritual state after death, you would be led to exclaim, "O God, how great the change!" And yet the change is so simple that a little child instinctively understands it. When a child is born into this mundane sphere, its first effort is to inhale the atmosphere. Nature acts in conjunction with the wisdom of the Great Infinite who rules in nature. The child breathes here because there is a necessity for it. One born into the spirit-land breathes in a different way, because there is need of a different way. There are other attributes added to the soul in the spirit-world than those it possesses here, because it finds it will need them in the higher life. As it advances, it receives more and still more. It passes out of the old; it instinctively embraces the new; and so on throughout all eternity. I believe it will be ever changing in the external, but in the internal remaining forever and forever the same.

Q. Does the controlling intelligence believe that there is any intelligent, eternal disorganized spirit distinct from man?

A. I believe that without the agency of matter in some state spirit could not express itself; therefore, I believe that spirit and matter will ever be so thoroughly wedded together that they will never be separated. If spirit is dependent upon matter for expression, matter then is of as great a necessity as spirit. Spirit passes through the realm of matter, changing its forms, and carrying it from one state to another, higher and still higher in the scale, but at the same time it progresses in its external characteristics in correspondence with the progression of matter. I believe there is an eternal, ever-existent ocean of spirit, but I believe that that ocean of spirit is dependent upon matter for expression. I believe that the two are inseparably connected together. I believe that although you may soar to the highest spheres that we have any knowledge of in spirit-life, even there you will find matter.

Q. Does not this go to prove that matter is self-created? If spirit is dependent upon matter, cannot act in the absence of matter, is not matter self-created?

A. When considered from one stand-point, it would seem so; but when considered from another, it would seem quite different. Remove spirit from matter, and it becomes inert. Connect spirit with matter, and it becomes full of life. Now may we not say, and truthfully, too, that matter is self-creating only by the agency of spirit? As absolute matter it is not self-creating, but when joined to spirit it is.

Q. Will the time ever come when this earth will lose its material body, and become exclusively the abode of spiritual intelligences?

A. The time will certainly come when it will lose the material body that belongs to it at the present time. This is a self-evident truth. It is exhibited everywhere in life. But we have no special evidence that the earth will ever become, as an earth, the special dwelling-place of disembodied spirits. It may be so. We do not know that it will not. But we have no special evidence that it will be so. It is even now the dwelling-place of millions of disembodied spirits. They walk the air, both when you wake and when you sleep. Therefore to them it is a spirit home. It belongs to them just as much as it does to you.

By Theodore Parker, Dec. 3, 1867.

Q. Will the intelligence explain this passage — Luke xxiv. 19: "Behold my hands and my feet, that it is I myself: handle me and see; for a spirit hath not flesh and bones, as ye see me have." If it was a spirit-body, why did he say he had flesh and bones? and why did he eat?

A. Concerning this particular case, we have no positive knowledge, for that is born only of one's experience; but judging from analogy, we suppose that if Christ had passed through the change called death, and if he was, after passing through that change, a dweller within a sufficiently condensed body as to be able to meet the senses of humanity, we are to suppose that that body was formed of material particles, and these were drawn from mediumistic bodies and the atmosphere. The same has been done in your day, is being done all over the land, and it is vain for the sceptic to cry out, "I do not believe it" — vain, so far as staying the light is concerned, for it will continue to roll on till all the darkness is dispersed. I suppose this body that the disciples handled, this body that he was said to have, was composed of flesh, and blood, and bones; was a material body, formed for the occasion, as I have before said, out of the atmosphere, and some mediumistic body or bodies. I do not believe in the resurrection of the body of Jesus after death — the material, natural body. Science gives that theory the lie. It is in no sense true. We are told that everything is possible with God; but we know that God acts by eternal, immutable law, and we know he never tramples upon that law. It is always the same. Now, then, if Jesus had passed through the change called death, there was an entire and distinct separation between himself spiritual and himself natural. Therefore, if he had such a body as could be handled, recognized by humanity, it was a body formed for the occasion.

Mr. White. Do you not suppose his disciples were very strongly mediumistic, as well as himself?

A. I believe they were. In fact, I have very strong evidence towards knowledge, in that matter.

Mr. White. Would not their being in harmony so long on the earth give him greater power to make a body to show to them?

A. Yes; and in all probability if the harmony between the disciples had not been broken by the unfaithfulness of one of their number, Jesus would never have been crucified. You would never have had a Calvary in the Christian religion; you would never have had a Saviour in Jesus of Nazareth. But one was unfaithful, and betrayed his Master, and what followed you all know; or, at least, you know what the record tells you. By and by you will learn much more concerning that.

Q. The progress and happiness of society in the world, in all ages, have been impeded and marred by bad men, — monsters, I would say, — from the unprincipled politicians in our midst to kings, emperors, popes, &c. Now, I desire to know if those frauds on mankind still hold their influence in the spiritual world?

A. To a certain extent they do. You should consider that all that this life has produced, all that belongs to it, either natural or spiritual, is in the imperfect state consequent upon the imperfect state of the earth. It has not yet arrived at that point of perfection by which it can sustain good men entire, or good women entire. There are poisonous plants everywhere upon the surface of the earth, and there are poisonous theories everywhere. There is spiritual poison, as there is material poison; and both, I believe, are legitimate children of this planet, the earth. Now, then, as the earth grows, becomes more perfect, more spiritually unfolded, and more naturally unfolded, it will give you a higher type, not only in the vegetable, mineral, and animal, but in the spiritual. But all these things come by slow degrees. The world was not made in six days by any means. Man was not created in the twinkling of an eye, but thousands upon thousands, ay, millions upon millions of years rolled away ere thought was born. Now you have just as good a class of men and women upon the earth as the earth can take care of. Be satisfied; work on, as the earth works on. The earth does not complain. It performs its mission, and I am very much inclined to think you will all perform yours, whether you desire to or not.

Q. Will not this world receive, ere long, some astounding intelligence from the spiritual world? Will not the gates of the spiritual world be opened, so that we shall have a flood of light that shall sweep away darkness, superstition, priests, popes, &c., in one general ruin?

A. That very thing is being done as fast as there is any necessity for its being done. You are receiving to-day all the light you can bear, all you are ready for. The spirit-world has, indeed, a great ocean of light, in the shape of truths that are new to you, to bestow upon you when you are ready to receive them. Milk for babes, meat for mature age.

Q. Would it not be better for Spiritualists to organize — I mean, the Spiritualists of this world and the spiritual — on some grand or universal platform? Such a thing could be done without being sectarian.

A. Yes, it would be better, in my opinion; and in my opinion it will be done.

Q. Is there not organized, in the spirit-world, a congress to control and direct the great spiritual movements in the earth-life?

A. There is such a group of spirits as your correspondent refers to, but they do not control the affairs of earth-life, — not by any means. They only exert as much influence over those affairs as they are able to, by and through the instruments that they find on the earth. Sometimes, although they may desire to influence largely in certain directions, they may be prohibited from doing so, because of the want of some instrument through whom to manifest. Sometimes the atmosphere is against them, sometimes the soil. Different localities produce different thoughts, as well as different material influences.

By Theodore Parker, Dec. 5, 1867.

Q. Does not modern Spiritualism make larger drafts upon credulity than paganism or Christianity?

A. Hardly, hardly. It is a very large draft upon credulity to believe the fable of Jonah and the whale — very large indeed. It is also a very large draft upon credulity to believe that a woman could conceive and bear a child by being overshadowed by the Holy Ghost; it is altogether out of the course of nature; and whoever believe it stretch their credulity to the very last extent. Spiritualism comes in plain attire. A little child can read it. If the mother comes to the little child, the little child knows the mother. You cannot deceive the child. And so it is with pure, simple, God-spiritualism. There is no superstition in it, and the credulity of a child need not be taxed.

Q. Is not the resurrection of Jesus Christ as well authenticated, and by the same witnesses that confirm his death?

A. No; absolutely, no. We know, by nature, that if he ever lived, he died. We know also, by nature, that if he ever died to the body, the body never was resurrected again. Nature never lies — always tells the truth. You cannot force nature into a lie. You may seem to, but it is only in seeming.

Q. The spirit of criticism is a questioning spirit. Is there anything wrong in this, *per se?*

A. Certainly not. On the contrary, something gloriously right. Honest, earnest criticism should always receive attention. It is one of the great levers, I believe, through which man marches up through the various sciences of life. Criticism ofttimes informs us of our mistakes, for it causes us to look deeper into self, deeper into our surroundings. It causes us to turn critics upon self, and therefore it is of the greatest possible service to us. Why, the world would be good for nothing without criticism. When I was here on earth, I was never satisfied when the voice of criticism was silent towards me. I always felt that my effort had been so small that it was not worthy of criticism. But when it was most severely criticised, I felt that I had agitated the waters, out of which some good would come.

By Theodore Parker, Dec. 9, 1867.

Q. In controlling this medium, do you possess the body, as the spirit of the medium possesses it in her normal condition?

A. No; that is not necessary. I surround the body. I obsess it as the musical performer obsesses the musical instrument. The instrument gives forth no sound unless the musician is there, and playing upon the instrument. So with regard to this control. I surround the subject, and in surrounding her, I create an atmosphere peculiar to myself, which is in nearly all respects unlike her own. Therefore, she finding it not at all in natural harmony with her, generally retires, goes forth into the outer spirit-world, and becomes cognizant of scenes in that world. Sometimes it becomes necessary to become thoroughly absorbed in the body. Then the mental atmosphere is created within, and not without. I act then from within. But in this case I act as the musician would act upon the instrument. I surround the entire body. It is under my perfect control.

Q. Then if the spirit of the medium does leave the body entirely, how long a time elapses that the body is devoid of spirit?

A. It may be devoid of intelligence, or conscious existence, for a second, hardly more. All things are so nicely arranged that there will be no intermediate time, or scarcely any; perhaps like the passing of a breath, but nothing more. I want you to distinctly understand that the animal life that is in activity belongs entirely to the animal form. That is distinct from intelligence. All the animal functions may be performed perfectly and harmoniously when there is no intelligence. Of that you are well aware. But I am speaking now with regard to the amount of time that will pass by the spirit here in unconsciousness. I say it may be like a passing breath, but a second of time.

Q. Then could you not, if you chose, retain control of this body, and thus prevent the spirit of the medium from returning to it?

A. I certainly could.

Q. Have spirits a fixed size? Does each spirit have its own peculiar form of organization, or are they all alike?

A. Every spirit possesses its own peculiar form of organization, its own peculiar stature. They are *not* all alike. You find here the child and the mature form. You find the tall man and the short man; all the different characteristics of form as well as of mind.

Q. How would the spirit of a tall man possess the form of a little child?

A. Generally by acting upon it by surrounding it as I do to-day surround this medium, or perhaps by influencing one or two organs. It is not always necessary to influence the entire organic system. I generally do, but it is not always a necessity.

Q. Then can a large person take control of the body of a small medium?

A. I did not intend you to so understand me. If a little child is sufficiently mediumistic to admit of my control, I can control the child as I can the adult, only I cannot give the same amount of intelligence through the child, because the organs are not fully grown. You cannot play the same tune, or rather you cannot give the same amount of power through the flute as through the organ, yet both are music. You may play "Home, sweet home" upon both, but there is a difference in capacity.

By Rev. Joseph Lowenthall, Dec. 10, 1867.

Q. What is the history of the institution of the Sabbath? How should it be passed, irrespective of sectarian prejudice?

A. During my earthly life I believed in the religious observance of the Jewish Sabbath. It was a part, and a very great part of my religion. But since I have ascended from earth to the spirit-land, I have learned that God has sanctified and made holy all days, and that he requires absolute service and divine worship at the hands and hearts of all his children every day in the week. I have evidence which causes me to believe that the observance of the Sabbath, both Jewish and Christian, originated with those heathen worshippers whose religious history dates very far back in the past. It belongs to those who look to the heavens, and behold there the only true representation of Deity; and finding the only true representation of Deity, — that is, to their conception, — in the heavens, they worship their Deity in all sincerity and truth, in accordance with their belief. So, according to my belief, the Jews and the Gentiles have received these Sabbath ordinances from those whom both Jews and Gentiles denounce as heathen and idolaters. You have much to learn concerning worship, and it may be that idol after idol will be dashed to the ground by the unerring hand of truth, in your case as they have been in mine.

Q. What is the distance of the second sphere from the earth?

A. The second sphere, so called, is the sphere of mind — that can act independently of flesh and blood and bones. It is the sphere where the mind can exhibit a larger degree of power than while attached to mortality, and that second sphere is by no means any particular locality. It may be here in your midst, and it may be ten thousand miles away. Some theorists have determined that the second sphere is a belt, which is about sixty miles beyond the earth's atmosphere. They tell us that it measures so and so. They tell us what its atmosphere is; but for my own part I have no evidence that the second sphere exists there any more than here. The mind becomes to a larger extent free after death, and in its second sphere of action it may take up its abode sixty miles from the atmosphere of the earth and still be in the second sphere, or it may dwell here among its kindred on earth, and still be in the second sphere. Special localities belong more to the things of time or material life than to spiritual life. You will all learn this when you pass out of the mortal, and become more free in the spirit.

By Theodore Parker, Dec. 12, 1867.

Q. It was recently declared, at a public meeting, that Theodore Parker, when in earth-life, was an opponent of the Spiritual Philosophy, whereas his writings are strongly tinctured therewith. What is the truth in the matter?

A. Theodore Parker, in the external, opposed modern Spiritualism, but in the internal he did not oppose it. There was a something within me which said, in plain, unmistakable terms, "There is a great truth in modern Spiritualism," but I could not accept the external manifestations. I saw so much of chaff mixed up with what little good there really might have been, that I was not ready to accept any in my external reasoning. Nevertheless, as I before remarked, in the internal I was a believer in Spiritualism, ancient and modern. Those who knew me best know that I often remarked that I believed there was a very great truth, a wondrous philosophy, underlying these crude manifestations. And I also believed that the world was not ready for such an exhibition of spirit-power. But I have learned many things since I passed beyond this human life. I have learned that God does not deal with his children according to their caprices. I have learned that nature and mind will march steadily on through the infinite law of progress, whether we will or no; and we may denouce the manifestations of mind and matter as much as we may, it is all the same. It will snow, whether we will it or not. The sun will shine, whether it scorches us or not; and so it is with regard to the manifestations of mind. Mind is free, and it will run on through the infinite law of progress just according to the law. We cannot change the law. We have not the slightest power over it. So these spiritual demonstrations I believe to be the result of law, infinite law, and that law does not only pertain to mind but to matter. It belongs to the growth of the earth as well as to the growth of mind. It is an exhibition of both mind and matter, and we can no more control it than we can control the sunlight. We may shut it out from our own reasoning powers for a time; but it will shine on all the same, and its power will be precisely the same, whether we close our senses to it or the contrary.

By Theodore Parker, Dec. 16, 1867.

Q. Can different individuals on earth be influenced by the same person or power in the spirit-land at one and the same time?

A. Yes; for instance, I can, through the power of psychology, psychologize any number of susceptible bodies at the same time. I can psychologize them upon one special point, or I can vary with them as I see fit.

Q. In the same way that the mesmerizer operates upon his subjects?

A. Precisely, only to a larger extent. A disembodied spirit has more power than one in the body: first, because they have a larger understanding of the laws controlling in the case; secondly, they are free from bodily diseases, and through the atmosphere and through the peculiar condition of the sensitive subject, can come in more direct and positive *rapport* with them than they could by any possibility do through the flesh.

Q. What constitutes a person a medium?

A. A medium is simply a body that is sensitive to the od forces in the universe — forces which you do not thoroughly understand; those that have not come within the sphere of human science; those with which human science has not yet dealt. A medium possesses a peculiar quality of magnetism and electricity. The nervous system is generally very finely attuned, and it is constantly receiving from the external world, and as constantly throwing out. There is a peculiar atmosphere, mental and physical, surrounding every well-developed medium, and whoso can enter that atmosphere becomes at once in *rapport* with the medium; and whoso cannot enter it, cannot, by any possibility, come into *rapport*, and are shut out as virtually as if there were a wall of fire between them. Mediums are, in other words, sensitive subjects, not only to the action of mind in the body, but to mind out of the body; and particularly sensitive to mind out of the body.

By Theodore Parker, Dec. 17, 1867.

Q. If the spirit of the mortal dwells outside of the body, why do not clairvoyants perceive the spirit, or double, of man before death as well as after.

A. Certain phases or degrees of clairvoyance have reached that point in science. Certain clairvoyants are able to perceive the spirit as well as the natural body.

Q. Do you mean to say the spirit is outside of the body?

A. No; I did not say so.

Q. That was the question.

A. A short time since I answered a question relative to spirit-control. I was questioned as to whether I entered the body of the medium, or whether I controlled by psychology. My answer was, that in my case, there was what I saw fit to term an overshadowing. I overshadow the subject, and act upon it instead of acting through it.

This is not always the case. The spirit that belongs by nature to the body, acts through it always; but the foreign spirit, who comes to use the body as a borrowed instrument, acts quite as often upon it as through it. You may call it psychology, or distinguish it by any other term you please; it is an acting upon the instrument, giving forth my ideas from the internal to the external. I overshadow and act upon the subject to those who may constitute my audience. The control is quite as perfect, sometimes more so; indeed, I think I am better able to control in this way than by absorption. I could control in that way, but I do not think I could do as well. Do not understand me to declare that all spirits act in the same way; for they certainly do not.

Q. Does the spirit of the medium still remain in the body, in the case of this overshadowing?

A. Sometimes; not generally. The spirit had generally rather retire, for there is an instinctive consciousness on the part of the indwelling spirit that there will be more or less jarring between my spirit and her own, and, in order to avoid that, she retires, taking that as the better course.

Q. It was said, at a late séance in this hall, that aged people require less sleep than the younger, because of a loss of magnetic force or life. Will the intelligence inform us whether there is any remedy for this loss, or any means by which an increased magnetic force can be had? If so, what is it? how and where is it to be found?

A. No; there is no remedy, except such as would go counter to nature. Nature has marked out her course for human life, and it is a very exact and wise course. As the body grows old, or becomes burdened by years, it parts with its magnetic life that it may the easier pass through death. Now, suppose it retained all its magnetic vitality to the last moment of its earthly life, what would be the result? Why, the most terrible struggle between the magnetic and electric forces; consequently a very hard death. See how wise and humane Nature is to make the body part gradually with its magnetic forces, that it may pass easily through the change called death. And in your ignorance you ask to retain it. It would be the greatest of curses if you could.

By Thomas Paine, Dec. 24, 1867.

Q. Is it positively essential to the welfare of any person whatever to return after birth to spirit-life, and reassociate, through mediumship or otherwise, with mundane life?

A. In some instances it is an essential to happiness in the spirit-world, and in others it is quite the reverse. Some find the path of duty leading directly to earth, others directly away from the earth and earthly conditions. The experience of one is not the experience of any other one. All souls progress according to their own inner capacities for progressing, and according to their own external and internal law. No soul can unfold itself in exactly the same way as any other soul, being constituted differently; yet the souls of all are essentially the same.

Q. Do the appetites, passions, propensities, — in a word, the character, in earth-life, of the individual, adhere to him when ushered into the spirit-realm, and render it unavoidable that he shall, through the mediumship of those yet in the body, perfect his character?

A. Precisely as death leaves you, so life in the spirit-world finds you. You are spiritually no different after death. You have only passed through a chemical change, which has affected the body and the spirit's relationship to the body, while the spirit itself remains precisely the same. The thief is still the thief, the liar is still the liar, the murderer is still the murderer, the drunkard is still the drunkard; yet all these lower stratas of mentality the spirit can and will outgrow — pass beyond. It is not always necessary that the spirit should return to earth to take its first lessons in spiritual progress. Sometimes it is, but not always.

By Father Henry Fitzjames, Dec. 30, 1867.

Q. Is intellectual force or power only a modification of physical force or power? Scientific men say that electricity, heat, motion, and light are only different expressions of one and the same force or thing. Now, the question I ask is, Are all expressions of force, both intellectual and physical, only modifications of the same power?

A. No; certainly not. You would not consider thought simply a result of electrical motion. If you do, you have mistaken its true character. There is a marked and distinct difference between intellectual and physical power.

Q. By the use of what instrumentalities can an individual most rapidly and permanently increase his intellectual activities and force? What special information can the controlling spirit give us on this very important matter?

A. Knowledge is power, and it can be gained only by earnest thought and earnest endeavor. If you desire intellectual power, you must seek to unfold yourself through all the capacities of your being. A harmonious or well-rounded unfoldment is certainly best. Nearly all our, or I should say *your*, great minds have been unfolded only in one direction,—perhaps two or three,—and this at the expense of all the others. Jesus possessed a very marked degree of harmonial development; all the capacities of his nature seemed to be rounded into use. He was conversant with the laws of Nature in the external world, with the laws of mind, and clairvoyantly went out into the spirit-realm. It is impossible to draw any lines by which the spirit, or mind, should be governed with regard to seeking knowledge. It should be sought from every source, and nowhere ignored. You should be willing to allow everything and every mind to be your teacher; and, in turn, you should be willing to teach all things and all minds. Seek to unfold all the latent energies of mind, and, in all directions, be harmonious in your actions, and seek for wisdom from God's eternal volume, that is open for all.

By Theodore Parker, Jan. 2, 1868.

Q. Is it well to disturb a medium in a circle, who is in a trance, quite unconscious and paralyzed, in order to wake her up? Would it not be best to wait for the same power to release her that placed her in that particular state?

A. Certainly. There is no power on earth, under certain conditions, that can arouse a medium from a thorough trance condition. It must be done by the same power that passed them into the state.

Q. Do the more progressed spiritual beings of our planet have the power to visit any of the other planets of our solar system? and have any of the spiritual entities of any of the other planets of our system been known to come within the spiritual realms of our planet? and, if so, has there ever been an interchange of ideas between such intelligences?

A. Yes; there are certain far-reaching minds that could no more be content to exist with the simple amount of knowledge that could be gathered from one planet, than they could be content to exist, if it were possible, within the confines of a nutshell. They desire to know all that it is possible for them to know; and finding that they have unlimited freedom in the spirit-world, they exercise it — they make use of it. It is not every soul that knows its powers. It matters not whether the soul be clothed with the flesh, or whether it have laid off the flesh, there are very few souls that fully realize the power that God has invested them with. The majority have no idea that they can go beyond the limits of this earth; therefore they never make the attempt. But there are those who tell us they have visited many of the planets besides earth, and have become quite conversant with their conditions.

By William E. Channing, Jan. 6, 1868.

Q. Is God a power or soul permeating the universe, or a self-existent being, having habitation and personality with inconceivable capacities of knowledge, wisdom, and happiness?

A. I have no belief in a personal God, except as I believe in God as being personified through every conceivable form. I believe God is a power permeating all mind and all matter, and forever and forever changing all according to his own divine life.

Q. Do the spheres exist as separate localities or one world, as the earth, presenting only a different aspect to different minds, soul-gravity and culture determining the society and scenery each one enjoys and earns?

A. The spheres spoken of by returning spirits are

not localities, by any means, but they are conditions of mind, states of being. The spirit-world proper has been derived from the spiritual emanations of this world, therefore it is like unto it, only superior to it.

Q. If spirits can or are to re-manifest in human form, can they choose as to that form, and to the extent of their past earth experience elect as to their hereditary and intellectual conditions?

A. The spirit-form changes according to the requirements of the indwelling spirit, and according to the powers and capacities of the indwelling spirit.

Q. What generally becomes of families in spirit-life after a few centuries? Do they clan and cling together as on earth, or separate and become absorbed in the great family of mankind, or spirit-kind?

A. Spirits are gathered together in groups, suiting their needs. Whatever kind of intellectual life I may be attracted to, there I shall gravitate; and what is true in my case, is true in the case of every soul. If there is no natural or spiritual attraction between persons composing earthly families, they will separate in the spirit-world.

By William E. Channing, Jan. 7, 1868.

Q. Will you give a scientific explanation and definition of insanity?

A. Medical men inform us that insanity is simply an unbalancing of the physical and spiritual forces. They inform us that the cause is seldom found in the physical organism alone, but it is found with the forces that play upon the organs. Therefore it is very hard to know exactly how to treat the different kinds of insanity. They tell us it is a very subtle disease, sometimes appearing to yield to remedial agents, and suddenly rising up again with more vigor than before. Medical men, in the spirit-world, not here, inform us that they are doing all it is possible for them to do towards enforcing their ideas of insanity upon the plastic brains of medical men on the earth. Those who are the most susceptible to spirit-influences will receive their ideas first. I believe that the foundation of their theory is here: Insanity, lying in the imponderable forces, should be treated not as you would treat organic disease, but as you would treat spiritual disease, or a disease running through the imponderable forces of the human body. Magnetism and electricity have been heretofore very little understood. They have been recognized as existences, but their wondrous uses have never been sought out. Now, medical men inform us that magnetism and electricity are the most powerful agents that can be used, if used understandingly, in all cases of insanity; but, inasmuch as medical men have so small an understanding concerning these forces, it would not be safe for them to seek to make use of them till they have learned something more of them. Magnetism and electricity stand as masters over humanity; but when humanity comes to know these agents, humanity will master them, bring out all their uses, and apply them to the needs of the suffering.

Q. Can those who know their ancestors have been insane, prevent the same defect from expressing itself in themselves by education and self-discipline?

A. Medical men tell us that it is almost impossible to prevent hereditary insanity; that is to say, unless you know just where to strike, you are very apt to strike in the wrong place. Now, as insanity, as I before remarked, is located upon and through the imponderable forces, it is a most subtle disease, and does not become apparent often until it suddenly bursts upon you in all its fury. Medical men tell us that the seeds of insanity are very frequently sown at conception. Then it is called hereditary. It is transmitted from the ancestors down through a direct magnetic and electric line. If you know that your ancestors have been thus afflicted, the only proper and sure course is, if you wish to stay its progress, to avoid marriage. Medical men tell us that when once the disturbances are in the imponderables of the body, you can very rarely affect them for good, except at the time when they have shown themselves the most violently; when they have reached a certain point, then you are able to affect them (if you know how to apply the agents), generally very successfully. But even if you know that you have the seeds of insanity implanted within your being, you can do nothing towards eradicating them till they have shown themselves outwardly. Now this seems rather hard; but those who seem to understand such things declare that it is absolutely true.

By Joseph Lowenthall, Jan. 21, 1868.

Q. During my experience of ten years as a healing medium, I have found many cases of disease induced by the close proximity of spirit-friends. And I believe a large amount of the physical suffering with which we meet is traceable in some way to this cause. I would ask if you can give us such an explanation as would help us to guard against such influences? Can we do anything, in conjunction with friends in the spirit-world, to prevent so frequent a recurrence of these cases.

A. The only sure method of prevention known to us is this. Make yourself acquainted with the influences by which you are attended, and, through reason, dispel the clouds. If they are injurious to your physical and spiritual well-being, if you reason with them, they will depart. Knowledge is the only safe way by which to reach and overcome all the ills of life. The various churches scattered throughout the land are perpetually sending forth their cry against modern spiritualism, but they know as little concerning modern spiritualism as the snail knows of the stars. Yet they are constantly sending forth their anathemas, expecting thereby to annihilate modern spiritualism. If they would be successful in their cause, they must first seek to understand it, and then they may have some guarantee for success. So it is with regard to all laws in life. You are compassed about by an innumerable cloud of witnesses, unseen attendants. Some there be who come for good, and some for what you call evil. Some come to gain for themselves; others come to give. Some come for the purpose of making themselves better — to find entrance to heaven. Others come expecting to wreak vengeance upon those who have done them ill upon the earth, or whom they fancy have ill-treated them. There are all classes of spirits who visit the earth. It is a great highway, and open to all. Now, then, it behooves you all, as spiritualists, as scientists, as moralists, as Christians, to seek to know concerning the powers by which you are surrounded. Then, if they produce injury to body or spirit, you will know how to repair it, and how to provide against it.

Q. Can you, or do you ever dart thoughts into the mind of man, and he at the time be unaware of it?

A. Certainly; that is a very common occurrence. Mind is constantly giving out of its thoughts, and as constantly receiving from some other mind; and as the disembodied spirit has more power than the spirit embodied, and can with greater facility fasten its thoughts upon some other brain, so, in that respect, they are superior to minds in the flesh, and can exercise a greater power over you than you can exercise over them.

Q. Is there any other judgment day beside the last day of a man's life here on earth?

A. Yes; every day of your lives is a judgment day. Every day which belongs to you as an individual, there is judgment passed concerning. All the acts of your lives are passed before the great judgment-seat, and each one determined upon. If they are evil, they bring their legitimate results. If they are good, they also bring their legitimate results. An evil tree cannot bring forth good fruit. Whatever you sow, that you will reap. There is no forgiveness for sins. You must pay the uttermost farthing for all the mistakes of life. You will by and by learn that it is well; for, did the great power in the universe suffer you to go without judgment when you make mistakes, you would hardly march on through the wondrous degrees of progress marked out for you as an intelligent spirit.

Q. Do we have the celestial body that is spoken of in the Bible as soon as we die?

A. You have it before you die. It is with you now. It forms an ethereal, mystic covering for the nervous system, and it passes out, or is expelled from the body, by the electrical forces. When the magnetic force has departed, it is the business of the electric force to expel this spirit-body; then you are born again.

By Rev. George Whitefield, Jan. 21, 1868.

Q. What *is* a proper, and what is an improper question?

A. All personal questions would be considered improper, at this place.

Q. Under what conditions are spirits able to move ponderable bodies, organic or inorganic, through the atmosphere?

A. Various conditions are necessary. First, it is necessary to bring the medium in spiritual or electrical *rapport* with the object you desire to move. Secondly, it is necessary to bring the will of the person who is the prime operator in the case in conjunction with the object to be moved, and with the medium. These three conditions, or parts of one, being perfect, any body, however ponderable, may be acted upon according to the capacity of the power that may be provided by the medium. Under some circumstances, a dry atmosphere is quite necessary; under others, a moist atmosphere seems to be better.

Q. It has been said by a certain author, that mediums are generally somewhat mistaken with reference to the personal presence of spirits at circles. He states that it is more the reflective than the real presence, like the shadow upon a placid lake. Is that correct?

A. Under some circumstances it is correct; under others, wholly incorrect. Sometimes the spirit is present, and holds absolute control, *in propria persona*, of the medium; at other times, the spirit may be thousands of miles away, and yet the medium may be under the control of that spirit.

Q. In the petition presented, as I understood, to the Divine Being, what is the nature of the repentance referred to?

A. It is a softened joy, which naturally follows the knowledge that we have been mistaken, and that we are now in the possession of truth.

Q. Does not repentance naturally imply that there is something to be repented of? something we have done wrong, that should be rectified?

A. So it would seem. Repentance may be called the avenging angel, who deals with us for all the mistakes that we may make in life.

Q. What is your opinion with regard to the nature of man? Is it a duality or a trinity? I have heard it said that we are three component parts — body, soul, and spirit.

A. I believe while you are on the earth you are three in one. You have the physical body, which is the outgrowth of earthly conditions, and you have the spiritual body, which is an outgrowth of your earthly body; and you have the divine life, which is the same yesterday, to-day, and forever.

Q. With reference to repentance, am I to understand that it is a punishment, and not an act on the part of the one who exercises repentance?

A. Some consider it in that light, but I believe it is a natural result which follows error. We are sorry that we have not seen the better way before, but at the same time we are glad that the light is now with us. This seems to me to be repentance. I have myself repented sorely and sincerely over the errors of my past earthly life; but at the same time I perceive a joy running through my repentance, which I believe to be the glorious light that has lifted me out of the darkness. I do not believe that repentance comes from the great and perfect Father of our spirit, in consequence of our fault itself; but I believe it follows our mistakes of necessity. If we infringe upon the laws that govern physical life, pain is the result, suffering is sure to follow. And so it is with regard to all spiritual things. All spiritual mistakes may be called, I believe, and justly too, infringements upon the spiritual law of our spiritual natures, and to the same extent we must suffer. We may call the suffering repentance, or by any other name.

Q. I observe that you call the suffering repentance. I would ask, What is the cause of that? What is the spiritual influence that operates upon our spirit to produce that sorrow and the subsequent joy?

A. I believe it to be the spiritual light which attends the consciousness of the soul who has attained a better state than the past. I do not know that it is shed from any particular source. I believe it is born of the divine life of our own natures.

Q. Are not sadness and suffering essential to the perfecting of the spirit under all circumstances?

A. I think so; just as much as the storms that sweep over the earth are necessary to the unfoldment of the earth.

Q. Can there be any growth without suffering?

A. I think not. If the most perfect beings that we have any record of were capable of such intense suffering as the record of their lives affirms, what have we the right to infer concerning suffering? Why, certainly, that it is a necessity. It may be called the key that unlocks the gates of heaven, and bids the spirit flee from past shadows.

Q. Will this suffering continue to the after life?

A. I have seen the keenest of all sorrow in the spirit-world. You have sorrow here on earth, but it is dull and stupid when contrasted with that of the spirit-world. O do not be mistaken with regard to your future life. Do not suppose that it is one continuous life of joy, for I tell you it is not. The suicide who seeks to escape the sorrows of earth, hoping to gain the joys of heaven, wakes from a mistaken dream, to find himself ofttimes in deeper sorrow than when on earth. The shadow that belonged to him while here has followed him to the spirit-land, and by natural and perfect law he must outlive it. When we know concerning sorrow, we know how to flee from it; but when it is a mystery to us, it lingers around us, and, like the shades of evening, refuses to depart till the morning light of knowledge streams in, and then, by natural necessity, it must depart.

By Theodore Parker, Jan. 30, 1868.

Q. What relation does Mesmerism bear to Spiritualism?

A. It bears a very intimate relation; so intimate, that you can scarcely tell where to divide the two. Mesmerism, or the mesmeric aura, may be called one of the most essential agents by and through which the disembodied or the embodied spirit acts upon any other spirit.

Q. A lecturer at Music Hall, Boston, a few Sundays ago, stated that a shower of fresh and various flowers fell upon his bed, on which he was lying, at midnight, in severe weather in midwinter, and that the stems of the flowers appeared as if *twisted* off, and not *cut*, and as if *torn* by a current of electricity, leading to the conclusion that they had been conveyed to him from a warmer climate, where they grew. It has hitherto been supposed by many that such and other productions were immediate formations, composed by spirit-power from the elements of our atmosphere. I would ask which process is the *true* one?

A. They are both true. Sometimes, under certain

conditions, those spirits who are conversant with the science of chemistry are able to form out of the atmosphere — your earthly atmosphere — flowers of different forms — their own spirit-forms. A great variety of flowers they are able to create out of the atmosphere. And sometimes we are told that the guardian spirits of mediums bring them flowers from your earthly gardens. They are sometimes twisted from the parent stem by the electricity that is thrown upon them by the spirits who desire to possess themselves of the flower. You should understand that there are many chemists in the spirit-world, and they take great delight in making chemical experiments with regard to all the things of this world. They never allow an opportunity to pass without doing something towards informing themselves with regard to the nature of the earth, and its relations to their spirit-home. They want to know how much power they can have over all things here, and how much, in turn, you can have over them; what they can do with the vegetable kingdom, the mineral kingdom, and the spiritual kingdom; what they can do with all things here that pertain to mind or matter. So their experiments are constantly going on.

Q. How do you explain the word "seer," as used by the ancients?

A. Seer is another term for clairvoyance, or the spiritual condition; a condition in which the spirit can enter the past and future, as well as the present.

Q. Did not these seers, being, as you say, "wiser than they knew," actually foretell events?

A. Perhaps so. At all events they were not styled prophets.

Q. Is anything impossible with God?

A. Certainly to me there is. The breaking of his own law would be an impossibility. He would destroy himself, and annihilate all the forms that are in being. I do not believe that God can step outside of himself. He must always live in his own being. To perform a miracle, according to my idea, he must step outside of himself; he must trample upon his own law; he must totally disregard all that which constitutes the law of life. No, I do not believe it is possible for God to create a world in six days, nor in six thousand years, nor in six hundred thousand years. No; to me there are many things impossible, even unto God.

By Thomas Starr King, Feb. 4, 1868.

Q. Is there a devil existing outside of the human mind?

A. The greatest, the most perfect devil that we ever knew, had an existence in the human mind — in that portion of it that is the result of human education. The devil, as a distinctive personality, is a thing of time, a something that has been wrought out through your defective educational system. You are here educated, religiously, morally, intellectually, and physically, and that portion which we call defective, which runs through the whole system entire, is that which has produced this personal devil. It has made his horns, and his hoofs, and all his various appendages, and it has called upon humanity to exercise a fear concerning him; but it is all the result of a false education. Those persons who have never been educated at all in such matters have no thought of a devil.

Q. Is not science one of the greatest and most important studies in the spirit-world?

A. It is the foundation of all true educational systems. It is the only true basis upon which intelligence can rely for information, whether here or there. All spirits, when they become divested of the mortal form, and have risen beyond the prejudices incident to human life; when they begin to desire to know more concerning themselves and their surroundings, at once start off, attended by science; and this attendant never forsakes them. They are never satisfied with any demonstration that is not truly scientific; that cannot be resolved to a clear point beyond dispute. And it would be far better for our religionists of earth, our moralists, and, indeed, far better for all classes of being, would they adopt a similar plan, and investigate therein by science. Let science be the basis of your religion, and worship at no shrine that is not a scientific shrine. When you do this, you will seldom have occasion to look back with regret over the many mistakes you have made.

By Theodore Parker, Feb. 6, 1868.

We have a few words to say with regard to these letters. (*The letters placed upon the table for answers by the invisibles.*) There seems to be, to some extent, a misunderstanding with regard to them. Persons who receive indefinite and vague answers cannot understand why they do not receive clear and satisfactory answers, as their neighbors perhaps may get.

The fault, in nine cases out of ten, lies with themselves. They, not understanding the laws governing in the case, fail to obey them, therefore they are disappointed in their answers. It should be understood that but a very short time, say a few seconds, can be devoted to any one letter, and for this reason: A certain amount of magnetic power is abstracted and used from the medium in the answering of the letters. Those who are in control know just how much can be taken without injury to the subject, and it must be divided according to the demands of each letter; some require more, some less. But if there is no power by which the letter can be answered, there certainly can be no answer. Now, in order to insure an answer which will be to any extent satisfactory, each letter should contain only one question, or two at most. And those questions should be of a character that can be answered by some one of the spirit-friends whom the writer may have in the world of souls. Many of the questions, we are sorry to say, are of a very frivolous character, pertaining more to the things of this world than to the things of the other; more to mundane circumstances than to the circumstances of the soul. For instance, Mr. B. asks, "Shall I marry Mrs. C.?" Now look at the absurdity of the thing. And *vice versa.* One man asks, "Shall I sell certain goods at such a price?" Another asks, "Will I be successful in such an undertaking?" Another, "Shall I go west?" Another, "Shall I go east?" And another, "Shall I receive a letter from such a friend at such a time?" All sorts of such questions are asked. Do you suppose the inhabitants of the spirit-world have nothing better to do than to return here as penny-posts in those matters about which you can better answer yourself than they can? In all matters of vital interest your friends will respond heartily, when they can come into *rapport* with the subject who is answering letters, and truthfully too. But where your question is of a vague, uncertain, lifeless character, the answer will of course be correspondingly so.

If you want good answers, write good questions.

Remember this. It is for your good that we speak. You want truth, and the highest, the best that can be given you. Then, in seeking for it, seek in the highest and best possible manner; for only through your own good efforts can good results be brought to you. Remember that you are of as great a necessity in this soul-communion as are those who stand out of your sight. You are at one end of the wire, they at the other. If you allow yours to drop, do not perform your part of the duty, how can you expect that they will be able to do theirs and yours also? You cannot do their part of the work, neither can they do yours. Now, understand us to say that all questions having a bearing upon your highest interests, asked in honesty, in sincerity, to gain wisdom, to get good or do good, will always be honestly, if not clearly, answered. Clearness will be in correspondence to the nearness and power of the spirit you have called upon to answer. If they can come within the immediate sphere, and control personally, then your answers can but be satisfactory; but sometimes they are answered by proxy. Those you call upon cannot come, perhaps, within even the outer circle, and many mediums may be used in transmitting their answer down to this mundane sphere. In some instances, again we tell you, they come into personal communication; then your answer is generally very clear. We hope we shall not be obliged to revert to this subject again. We want to do you all the good we can. We want to open the way for you just as fast as you are ready to walk in it. We want to lead you gently over the rough places of life. We ask, in turn, your love, your good wishes, not only to us, but to all by whom you are surrounded.

By Theodore Parker, Feb. 10, 1868.

Q. Are we subject to changes in spirit-life similar to death in the earth-life? If so, what is the length of a spirit's life up to that change?

A. The spirit is constantly passing through different changes, gradations of mind, as well as matter. There seems to be no special time appointed for any definite change to come to any spirit. These come in accordance with the needs of the spirit always.

Q. What is the law of classification in spirit-life? Is nationality the distinction, as on earth? In other words, are we distinguished as English, French, German, &c.?

A. The peculiar characteristics of the mortal dwelling-place of the spirit are carried by the spirit to the spirit-world, consequently the American is the American still, the Scotchman is the Scotchman still, the Negro is still the Negro, the Indian is still the Indian. To be sure there is a very great difference between American spiritual and American physical life, yet when resolved to characteristics, we find them almost identical. It will be very easy for you to detect one of your own nationality even after death.

Q. What is the language of spirit-life? Surely if spirits have vocal organs they must have language.

A. The language corresponds to the needs of the spirit. In the spirit-world sight is changed to perception. Language, to a very great extent, is bound to the law of perception. And yet it is a distinctive feature. There is sound in the spirit-world. It is not all silence, by no means. There is form. Forms change. There is a great variety of sounds. All the different languages of earth, as of all the inhabited planets, are represented in the spirit-world. Language has a spirit, as the flower has a spirit. The spirit of the flower is the fragrance or peculiar exhalations of the flower. Language has its exhalations, its atmosphere, its spirit, and it is that that exists after the spirit passes out of the body. It is that that goes with the spirit. It is that that the spirit employs in communion with its fellows after death.

Q. You say there are sounds in the spirit-world. Are they echoes from the earth, or are they caused by spirits in the spirit-world?

A. They are not echoes from the earth, by no means. Sound also has its spirit, its pure, its more glorified part, and it is that that the spirits make use of. You have your musical sounds here. We have ours there. Ours are the more ethereal, the more glorious, the more beautiful, the more perfect. Every peculiar sound on earth sheds its own peculiar atmosphere, or light, or spirit, and it is that that spirits make use of in the spirit-world proper, or in that condition of life which follows the change called death.

There being no further questions, the intelligence remarked, —

We have received a question from certain parties who had rather an extensive part in the late rebellion. The question is this: "What do the spirits — that class of spirits who, we are told, are watching over the destinies of this nation — believe with reference to the right of Congress to legislate for the Southern States? In their opinion, is it right or wrong?"

A very few plain common sense words will define our position. In looking beyond the mere external of the question propounded for our consideration, we find that those who have propounded it are standing still upon rebellious ground, so far as this government is concerned. They still hold to their peculiar notions which plunged this nation into civil war, and they are as loath to give them up as a mother would be to consign her baby to the flames. They seem to hold it as something sacred to themselves, a something they have a right to hold. Well, no one questions the right, when considered from one stand-point; but when considered from another, every honest, loyal heart will question the right.

Let us pause and consider, for a moment, what was surrendered when General Lee and General Johnston surrendered to the Union army. Was it merely a few military traps? Or was it something deeper, something of more value, something of more vital importance? To my mind it was the latter. One of the chief notions held by the South before the rebellion — and it is holden to-day as then — is this: the right of state sovereignty; that every state should make its own laws and govern its own internal affairs; but they seem to forget that this can be done only in harmony of the national constitution with the general government. Now, as this notion of state sovereignty was one of the chief features leading to civil war, one for which they fought, — so they tell us, — of course that, with other rights, was surrendered at the time that Lee and Johnston surrendered to Grant. The rebellious states virtually said, "We lay at your feet, subject to your disposal, all that which has fed this civil war, and that which bred it. We are civilly and politically at your disposal." The surrender, in plain words, meant this: "You are the strongest party; we are the weakest. You consider that we have been in rebellion against the government. You have fought against us. You have won. We can fight no longer. We surrender. Do with us as seemeth good to you."

Now if the right of State sovereignty was surrendered at that time, the loyal people of the North and Congress *have* the right to legislate for the States at the South that have been in rebellion. Who gave them the right? Why, the South gave it to them. It is vain to argue that the Constitution provides differently; we remember that those who have been in rebellion were outlaws to the Constitution. The Constitution has been set at nought by them. They have trampled it under their feet. They have not recognized the demands of the government. They have gone to war against it; and because they did, they became outlaws. They have no right to make laws, not even for themselves. They have, so far as politics are concerned, cut themselves off from the government, and they should be willing to wait and see how government will dispose of them. So far it has been very lenient, almost too much so. We see that Congress is right in the course it has taken in that matter. Congress has the right to legislate for these rebellious States. They have no right to legislate for themselves. They have given no proof that they are loyal, or that they will be — none that is sufficient. Time and good works, unbroken faith, are the only remedies that can be looked for with any degree of hope in their case. The nation is to-day passing through a greater struggle than it was passing through three, four years ago. Clouds hang more heavy to-day than they hung then. Notwithstanding one great cloud, one mighty stain, has been wiped away, yet there are others to be disposed of. The war of mind is more terrible than the war of the sword.

Before closing, we would request that the friends who

have forwarded us the question we have just briefly considered, if they are not satisfied with our answer, continue the subject farther. Let us see what they have to say — how far they can defend themselves. It is possible we may change tactics, but we do not expect to.

By Father Henry Fitz James, Feb. 11, 1868.

Q. If this Spiritualism is what it purports to be for the uplifting of humanity, ought not our mediums to be surrounded by the highest type of intellectual and moral civilization, so that spirits of the highest order can manifest through them?

A. That condition is certainly something to be desired, but it is not absolutely a necessity. The returning spirit does not make use of the moral law belonging to the media. It only makes use of the physical law. The physical body only becomes an instrument in the hands of the foreign spirit. But if all mediums were surrounded in their earthly lives by good influences, — those that you call high and holy, — then they would always attract to themselves, by virtue of those surroundings, the higher; but the lower would find it very hard to come. That which would prove such an excellent agent for the one, would prove a most formidable obstacle to the other. A wise Providence has made selection of its subjects you call mediums from the middle strata of life. Jesus was found eating and drinking with publicans and sinners. So frequently was he in their company that his opponents called him a wine-bibber. He stood between the high and the low. Angels ministered unto him from above, devils came unto him from below. He preached to the one, he received from the other. If you will observe closely, you will find that it has always been thus.

Our mediums are carefully selected from the middle strata of human life, for from that plane they can be made capable of doing the most good. They can receive the most, they can give the most from that plane.

> "There is a divinity that shapes our ends,
> Rough-hew them as we may."

There is a power behind all life which shapes and fashions all things, all thoughts, all exhibitions of mind and matter, and whether we trust it or doubt it, it will move on its mighty course just the same.

By William E. Channing, Feb. 13, 1868.

Q. What are the claims of Spiritualism, when viewed in the light of a common test, which is as fair for one class as for another, viz.: "the tree is known by its fruits"?

A. The claims of Spiritualism are as wide, as deep, as high, as Spiritualism is itself. Spiritualism claims homage from all things — true Spiritualism, not that which is such only in the exterior, but that which is such in its internal life. The opponents of Spiritualists and Spiritualism sometimes determine very harshly concerning the "ism" and the "ists." They tell us they have not determined unwisely or unrighteously, for they have judged by their fruits which they perceive. That is right. Spiritualists should be judged, and should expect to be judged, by the fruit they bear, by the moral light which they are able to shed upon humanity, by the golden age which they are expected to usher in. Spiritualists should expect to be weighed in the balance of public opinion, and if they are found wanting they should remember that not they alone will suffer, but the holy cause which they represent.

It behooves every one who claims communion with the angels to walk honestly, uprightly in that faith, keeping the golden rule where they can see it, making it a part of their lives, ever being in harmony with it, and never at any time suffering themselves to be in antagonism to it. When considered in conjunction with the external unfoldings of some Spiritualists, Spiritualism will bear no test whatever. If it were dependent upon some of its exponents for merit, for real value, it would be found sadly wanting; but thanks be to God, it does not depend upon any "ist" whatever. Inasmuch as it is pure and undefiled itself, it can march through the ages unsoiled, and those persons who are able to look beyond the mere bubbling, foaming surface, can see it in its purity. Spiritualism, or spiritism — and Spiritualists differ — there is a wide line of demarcation between the two. One is a mere shadow, the other is the reality. In order to test Spiritualism, in God's name do not test it through Spiritualists. Throw it into the scale in all its purity, and weigh it, and it cannot be found wanting.

Q. Is the mind, or that power or principle called intellect, a separate organism, or does its action or growth depend on the spiritual organization for its objective expression, as spirit depends on matter for its medium of expression?

A. Mind is almost entirely dependent upon the formation of the external body for expression. It is the medium between spirit and crude matter. It is a mirror through which the spirit reflects itself upon matter, and its capacities are increased or decreased in correspondence with the increase or decrease of harmonious matter. It belongs to matter.

Q. Can you give me a clear, perspicuous definition of

the connecting relations of the three principles, matter, spirit, and mind?

A. Spirit I believe to be the all-pervading presence called life. Mind, as I before remarked, I believe to be the medium between spirit and matter; matter the machine through which the spirit manifests — through the medium of mind — while in the external life. As the spirit passes on, or changes states of being, it becomes less and less dependent upon crude matter for its expressions. It is dependent upon matter for its expression even in the spirit-world, but not the class of matter that it is dependent upon while here. It is so refined that human senses take no cognizance of it whatever; but yet it is matter.

By John Pierpont, Feb. 20, 1868.

Q. Is a spirit, after leaving the body, as emphatically an independent individuality as when in the body?

A. It certainly is. There are two distinctive individualities; one belonging to earth and earthly experiences and conditions, and the other belonging exclusively to the soul, to spirit experiences and conditions. The spirit carries with it the effects of its individuality here — that which belonged to it while here in the body. These effects it outworks in deeds in the spirit-world. But the individuality that belongs more properly to the spirit in its spiritual condition is more fully expressed after death than before. Here in this life the earthly individuality is in the ascendant. After this life is passed, and you take on the second sphere of change, then the spiritual individuality gains the ascendant over the material. It is not sudden; it comes by slow and distinct degrees, but it is sure to come — the individuality, understand us to say, that belongs to the soul, through which the soul proper, or spirit, expresses itself, that gains the ascendency after death. Before death the earthly individuality is in activity. Its power is superior to the individuality of the spirit, because of earth and its laws. Earth calls for earthly individuality. Its laws demand it, and they are just as exacting and unerring as are divine laws.

Q. Then I infer that the earthly individuality must gradually lose its identity.

A. Yes, that is true. The earthly individuality gradually loses its identity, precisely after this fashion: You have lost the identity of childhood; it has gone from you. You have another, the identity of manhood. So it is with regard to the spirit. You do not suddenly pass from childhood to manhood. No. The degrees come slowly and steadily upon you. So it is with regard to all individualities. Individuality is but a succession of states of being that belong either to the spirit or to the material life.

Q. Then is not this the reason why our friends who have passed away do not in their communications give us more positive evidence of their earthly individuality?

A. It certainly is the reason. If they give you any evidence at all of their earthly individuality, they give it through memory and in symbols. Those who have not outlived their earthly individuality can give a very clear expression of it, because they still retain it; but when they have done with it — gone beyond, outlived it — it is quite another thing. You cannot talk to me as you could in childhood. I cannot talk to you as I would in childhood, but yet you say you are the same person. Now, that is not so. You are quite another being. If your identity depended upon outward expression, surely the identity which belonged to you and to me is ours no longer. We are constantly passing through changes, and each one takes something of what we had and substitutes something we have not had before.

Q. Then are we not changing our individuality every day?

A. You certainly are. For instance, a man may this season live in a certain political individuality; he may be wedded heart and soul to the republican party. All his political interests may turn in that direction. By and by he begins to see that there is a something better. He begins to change his views, again to revolve, and he at length loses that particular individuality and gains another. And his friends who knew him last year as a republican, this year know him as quite another thing. O, yes, you are constantly changing; and for my own part I thank God for it. I would not revolve in a half bushel throughout eternity, not if I could. I do not expect to retain the same views of anything — of heaven, of myself, or of God — years in the future that I retain now.

Q. I would ask, in regard to the letters addressed to spirits, whether those answers are generally given by the one addressed, or by some other spirit?

A. This is almost always done by proxy. For instance, one spirit is selected who can, at the time, best come into *rapport* with the medium. That spirit receives the answers that those called upon may be disposed to or can give. In some instances they are very indistinct, because they cannot understand what they should do in the matter. Others are very distinct, because they know all about the *modus operandi*, and come very near, or in *rapport*, with the medium. Sometimes the spirit called upon in the letter comes in direct *rapport*, and answers the letter; but this is the exception, not the rule. Let me illustrate more perfectly. Fancy yourself in an assembly acting as scribe, receiving answers to questions that may have been put by some one in the assembly or out of it. For instance, Mrs. B. says in her letter, "My dear husband, can you respond to my call?" The spirit scribe calls upon that person. If they are present and can answer, of course they do. If they are absent, generally no reply is written upon the letter. Or, if present, perhaps they give an indefinite answer. Sometimes they do not know how to answer the questions half so well as any one in the audience would; and yet you suppose, many of you, because they are freed from mortality they are endowed with wisdom concerning all matters that belong to you here. It is not so. Whatever they know concerning your earthly affairs, they must know through distinct mediumistic lines of thought and intelligence, and in no other way. Now, then, considering this to be a scientific fact — which it is — you should not wonder at the vagueness and indistinctness of many of the answers that are given to your letters. It depends entirely on the condition of the subject, the person called upon, and the person who has dictated the question. It is a triune affair, and if one happens to be faulty, the others must be correspondingly so.

Q. If there are two distinct individualities, one material and the other spiritual, of course the sounds that emanate from spiritual forms do not reach us externally. How, then, do we take cognizance of them?

A. You are all spiritual mediums, every one of you, and in this sense: Your spiritual individualities are constantly taking more or less cognizance of the things that belong to the spirit-world. That individuality is more in *rapport* with the spirit-world than with this, more in *rap-*

port with higher things than with the things of this life. Therefore when holy thoughts steal over you, thoughts of some dear, absent one, there is a communion then going on between two spirits. The individuality of your spirit has called to the individuality of the friend in the spirit-land, and nine times out of ten there must be a response.

Q. I do not understand these two individualities clearly. When I attach my individuality to the things spiritual, I am spiritually conscious of that fact; but when to things material, my individuality becomes material in consequence.

A. O, no. You do not understand us. You have two thoroughly distinct individualities. One takes cognizance of the things of the other life — is shaped by those things; the other takes cognizance of the things of this life, and is shaped by these. Both are distinct. One belongs to your spirit, the other to your animal existence.

By Theodore Parker, Feb. 24, 1868.

Q. Do male and female spirits mate in marriage, as on earth, or analogous to it?

A. Yes; notwithstanding it is said in the hôly Scriptures that "in heaven they neither marry nor are given in marriage." It is true that there is not that kind of marriage that is current here, and I thank God for it. But there is a kind which is in itself so divine and so perfect, that two souls are merged in one, and the harmony is complete.

Q. One man passes from earth well developed in his moral and spiritual organs. Another passes away in an undeveloped condition. The first returns to earth full of joy, and tells us that he moves in an atmosphere of light. The other likewise returns, but complains that he dwells in darkness. Is the light and darkness spoken of an actual local condition of the atmosphere, applicable alike to all soul existences, or does it grow out of the condition of each individual spirit?

A. It is a mental condition, not an atmospheric condition. You have thousands, millions of souls on the earth who are in darkness, just the same kind of darkness — notwithstanding the sun may shine ever so brightly — that exists with souls after death. It is precisely the same. They do not understand themselves; thay do not understand their surroundings; they do not seem to know what they had better do to gain happiness. They desire it, but know not how to reach it. That is the very worst kind of darkness.

Q. Will you explain the difference between trance and inspirational control?

A. The difference is in degree. If I wish to control a subject inspirationally, I do not obsess that subject, either from the external or the internal, but I simply come in *rapport* with the subject, and through that magnetic *rapport* I give the subject my ideas, and they are given out by the subject in his or her own clothing after the capacity of their own intellect. Do you understand?

Q. Yes; but it only answers half my question.

A. There are also different degrees of what is called trance control. Sometimes the spirit controls by overshadowing or surrounding the subject, as I do to-day. Sometimes they are absorbed by the subject, and express themselves from the internal to the external. Sometimes one organ, or two, or more, as the case may be, is controlled, while others are left in an entirely normal state. Sometimes all the organs are controlled thoroughly. I do so to-day, although I surround the subject, and control through the external, as the musician controls the instrument. He does not enter it in the external; he controls it, and it answers his purpose, becomes his agent.

Q. When you enter or obsess the medium, is the spiritual part of the medium externalized from the form?

A. Yes, it is very often the case. The animal magnetism is never absent from the body. It is a part of the body, and cannot be absent without producing the chemical change called death. But the intelligent magnetic part, with its organic structure, that which belongs to it as a spirit, can absent itself from the body, and very often does, particularly when the body is under the control of a foreign spirit.

By Theodore Parker, Feb. 25, 1868.

Q. In the Banner of Light of January 11, the controlling spirit says, "Many of the planets have passed out of their material into their spiritual orbits, as the earth will do by and by." Will you give a more definite explanation of this statement?

A. Planets, as well as spirits, have an inner and an outer life. It has been said, and truthfully too, that all things have a soul. This being true, the planets cannot be an exception; it pre-supposes that there will come a time in the experiences of planetary life when each shall pass out of the material orbit into a spiritual one — one which shall become so ethereal, so spiritual, so far removed from crude matter, unrefined matter, as to be able to sustain only spiritual existences. It is a well-known geological, scientific fact, that the animals that existed upon this planet thousands of years ago could by no means exist here to-day, because the planet has grown more spiritual. It has ascended from a rude, undeveloped material, into a more refined spiritual condition; and it will continue to ascend — that is the law. It is the law of all things, planets and souls. This has been proved beyond question; not by souls on earth, surely, but by those who have passed beyond earth. But everything moves on in slow and distinct degrees, so slow that your human senses can scarce take cognizance of the movement, except by comparing past and present. You cannot understand that this earth is not to-day what it was yesterday. But it is so much nearer the spiritual plane. You say, "Why, it seems to me to be just the same." So it is, when weighed and measured in the balances of finite reason; but when weighed and measured by infinite, immutable law, it is not the same. Understand us to affirm that all planets, all things — it matters not what, from the grain of sand under your feet to the worlds in the spaces — which you cannot reach with the external vision, are all possessed of souls, inner lives, germs which propel them out of crude materialism into spiritual existence. They change their forms and their conditions to correspond with the needs of their inner being. When the soul, the germ that exists despite all the storms of physical life, which outlives all, when it can no longer manifest itself, unfold itself through these physical forms — then — what then? Why, it enters another orbit, and revolves there till it has performed its mission; then it enters another — and I believe there is no bound to it. I can find no starting-place for matter; I can find no place where it ends.

By Theodore Parker, March 2, 1868.

Q. I notice in many of the communications to your circle, and published in your paper, the spirits say it is hard to come back — to communicate to us here, I suppose. With some it costs them great exertion and much trouble or labor; others study a long time the way to get back before they learn it; some have just learned that such a thing was possible, &c., &c. I wish to ask how this is, when they have been communicating with us here for so long a time, and all over the world?

A. While an idea is struggling through its imperfect or incipient stage, that idea finds it very hard to express itself, even though under somewhat favorable conditions. All kinds of growth are such by virtue of the struggle they pass through. Everything that is growing is struggling. The little shoot that comes up out of the ground in spring struggles to break through the surface of the earth, that the sun may warm it into greater strength. So it is with regard to all kinds of growth — mental, moral, vegetable, physical, animal, spiritual; every kind of growth is subject to this rude experience. Now, it should be remembered that nearly all the intelligences that come to this place to communicate, are such as have not the sympathy of their friends to whom they come. They do not believe that they can return. They come and throw their wish upon the waters of human life, praying that it may receive a favorable answer. They know that they shall meet cold unbelief in most cases; and, knowing this, it is very hard for them to communicate. When the desire on the part of the earthly friend is earnest for them to come, it is generally far easier for the spirit to come *en rapport* with the medium and communicate; but even under the very best conditions it is sometimes hard. The returning spirit fears to pass through the struggle, which is in some respects like unto death. This return, this being clothed upon with mortality again, is by no means an easy thing. It is generally fraught with fear, encompassed about with a certain doubt and fear that the spirit cannot at first overcome. Indeed, there are a variety of conditions that the spirit is obliged to come in harmony with, in order to communicate with the friends it has left on earth, and sometimes, as often as it overcomes one, another, and a still greater, presents itself, till the spirit gets weary and retires.

By Lorenzo Dow, March 3, 1868.

Q. Does Lavoisier continue his experiments on the crystallization of carbon? and did he arrive at a satisfactory result? If so, is he willing to communicate his experiments to mortals?

A. Here you are again, as of old, you mortals, asking to know how you can enrich yourselves with the things of this world — with the toys that pass out of your hands perhaps at the next breath. "How shall we crystallize carbon in order to make it valuable?" This chemist, who threw away a large portion of his best energies in this direction, is in one sense very sorry that he did so, because he did so from wrong motives; and in another he is very glad, because it has led him out of certain dark places into lighter ones. He would inform you, were he here speaking, no doubt, that if there are any individuals on the earth who desire to know what he knows with regard to this subject, simply because they desire to gain good and to do good, he will exercise all the powers of his being to transmit that knowledge to them. But if they desire it from selfish, unwise purposes, he would be the last spirit to return, giving that knowledge. Carbon in the coal and carbon in the diamond, we are told, are precisely the same. But the crystallization depends upon the peculiar soil in which it is found, upon atmospheric and climatic conditions, upon the peculiar condition that exists between the rays of light and the soil where the carbon exists. If you can ascertain just how to regulate this natural machine, you have effected your desire. If you can talk to the sun, and find out how he will send down just such a peculiar kind of light and shade as you need to crystallize the carbon here in this northern clime, perhaps you can make diamonds. But if the sun could speak, I rather think he would be pretty likely to tell you that he and the soil — for instance, of Brazil — can do far better in that way than all the chemists on earth, or in the spirit spheres.

By Theodore Parker, March 5, 1868.

Q. Will you explain the difference, if any exists, between the will-power and mesmeric influences? also their different modes of operation?

A. The will-power in each individual differs according to the capacities of the individual, and yet it is will-power, after all. The will-power that the mesmerist exercises over the mesmeric subject is simply will-power. It is his or hers. The will-power that belongs to the subject is will-power; nothing more nor less. But it belongs to the mesmeric subject, not to the mesmeric operator. Will-power is that force by which all spiritual motion is made. It is the life of intellect, mental motion; without it there could be no exercise of mentality.

Q. The material universe, and, as far as we can understand, the spiritual universe also, are governed by fixed laws. Now, law implies a law-maker, or, in other words, an intelligence. Is that intelligence an individualized intelligence? If not, in what sense are we made in the image of God, and after his likeness? God being assumed to be the name of the author of these laws by which all things are governed?

A. Your correspondent, like thousands of others, is laboring under a great mistake when he confounds God's laws with human laws; for human laws pre-suppose the existence of a law-maker, but it is not so with divine laws. To my mind, the law of life is the God of life; the power by which all life is expressed and perfected. It is the personification of the divine power; wherever you see it, under whatever conditions it manifests, it is God. The law operating in soils, in minerals, in the atmosphere, in the water, in the skies, everywhere is God. There is no power outside of this law that we can recognize as God. No great-intelligence fashioned with a human body. By no means; and the sooner you cast off this mental and theological darkness, the sooner you will rise into clearer light. I know it is almost impossible for the human mind to conceive of law without conceiving of a law-maker; but I know, also, that the impossibility arises from your education here, and from nothing else. You go to work here, and you make laws for the various departments in life. There is the maker. There is the law. It is not so with the law that governs in the universe. It is not so with the law that holds you and me in our proper places. It is not so with that power which determines concerning our well-being. It is a power, an all-pervading existence, that has all forms for its own, but claims no speciality of form whatever. Man is made in the image of God simply because he holds within his physical form all the elements that exist in the universe. There is nothing, no kind of life, that man in the physical does not hold within himself. He is a microcosm of all beneath him, and stands as the crowning glory of creation. In this sense, and in this alone, may he be said to be created in the image of God. Because created in the image of all things beneath him, he represents all things, holds all things, embraces everything. In this sense is he in the image of God.

By Rev. Joseph Lowenthall, March 9, 1868.

Q. Was the organization known as the Order of Eternal Progress organized alone by mortals, or did spirits out of the form favor and assist?

A. An organization corresponding to that which has lately been instituted in your mortal world, has been in process of action in the spirit-world for a long, long series of ages, and through certain mediumistic minds certain ideas have been transmitted to you in mortal, and you are just beginning to put forth in active life.

Q. Does the prevalence of Spiritualism tend to lessen the proper appreciation of human life? The question is asked in all sincerity, in view of some of the terrible crimes, involving murder, sometimes perpetrated by persons professing to be Spiritualists.

A. Spiritualism, pure and unadulterated, teaches us that the gift of life, in all its many phases, is the greatest and best boon that the Creator has conferred upon his children, and that none has the right to seek to change the conditions of time for those of what you call eternity. It is the duty of all to seek to prolong their lives here, till the spirit can no longer express itself through the mortal form. Then, in a natural, harmonious manner the spirit will pass out and enjoy the glories of that higher life. Spiritualism teaches that the suicide and the murderer find more unhappiness there than they can by any possibility find here. Spiritualism proposes to enlighten the soul concerning its highest interests, whether of time or of eternity. Spiritualism does not teach that you shall infringe, or seek to, upon any law of your mortal or spiritual being. It teaches how you may become in harmony with the law, and by becoming in harmony, you learn the way to heaven. It is only when you are in harmony with the laws that are governing you that you are in heaven, or can by any possibility know what true happiness is. And if you seek to infringe upon the law, it will rebuke you always with the sternest severity. It matters not whether you are here or there. The law does not leave you at death. It follows you beyond the tomb.

Q. It seems to be the opinion of a large number of Spiritualists that woman is entitled to exercise authority equally with man, in all the duties of life. What would be the result, in a case of man and wife, where there was a difference of opinion in matters of business?

A. That woman is mentally, morally, socially, and spiritually the equal of man, we do certainly know. Physically, she is his inferior, and by being physically inferior to man, she is raised just so much higher in the spiritual scale, has become just so much more spiritual, just so much more intuitive, just so much in advance of man, with regard to the things of the real life. Now, with reference to the question that you have propounded, your speaker can perhaps give very little valuable advice, and yet what I am able to give will be given in all sincerity, with a purpose entirely honest, and I should hope entirely separated from all favoritism with regard to the man or woman. In matters of business, that which relates to things of this world, that which takes in the merchandise of human life, deals with those forms that are current here, the man knows generally more about than the woman. Why? Because he has lived more in that atmosphere than she. He has dwelt more steadily there than she has. He has become more accustomed to and assimilated with these conditions than the woman has; therefore, considering the case in that light, he should stand pre-eminent to the woman in regard to this particular kind of wisdom. But when considered from another stand-point, the woman rises above him; and it is from this stand-point that we behold her spiritually his superior, even in this respect. Her intuitions being more unfolded, it is sometimes very possible that the intimate friends of the man, in the spirit-world, may be able to shed their influence upon the woman with regard to what is best to be done even in the things of this life. The woman may be able to receive the very best portion of spiritual knowledge with regard to the things here, while the man's senses may be entirely closed to them. And as man stands side by side with woman, and as God recognizes them both as standing upon one plane of life, it behooves both to seek to understand each other, and in seeking to understand, you seek to improve each other, too. Woman should lend of her wisdom to the man, and the man should lend of his physical strength to the woman. There should be an harmonious action between the two, else there is no heaven for them. Nothing but hell can dwell with the man and the woman who are inharmonious to each other, in any sense whatever. The time is coming when the man and the woman will learn how near they stand to God, and how God is speaking to them through all the different forms of life. And when they understand this, they will hearken unto the voice, and harmony will come where inharmony now reigns supreme.

By Lorenzo Dow, March 10, 1868.

Q. Have spirits, besides thought or mental communion among themselves, also the audible voice sound which some seem to affirm?

A. The law of correspondences is an absolute and perfect law everywhere, not only here, but in the spirit-world proper. Yes; we do have that which is equivalent to sound. It is such to the disembodied spirit. It would not be such to you, because the applications could not be made successfully to your human senses. The auditory nerves would not vibrate under the sound that belongs to the spirit-world proper, but the auditory nerves of the spirit-body will vibrate under the sounds of the spirit-world. Every condition of life is regulated by its own special laws. There are laws pertaining to Nature, laws pertaining to mind, and laws pertaining to every degree of mind and matter, and governing each in their own proper sphere.

Q. It has been said that all things in Nature must take upon themselves a second life, that is, the spiritual. Does not the earth — this planet, which we inhabit — come under the same law? Will it not enter a more spiritual or ethereal life?

A. It certainly will. This planet is dying constantly. By and by the death change will become so complete that it will pass out of its material orbit and enter a spiritual orbit, or become the dwelling-place of ethereal beings, and not the dwelling-place for material beings. All things, all forms, every condition of being of which you can conceive, has its inner and its outer life. The inner is the propelling power, the outer is the expression of that power. The outer changes constantly. Through an infinite number of degrees it passes till it becomes so etherealized or spiritualized as to be no longer recognized by material senses. Mark us: everything has its inner and its outer life.

Q. Is it not probable, then, that these spiritual forms that have passed from the earth-sphere will finally return to inhabit the same places again as they once inhabited in the body?

A. It is certainly not impossible.

Q. I would ask, as bearing upon the first question, what is the philosophy of spirit-influx? Ideas are communicated by sounds or words, in which case the ear is the medium — also through forms, as by letters, &c., where the eye is the medium. Now, what is the philosophy of spirit-influx where the senses are not appealed to?

A. Sometimes the perceptive faculties are made use of as agents to convey thought from one mind to another. Under some circumstances a thought is no sooner rounded into form in one mind, than another catches it up, and another and another, and so on till it is lost in the distance.

Q. You say thought is rounded into form. I can conceive of a bubble being rounded into form and then vanishing into air. Is it the same with a thought?

A. It certainly is. You cannot conceive of the reality of thought simply because you cannot measure it by your human senses, you cannot weigh it, you cannot materially deal with it. Now, thought is to humanity the intangible, the unreal; it is the fleeting. But to the disembodied spirit it is the real, the tangible; it is *the* life.

Yes, thoughts are rounded into form just the same as bubbles are, as worlds are, as dew-drops are. Everything begins with a cycle and ends with a cycle.

Q. Has not man a direct destiny placed before him, a road in which he is compelled to walk, a destiny marked out for him by an infinitely wise and good power, which governs all things?

A. Yes, I believe so. I believe that we are just as much the creatures of destiny as this world is. It performs its revolutions in perfect harmony with the law of its destiny. We do the same. We may think that we can do this or that, as we please. We may suppose, in our ignorance of the great law by which we are controlled, that we have an all-sufficient and omnipotent will of our own; but, after all, it is very insignificant, and of small account, when measured by the great governing power of the universe.

Q. How far, then, is man a free agent, responsible for his actions on the earth?

A. That is a question very hard to answer. Because man is subject to the law of a certain destiny. I believe that law does not infringe upon his freedom — upon all the rights which belong to him as an individualized being. I believe that the judge of every intelligent being is within themselves, and I believe they are accountable only to that judge; and in this way: for instance, suppose the mercantile man makes a mistake in his mercantile operations to-day; he looks over the ground, and sees where he might have done better; he regrets what he has done, and in the future he avoids taking the same steps under similar circumstances. Now, he has judged himself; he has paid the penalty through regret, and he has come out into a newer light in consequence of the mistake. He knows more than he did before; he would hardly do the same thing over again. So it is with regard to all things in life. If a child burns its hand by putting it into the flame, you will hardly get it to do the same thing again. It will fear the flame. The old adage, "A burnt child fears the fire," is a very true one. It holds good in the intellectual realm, and in every other.

Q. With reference to my former question, I would ask if there are not conditions in the life of man over which he has no control, which prevent him from doing otherwise than as he does?

A. Most certainly. There are conditions surrounding humanity over which humanity has not the slightest control. The fire possesses destructive properties, and so long as it is the fire it will possess those properties. If you place yourself in a position to be burnt by it, it will burn you. You cannot control it. And throughout all the circumstances of life, conditions are constantly coming up over which we have no control. For instance, you had no control over the way and manner of your birth — no control over the organic life which you possess. You found that you possessed it when you came to a certain standard of intelligence. You had no voice in the matter whatever. The law, or nature, operated without even asking if it might operate in your case, and that same law goes with you all through life. Just so far as you understand the law thoroughly you can make it your servant, and no further. But you never can thoroughly understand the law; therefore there will always be conditions over which you have no control.

Q. Does not man's assertion of his free agency spring from his ignorance of the forces which control him?

A. I think so.

Q. Have not good and evil always co-existed? Could we understand one without the other?

A. No, certainly not. Why, if I thought that the devil was going to take his leave from the world of mind and the world of matter, I should be miserable indeed, and for this reason: I should know that God, or the great, good power, would be robbed of half its glory. What would you know about good, fine, pleasant weather, if there were no storms? You would weary of it very soon. What would you know about appreciating the sunshine, if there were no clouds that passed over the sun's face? Why, I think the devil is one of our very best friends, and instead of putting horns and hoofs to him, we ought to array him in garments of light, and call him what God calls him — very good.

Q. Are we not placed here in order to gain knowledge from adverse circumstances, that we may be better fitted for the life which is to come?

A. Why, certainly. Do you suppose you would appreciate the joys of what you call heaven, the heaven of the spirit-world, if you had always passed through a sort of an easy, free life here? Why, no. You would say, "I had about as good as this on the earth." You would hardly know which you liked best. They who have been crushed under the wheels of adversity are the souls who know how to enjoy heaven. Why, I am only sorry I did not have more adversity when here. I am only sorry I did not drink deeper of the cup of bitterness, because if I had I should have a keener relish for the joys of heaven. My relish is very keen now, but it would have been enhanced a hundred fold if I had only suffered more when here. That is why the returning spirits always tell you that though they suffered much here, they cannot afford to part with the remembrance of it — they are very glad to have passed through it.

Q. This being the case, then, in order to secure the future happiness of our friends, ought we not to begin to torment them all in our power while here?

A. By no means. And you could not if you would, for the law of your destiny has you in its grasp, and you cannot escape it. You can torment them just so far, but no farther. If you have a mind to, you may try it, and see how far you can go. You would very soon weary of it, for you would find the torment reacting so fully upon yourself, that you would get sick of it.

By William E. Channing, March 12, 1868.

Q. What is experimental religion? or, in other words, what is the influence spoken of as being the workings of the Holy Ghost? for there is evidently some unseen, moving power.

A. Every kind of religion is in itself experimental. There never was a religion that was not an experimental religion, that I have had any knowledge of whatever. This Holy Spirit spoken of by your correspondent is the power which determines concerning the particular cast and color of the religion which we shall possess, and it gives a very great variety, no two possessing the same kind of religion. A thousand persons may worship at the same religious shrine, and yet in essential individual worship all differ from each other. This Holy Spirit and this Divine Power which determines between good and evil is the power that will unlock the gates of heaven to every soul individually, not collectively. Strait and narrow is the way. One soul cannot come into heaven by any possibility by any other way except its own — the way that God has marked out for it. You cannot go to heaven by my way. I cannot by yours. It is no use trying. You may try to climb up by my way, but you cannot do it; you will find that you have mistaken your power. All must knock at the gates of heaven through the law of their own holy ghost. They can by no possibility enter heaven in any other way; and as all souls enter heaven, or suppose they do, by some religious light, so all must enter by their own particular religious light. The man or woman who is not ready for a spiritual religion, and is ready for the religion of Catholicism, will go to heaven in that way, and you cannot help it.

By Theodore Parker, March 16, 1868.

Q. Do all spirits take cognizance of their surroundings immediately on being dismissed from the body?

A. No.

Q. Why not?

A. It is impossible to tell why not. We cannot always account readily for this phenomenon of Nature that is presented to us; though we may master it in time, yet we may not be able to do so at once. Many spirits who pass from this sphere to a more spiritual state of being, who lay off the mortal and are clothed upon with immortality, pass through the chemical change called death, perhaps under the influence of ardent spirits, perhaps under the influence of narcotics. Such are not readily awakened to consciousness of spirit. For instance, a man dies dead-drunk, and while in that state he passes out of the body. What is it that is dead-drunk? Is it the body? No, it is consciousness. It goes out into the spirit-world dead-drunk, and it remains so till by natural law the condition passes off, and he is roused to a state of consciousness, takes cognizance of his surroundings, measures himself and that by which he finds himself surrounded by his own inner consciousness. All souls are in their external specially aggregated; yet there are no two alike. One perceives very readily all the conditions that surround him and in which he seems to live, while another is very slow to perceive them. One spirit hears that the way is open to return to earth, and straightway he comes back. Another hears of it, but his ears are not attuned to the truth of the sound; he does not believe it. It cannot appeal to him as a truth, and he does not come back for years — ages, perhaps. All are differently made up in the external, yet in the internal the Bushman, the Hottentot, the Anglo-Saxon, are all the same. Now, do not fancy that you are any better than the savage of the Western wilds, for you are not. In essence they are one with you.

Q. Does that state of unconsciousness generally last long after death?

A. It is generally governed by the internal power, the internal capacity of the individual to throw off inharmonious external conditions. Some can do it more readily than others. It is governed by their internal state. With some it lasts only a few hours, with some, years.

Q. In your answer to the previous question, do I understand you aright that the consciousness, the soul and the spirit, are one and the same thing?

A. No; did I say so? O, no.

Q. Do not some kinds of disease produce the same effects to deaden consciousness?

A. Certainly. Whatever will render individual consciousness inactive here, renders it so there. It carries the impression there, and time must be given it to outlive that condition there, as well as here. There are no miracles performed anywhere, not even with the great God himself. Everything is done by law. You may talk of breaking laws here and breaking laws there, but God's laws are unbreakable.

Q. How much does learning benefit the spirit after death?

A. True learning benefits it a great deal. It draws out the inner powers of the spirit and makes them strong, brings them in contact with external things, gives them that active strength that corresponds to the strength of the body, which you receive by action. How strong would you be if you were to take no active part in the external physical world? For instance, suppose you sit down, or go to bed and lie there two months; would you get up strong? No, you would be very weak. Why? Because your limbs had been deprived of their natural activity. So with regard to your mental powers: the more you use them without abuse, the better it will be for you here and hereafter.

By Sir Humphrey Davy, March 17, 1868.

Q. What is the meaning of the great seeming difference in the condition, growth, and progress of man? Some learn much faster than others and with very little labor, and that a pleasure; others have to toil hard with suffering and distaste, but persevere from necessity or a sense of duty. These, contrasting their condition with that of the more favored, must naturally feel neglected by Nature, or the creative power. They cannot emulate the ability they witness. Success seems to be the result of certain endowments. One, mentally, is an antelope in speed, another a tortoise. One acquires wealth rapidly and easily, another fails, though he uses every effort. So in all departments of life there seems a distributing and directing power. Two rivers, starting from the same point, may, by the apparent accident of a pebble in the path of one, take widely different directions; one coursing through a land flowing with milk and honey, the other through a desert. Is the advantage or disadvantage we have seen, real or apparent? Does the credit or discredit belong to the stream, that its bed should be by green pastures or through burning sands? Will there be an equalization at some time? — the soul, crippled and withered by adverse conditions, be released and made to progress proportionately faster for its delay, and overtake or outstrip the comrade whose beginning was brighter than its own, to be in turn, perhaps, surpassed again, but to demonstrate to life at large, by these different phases of destiny, that there is not in the progress of spirit the inequality that appears; that soul is but as a wide-tossed ocean, every part of which is in turn elevated or depressed, but the average level is maintained the same — each drop knowing the giddy elevation and the corresponding abyss, and destined to find between the two the golden mean that constitutes the real victory, peace and joy of life?

A. In consulting the heavenly bodies, we find that they vary in magnitude, therefore in power, in condition. Every star seems to differ from every other star. In fact, there are no two forms, either in mind or matter, that are created precisely alike. A vast variety exists, and it is very fortunate for the soul that it does, for if the contrary were true, a vast monotony would be the result. Indeed, with all the beauty that meets all the senses at every turn, in mind or matter, we should find nothing to delight us, and also nothing to depress us, but mediocrity everywhere. Nothing to aspire to, nothing to dread. As we look abroad everywhere we behold this variety, and it is exhibited with no less power in the human organization than elsewhere. We find one man laboring hard to attain his desires here. He goes yonder, and still he labors hard through centuries, through cycles of years; still he labors hard. By and by a change comes. On the other hand, we behold a man whom we see accomplishes his purposes, and seems to be riding to heaven in the chariot of ease. All goes well with him. One enjoys almost uninterrupted physical health, while another suffers almost uninterrupted physical disease. So on through the great calendar of Nature. We find that all this variety may be blended into one grand scale of harmony in the life of our God. It is well that these differences exist. The soul has absolute need of their existence. Some souls would hardly unfold themselves under pleasant, harmonious conditions. They need the hard friction of affliction. They need to be brought in contact with the rude scenes and storms of life, so that the soul may grow thereby; so that it may unfold itself in a different manner from all other souls. A wise power hath fashioned us; that same power governs and guides us, and that same power will bring order out of chaos, harmony out of inharmony, perfection out of imperfection, and the great law of compensation will exempt none.

Q. Why are some persons subject to singular acts while sound asleep? as in the case of a young woman rising at three o'clock, making a fire, filling a tea-kettle, and setting the table ready for breakfast, then returning to bed, leaving the doors behind open, even to the open air, and surprised at the breakfast table with the relation of her unconscious services for an early meal?

A. There are some persons who are furnished organically with a double motive power, each perfect in itself. These persons are capable of being used by those intelligences or minds who have laid off their own external organizations, or physical bodies. While the indwelling spirit has possession of the inner motive power, the inner nervous structure, the outside and foreign spirit may have control of the external motive nervous power, and there may be no consciousness transmitted to the indwelling spirit, because these two nervous systems, or powers, are each distinct in themselves. Though in one body, they are distinctively separate. The one conveys no intelligence to the other. The foreign spirit controls the external, while the indwelling spirit controls the internal. Here, then, is a double control of one body, each perfect in itself. Those persons who are possessed with this double nervous system you call mediums, somnambulists. You give them various names, but they are simply extraordinarily sensitive persons. Their sensitiveness consists in their having this double nervous system — nothing more, nothing less.

By Theodore Parker, March 19, 1868.

Q. What is God essentially?

A. Everything. Essentially you are God, I am God — the flowers, the grass, the pebbles, the stars, the moon, the sun, everything is God. Now, that may seem to be a very material idea of God, but in reality it is not. If you can show me where God is not, then you can force me to believe that God in essence and God in form is not everywhere present to our understandings. God to me speaks through the water and the dry land; through the skies, through the flowers, through the mountains and the valleys. I cannot understand God as existing outside of Nature.

By Abner Kneeland, Thomas Paine, Robert Hare, and Theodore Parker, March 23, 1868.

Q. Please explain the following paragraph:—

"VEGETATION IN THE MOON. — It was for a long time the common conclusion among astronomers that the moon was without any atmosphere, and destitute of water; and that, consequently, neither animal nor vegetable life could be supported on its surface. But several eminent modern astronomers have maintained the moon has an atmosphere, though of a very limited extent. And quite recently, Mr. Schawbe, a German astronomical professor, thinks he has discovered signs of vegetation on the surface of our satellite. It is well known that there are certain dark lines, or scratches, as they appear, extending across the slopes of the highest mountains in the moon. These have been variously explained, some regarding them as the beds of dried-up streams; others as the channels left by torrents of lava; others as having some other origin. Professor Schawbe claimed to have discovered in these lines a greenish color, which appears at certain seasons, lasts a few months, and then disappears. He therefore regards these lines as belts of vegetation. If his observations should be decisively confirmed by those of other astronomers, it will settle the question that the moon has both air and water, and will therefore remove any presumption against the existence of animal life on its surface." — *English paper.*

A. Professor Schawbe is correct in his astronomical conclusions with regard to the moon. It has an atmosphere. There are land and water upon its surface, and vegetation exists, although, it is believed, in a very primal form. Astronomers are very fast becoming acquainted with

11

many points of their science, which they have hitherto overlooked; for the world grows, and so do astronomers. The great influx of light which is being shed from the spirit-world in this age, at this time, cannot fail to reach, more or less, all classes of mind, and it reaches with particular force that class of mind which is in itself scientific — those minds that desire to solve the great problems of life. It is to them that this spiritual influx descends with great power, and although they do not recognize it or understand its bearing, it is with them, impressing them with the great truth that is in the atmosphere, that is in the earth, that belongs to the stars, and to them also. The geologist is quickened by the spirit to know concerning what is entombed in the earth; the astronomer is quickened to know what is to be revealed from the starry heavens; and so on through all departments of science. Each one does not fail to receive a due portion of this light which you Spiritualists call your own.

"A. E. G." presents the following: —

Q. Has any human soul had a conscious existence prior to its incarnation in the flesh?

A. I myself have no recollection of an existence prior to the one which I passed through during the earthly life; but I have conversed with very many spirits who tell me that they have a distinct remembrance of having lived and acted through human life prior to their existence on the earth. These minds are, at present, the exceptions; but how long they will remain so we cannot tell. Judging from the great progress that has been made in this direction during the last fifty years, I should myself determine that in the course of the next two hundred years, these minds, with their seemingly mystic theories, will be the rule. Other minds will add their testimony, till the majority is with them, not with us. Perhaps you and I, long ere that time, will have been awakened to a consciousness of a prior existence to the one we enjoyed on earth.

A. E. G. — I will present a statement of facts bearing on the same subject.

"Rev. David Brainerd, who labored among the Indians of New Jersey in 1745, in a diary of his experience which he published at that time, mentions some of the wonders or marvellous deeds wrought by, or through, certain of the Indian diviners, conjurers, or powwow, as they were called. He says they are supposed to have a power of foretelling future events, recovering the sick by making passes upon them, charming persons to death, and that their spirit, in its various operations, seems to be a fanatical imitation of the spirit of prophecy that the church in early ages was favored with. He became particularly acquainted with one of these diviners, whom he represents to have been sincere, honest, and conscientious, and some of whose sentiments, Mr. Brainerd said, seemed to him to be very just.

"This Indian, in describing to Brainerd the way in which he obtained this power that he had of foretelling future events, knowing the secret thoughts of men, restoring the sick to health, &c., said, that before he was born he was admitted into the presence of a great man, in a world above, and at a vast distance from this world, who informed the Indian that he loved, pitied, and desired to do him good. This great man was clothed with the brightest day he ever saw, yea, a day of many years, of everlasting continuance. This whole world was drawn upon him, so that *in him* the earth and all things in it might be seen. By the side of this great man stood his *shade*, *shadow*, or *spirit*, which filled all places, and was most agreeable and wonderful to him. . . . . This great man told him he must come down to earth, be born of such a woman, meet with such and such things, and that once in his life he should be guilty of murder. At this the Indian was displeased, and told the great man that he never would murder; but he replied, '*I have said it, and it shall be so.*' All of this afterwards happened to the Indian (*i. e.*, he afterwards came upon earth, was born of that particular woman, met with such and such incidents, as had been predicted, and had also, on one occasion, committed murder, wholly unconscious at the time that he was fulfilling a prediction made in reference to him prior to his birth).

"The great man asked him what he would choose in life. He replied, to be a hunter, and afterwards to be a powwow, or diviner; whereupon the great man told him he should have what he desired, and that his shade, or shadow, should go along with him down to earth, and be with him forever. There were no words at this time spoken between them. The conference was not carried on by any human language, but they had a kind of mental intelligence of each other's thoughts. After this, the Indian says, he saw the great man no more, but supposes he came down to earth to be born. The spirit, or shade, of the great man still attended him, and ever after continued to appear to him in dreams, and in other ways. . . . There were times when this spirit came upon him in a special manner, and then, he says, he was all light, and not only himself, but it was light all around him, so that he could see through men and know the thoughts of their hearts."

Who or what was this great man that the Indian conversed with in his pre-existent state, and who marked out a definite, precise, and, in some respects, unpleasant work for the Indian to perform on earth? Does he resemble the Grand Man of Swedenborg?

A. I should say that this great man was none other than some guardian spirit, whose mission was to watch over this Indian, and perhaps to watch over many others.

Q. Jesus, a day or two before his death, said, "Father, I have finished the work which thou gavest me to do, and now glorify thou me, Father, with thyself, with the glory which I had with thee before the world was, and now I come to thee." I would inquire whether these and other words of Jesus connected therewith do not imply that he had the idea of his pre-existence?

A. Jesus tells us that he clearly and distinctly remembered a long existence prior to the one that was crossed by so much sorrow. He tells us that he knew it when here, but that he was not permitted to speak in the fullness of wisdom, because of the ignorance of his followers. He was permitted to give them just such mental food as their condition demanded, and none other. He says he knew that he had existed through all the past as a distinct individuality, moving through different spheres, and acting under different conditions, but never once losing his own particular individuality. He tells us this in our spirit-spheres, and it is upon his testimony that thousands of spirits are seeking to know if they too are not, in this sense, immortal. Immortality, to the spirit, does not simply mean the future, but it implies that the soul has come through all the past; that its immortality rests upon the past as well as upon the future. It embraces all of eternity. If the soul was not a conscious spirit in the past, then it was not a soul. It did not possess that birthright to immortality which we suppose it to possess. Although I myself have no consciousness of a prior existence, yet I have the utmost faith in the testimony of those who have.

Q. Brainerd further represents the Indian as saying, "that the spirit, or shadow, of the great man continued to appear to him in dreams and other ways until he felt the power of God's word upon his heart; since which time it has entirely left him." I would inquire what, in the opinion of the controlling intelligence, was the cause of the cessation of the Indian's mediumship, as I suppose his peculiar power would be called in modern phrase.

A. It is impossible to tell what the cause was. You and I may both suppose what it may be, but we cannot know. Modern media are watched over and guarded by a certain class of spirits for a certain time. Suddenly they leave them. They never hear of them again. They cannot tell why it is that these things are so.

Q. You say that all spirits, that everything, is eternal, yet I find that Spiritualists, as well as all religionists, pray to a great First Cause. If *everything* is eternal, what need of this?

A. We use certain terms here upon earth to convey certain ideas. They are, perhaps, the best that we could use, under the circumstances, and yet they fail to convey half that we wish to convey to you. In our prayers to the great God, the Father and Mother of us all, we do but pray to that intelligence which is superior to our own; to that good which is beyond us in goodness; to that something which we feel that we must rely upon in our own individual weakness. It is like the atom praying to the mountain. It is like one drop of the great ocean praying to all the other drops. Prayer lifts us in the moral scale of being. It never fails to; for we never give birth to an honest prayer without leaving some of our darkness below us, without rising somewhat spiritually. From the very fact that we have desired to pray, we know that we are ascending, that the darkness is passing away. When we pray, we draw to ourselves a higher class of intelligences; and because they are higher they are disposed to aid us, for the better always lends of its aid to that which is below it. It is the order of life. We pray simply because we feel that there is a necessity for our praying. We cannot tell from whence the necessity comes. We cannot tell where the prayer will find its stopping-place; but we pray, and the answer comes by our own moral elevation.

By John Pierpont, March 30, 1868.

Q. You say that spiritual forms are matter?

A. Certainly they are.

Q. Then how is it that they can pass through other matter, as, for instance, when a spirit enters a closed room? Why does not the matter, more dense, oppose them?

A. It certainly does oppose them.

Q. But does not hinder their entrance?

A. No, because the spirit is always not only superior in point of beauty and excellence, but superior in point of power. I have a certain control over this crude matter because I am superior to it. As a disembodied spirit, I can pass through the walls of this room, because I am superior to them. They are but servants, so to speak, to me. They offer a certain amount of resistance. So do the waves of the ocean; so does fire; but they are not impervious to spirit.

Q. In passing through the waves of the ocean, or through fire, there is a displacement of the particles of matter. When spiritual matter passes through a denser medium, is there also a displacement of the particles?

A. No; there is no need of it.

Q. We call a spiritual form etherealized matter. Suppose you enclose an object in a glass case; could spirit pass through that?

A. There is nothing in all the universe that is impervious to spirit.

Q. Yet you say that spirit is matter.

A. It is matter, but so etherealized that your senses cannot grasp it. You have many conditions of matter impervious to the gases by which you are surrounded, but you have nothing which is impervious to spirit.

By Bishop Fenwick, April 6, 1868.

Q. Is life, or human life, the result of chemical action?

A. Yes; the whole universe seems to be a vast chemical laboratory, turning out its multitudinous forms, never ceasing to labor. And these physical bodies come within the realm of Nature. They are the results of a chemical power that is at work in the universe. Certain chemical combinations keep them in their proper spheres. They are chemical machines upon which the spirit plays, that it may express itself during its sojourn in the earth-life.

Q. Can all spirits communicate here?

A. If you mean to ask if spirits of all grades of intelligence can communicate here, I shall answer in the affirmative. It would be absolutely impossible for all spirits to find access here, to be able to communicate here, inasmuch as the channel is very limited, while the demand is very extensive.

Q. Does spirit ever lose its individuality?

A. No; I do not believe that it ever does.

Q. Is there not a time, at death, when it does?

A. No; certainly not. Death has no more power upon the spirit than it has power upon the sun. It has no effect upon it whatever. Death is a chemical change that takes place in the physical body, but it does not affect the spirit, only that it separates it from the physical body. The spirit goes forth precisely the same that it was while in the body. It has lost nothing; it has gained nothing.

Q. Are we to suppose that media who claim to be under the direct influence of Jesus Christ and other ancient spirits are correct? Can those ancients come and influence the media of the present day?

A. Yes; you are at liberty to suppose whatsoever you will. It is by no means an impossible thing for those ancient spirits to return, manifesting through modern media.

By Joseph Lowenthall, April 9, 1868.

Q. It has been stated here that there are vast regions of the earth's surface yet undiscovered — almost limitless regions. If so, our geographers are greatly at fault. They represent the earth's surface as pretty well explored, save a small space in the arctic and antarctic regions which is yet unknown. Will the intelligence localize the boundaries and extent of those regions?

A. You have no right to determine that your scientific minds who have explored certain parts of the earth are not right, so far as they have gone. So far as they have been able to reach, so far they are right. But in their ignorance they determine, because there is a boundary to their progress, materially, there is nothing beyond that boundary. Now, those who have made this matter a subject of deep observation in the spirit-world — not here on earth — inform us that beyond what is termed by you the arctic and antarctic regions there are almost unlimited stretches of land and water, varying in climate according to the conditions by which they are surrounded, according to the planetary influences that act upon them. This world, they tell us, this floating sphere, is by no means so small as you suppose it to be. It is small when compared with the vast universe outside of itself; but it is not so small as scientists of earth have determined. They tell us that, as mind changes its base of operations, so the earth changes correspondingly; or as the earth changes, so mind changes, and there will come a time when the scientists of earth shall be able to investigate still further, still more deeply, still more perfectly than at present, and it will be because of the change of climatic influences. That portion of the earth that is now so cold and rarefied that you cannot approach it — you cannot go beyond a certain climate and boundary line — will be changed to meet the needs of growing intelligence. Everything, we find, is finally subservient to the human will, and that all-powerful probe, human intelligence, that is never satisfied with the present. It is impossible to give the exact latitude and longitude of those localities. The time will come, but not in your day, when that which is now but a spiritual theory will be a fixed and demonstrated fact, just as much so as the fact that the world moves, or that it is nearly spherical in shape.

Q. Do heat and cold affect spirits in the spirit-world?

A. Only when they enter earth's atmosphere. That

is to say, that heat and cold which belong especially to the earth's atmosphere. That affects them when they return here, because they then come under the laws that belong to the earth, by which the earth is governed. For instance, if I am in this room, as a disembodied intelligence even, I feel the peculiar quality of the atmosphere. I am affected by the heat and the cold.

By William E. Channing, April 13, 1868.

Q. Do all grades of animal spirits exist visibly in the spirit-land?

A. Yes, but that spirit-land is right here on the earth, and those animal spirits are inhabiting animal bodies here on the earth. It is the tendency of matter to unfold, to perfect itself, to grow into higher and more perfect forms, and therefore the animal forms that have an existence on the earth to-day will by and by become extinct, to give room to higher forms. Life expresses itself always through form, and the form depends upon the condition of the life for its expression. For instance, all the lower orders of animal life reveal to us a certain amount of animal life, and nothing beyond it; there is no reason, no higher grade of intelligence manifested anywhere except through humanity; and by and by even these human forms will give place to others more perfect, better adapted to the life that is to come. They serve well the life that is, but they will not answer the purpose of that which is to be. So do not expect that throughout all the future you will retain the semblance of these forms, for you certainly will not.

Q. Perhaps I shall be better understood, if I put the question in this form. Take the case of a horse. It dies. Does that spirit appear in animal form in the future state, or does it vanish?

A. No. I believe that the spirit of animal life belongs, so far as its outward expression is concerned, to the earth and all other planets that have given birth to animal life. They have a spirit, to be sure, but that spirit, so far as animal expression is concerned, is non-immortal. You may rest assured of that.

By William E. Channing, April 14, 1868.

Q. Do spirits use vocal language in the spirit-world, as they did on earth? If not, by what means do they converse with each other?

A. Yes, they do use vocal language, but it would not be vocal to human senses — to those senses that belong to the physical body. It is only vocal to the senses that belong to the spirit-body. There is sound — all the different varieties of sound — in the spirit-world proper, as here.

Q. In what does God exist?

A. In everything. Tell us in what he does not exist.

Q. In all form?

A. In all forms. He exists in you, in me, in all these different forms — in everything.

Q. Is he, then, a personal being?

A. Yes, so far as form is concerned. He is personified in all forms, having no special form, but taking all. That is my belief.

Q. Do you recognize him as distinct and separate from human beings?

A. No, certainly not. I recognize him as one with them.

Q. As we become more spiritual, are not our perceptions more clear in relation to him?

A. Certainly.

By Father Henry Fitz James, April 16, 1868.

Q. Is it not probable that before many years electricity will be the motor of machinery, instead of steam?

A. It is, so scientific minds inform us, very probable. Franklin is largely engaged in impressing, or seeking to impress, the knowledge that he has gained during his residence in the spirit-world upon those minds that are able to receive it. He makes advance as mind advances on the earth. No faster.

Q. A scientific explanation of idiocy is requested.

A. There are various theories concerning idiocy. A certain class of scientific minds, with us, have recently determined that the cause of it may generally be found in the imponderables of the physical form — an unequal distribution of the electric and magnetic forces. In consequence of this unequal distribution, the spirit is unable to manifest itself. They determine that the spirit, the essential life, the intelligent part, is, of itself, perfect, and in many instances the external physical is, of itself, a perfect machine. But the cause lies between the two, as I before said; in the imponderables, those gases that keep the machine in motion; that power by which the spirit manifests through the physical body.

Q. Do not the signs of the times indicate that ere long great and revolutionary changes may be expected, both in material existence, and, more particularly, in human and political life?

A. Yes, and more than this, the signs of the times not only indicate such an experience, but it is already with you. The revolution in mind has already commenced all through the world, and modern Spiritualism is the great lever that is producing it.

By William E. Channing, April 20, 1868.

Q. Please explain the law that produces physical manifestations, and why they are more frequent than in former times.

A. It would be absolutely impossible to give a full, clear explanation of the law by which these manifestations are performed, without demonstration, and as the conditions are wanting here by which we can demonstrate the law, we, of course, must fail in the answer. They are of more frequent occurrence in these days, perhaps, than in past time, because man is more unfolded, and the earth is also in a state more fitted to receive such so-called occult manifestations. The earth is ready for such, mind is ready for such. A few years in the past — a few when compared with eternity, certainly — a certain band of disembodied spirits returned to earth for the purpose of demonstrating the reality of life after death to those who remained on the earth. They came, a certain portion of them, very near this locality; and what was the result? Why, the darkness swallowed up the light, absolutely crucified it, and therefore, as a matter of justice to the instruments through which the light was to shine, it retired to wait till the darkness should by a natural process be dispelled. The same light has come again; the same class of manifestations that were given then are given to-day, but under different circumstances. The darkness of night has passed away, therefore the instruments through which these manifestations were made are no longer crucified, as they were in those days; but the time is coming when the light will shine still brighter; when these manifestations, both physical and mental, will have reached an altitude far beyond the present, and you will look back upon the present, doubtless considering it as the infancy of spirit manifestations.

Q. In case of destroyed manuscripts or of typed works of literature, or of records important to us here on earth, have you, in the spirit-world, those ideas in record unobliterated? If so, are they where you can consult them, and impart their purport to us, when of importance to the development of science?

A. An accurate record of all written or unwritten thoughts that have found expression upon this planet is kept in the spirit-world proper, that belongs to this planet. Not a single thought is lost. All the old ideas are carefully kept in the spirit-world. Nothing is lost, because everything has an internal or immortal life. All those valuable records that the past had, but the present has not, so far as human life is concerned, are all kept in the spirit-world, and every soul that desires to inform itself concerning those records is at liberty so to do. They are free to all. The spirit-world is one vast public library.

By Joseph Lowenthall, April 23, 1868.

Q. "God sent his only-begotten son into the world that whosoever believeth in him shall have eternal life." My mind dwells on the "only-begotten" as the point at issue with the belief of Spiritualists.

A. Your speaker has no belief in an only-begotten son of Jehovah. He never did have any — therefore in all probability will fail to do justice to the subject according to the comprehension of the Christian world. Your speaker believes that every son and daughter of humanity, whether they had an existence in the past, or existing in the present, are the begotten sons and daughters of

Jehovah, every one of them, not one any more than another. The breath of the Infinite is with all, and all are created in the image of God, which meaneth in the image of all things that have been, of all that are, and all that can be. This only-begotten son of God, whom the Christian Church reverences, so much, was doubtless a most excellent specimen of humanity, but nothing more. It may be determined that your speaker still lingers amid the shadows of the Jewish Church. It is not so. No shadow of any Church, Jew or Gentile, lingers around the opinion of your speaker. I believe in the greatness, in the omnipotence of God. But I do not believe that one child is more specially blessed by him than all others. I have more faith in his justice than to believe him to be a partial God. I believe him to be the Great Spirit pervading mind and matter, acting through all things, at all times, in all places, and I believe he finds expression more perfectly through human senses than anywhere else, but no more perfectly through a Jesus of Nazareth than through any other good man or woman.

Q. Is it not necessary for a person to become weak in the physical being, in order to be in the proper condition for spirits to manifest through? And is not the medium generally very weak and susceptible to all influences, good or bad?

A. Weakness is sometimes a necessity of these manifestations, but not always. It is not a general rule. It is an exceptional one. There are some mediums whose bodily health is very excellent, while there are others who seemingly flutter between the two worlds. Sometimes the weakness of the body can be made use of by a foreign spirit in giving these manifestations. Sometimes sound health will answer their purpose much better.

Q. I would like to ask, if it would not be better to resist spirit influences, to keep away from them, and not allow one's self to become a medium. I am somewhat under the influence myself, and have been reduced from a strong and healthy to a very weak condition. Would it not be better for me and many others to keep away from circles where we are subject to those influences?

A. Your Bible teaches that you should not resist the spirit. It is ofttimes this very resistance that produces this inharmony between the indwelling spirit and the physical body, therefore inducing disease. There are times, no doubt, when it would be well to keep away from these promiscuous gatherings — those gatherings where any and every spirit is licensed towards any and every individual. There are some physical organizations so susceptible to spirit influence that under certain conditions they will be controlled, whether it is their purpose to be, or the contrary. It should be remembered that the spirit-world proper is the more positive world; that the spirit out of the body is more positive than the spirit in the body, and therefore has the advantage over the spirit in the body. All those subtile wires of electric and magnetic life that pass from your physical bodies out into the atmosphere, are all agents in the hands of unseen intelligences, every one of them. They can be used to your detriment, or the contrary. If you desire to retain your health, and at the same time give yourself to the use of foreign intelligences, it is your duty to make yourself as harmonious as possible — to study the laws of life and harmony — those laws which pertain to you as an individual, not those which pertain to any one else.

Learn what is best for *you*. No general rule can be applied to all; there is a law of life for each individual. For instance, one person is obliged to appropriate to the physical a certain amount of animal food each day, in order to keep the machine in good trim, while another finds that animal food is not adapted to him. Vegetable answers his purpose much better. You should study what is best for you. If a certain class of spirits come to influence you, to the taking away of your health, and substituting weakness and disease, you should learn what the characteristics of those spirits are, and how and why they injure you, and then seek to educate them as well as yourself. When they are satisfied that they are unjust to you, believe us, they will be unjust no longer. I have that amount of faith in humanity, either as it is in mortal or beyond mortality, that makes me feel that no soul will ever practise injustice when it is once satisfied that a thing is unjust, absolutely.

By Rev. John Murray, April 27, 1868.

Q. Will the controlling spirit give a full and complete definition of "mesmeric aura," in order that the unlearned reader may understand the intimate relation such an agent bears to Spiritualism? Give us a scientific analysis of the whole idea, if you please.

A. That would take a very long time to accomplish, for it is of itself very great. The science of mesmerism is embraced in the science of life; life here and life hereafter. All the emanations of these animal bodies may be called animal magnetism, or the animal or material sphere in which you, as beings of this world, live, move, and have your being. You are constantly taking on magnetic influences from everything that you come in contact with, and you are as perpetually shedding that magnetic life upon all things that you come in contact with. When disembodied spirits desire to communicate through organic life to organic life, they of necessity come into communication or *rapport* with the magnetic life of the spirit. Sometimes it is exceedingly antagonistic; then there can be no perfect communion. At other times it is all that could be desired. This magnetic aura is simply thought impalpable, yet all-potent, that is exercised by the mind and projected through the animal life. You cannot see it, you cannot feel it, except with the perceptions of the spirit; you cannot handle it, you cannot analyze it, and yet it is all-potent to the spirit. So far as the spirit is concerned it is all-powerful; it sometimes prevents you from uttering a single word, or giving birth to a single thought. It is the grand agent that acts between mind and matter. It is the power that holds worlds in their places, and holds thoughts in their places; it is the power that forms thought, and it is the power by which thought is expressed. It is infinite in itself, and it would be absolutely impossible to analyze it, because of its infinitude.

Q. Do departed spirits have any agency in mesmerism, or is it simply the action of mind upon mind in the flesh?

A. A departed spirit may mesmerize a subject, or the spirit that still retains its hold upon this organic life may mesmerize a subject. Each can do it. A disembodied spirit has a certain degree of advantage over the embodied spirit, but both are able to perform the same thing. It is something that both the embodied and the disembodied can deal with.

Q. What is the advantage of disembodied spirits praying through a human organism?

A. The same advantage is derived by the disembodied spirit that is derived by the spirit that is embodied. Prayer always elevates the spirit, whether it is here in the flesh or passed beyond the flesh. It always lifts the spirit beyond or outside of its present cares and perplexities. It sheds a newer and diviner atmosphere around it, and attracts to itself higher and more powerful, more holy, more perfect intelligences, and by the presence of those intelligences the praying spirit receives benefit. You cannot remain in the presence of one that is holy, good, and true, without receiving benefit, for the good always shed a holy influence which every soul that is in *rapport* with it must feel. Prayer is of use always, and all souls are constantly at prayer. Now, this may seem to be a very wild, erratic statement, but it is nevertheless true. All souls are constantly at prayer, because all are constantly aspiring towards a better state. This is prayer. One kind of prayer is embodied in words, another kind in deeds. There are many kinds of prayer, aside from those that are clothed in words.

By Theodore Parker, April 28, 1868.

Q. Is there not a transitional condition of the atmosphere, during the months of March and April, which is more unfavorable to health than at other seasons? and how can we avoid or repel such influence when exposed to it?

A. I am not sure that this transition state of the seasons is absolutely inimical to life. Experience and observation have taught us that during these months certain planets seem to have, and do have, a direct influence upon the earth — an influence to call out from her centre what the surface has need of; consequently the elements, magnetic and electric, all the atmospheric elements will be in a state of unrest — in a state of labor — to bring forth renewed life. And as man is but an animal upon the surface of the earth, and an animal made up of mineral and vegetable, as well as animal and spiritual substances, of necessity he must feel these changes. But it would be unwise to determine that they are absolutely unfavorable to him. On the contrary, I think that were we to dispense with those conditions which these months bring upon us, we should find ourselves very much worse off than at present. These bodies that are upon the earth to-day are peculiarly adapted to the atmospheric conditions by which they are surrounded; and should you, if you could, bring about the change which many desire in these atmospheric surroundings, the result would be, I think, in very many instances, fatal to human life. You have absolute need, as the earth has need, of your March winds, of your April showers, and of all the quick and successive changes that these months bring. You could not well spare them, and though they are, in one sense, the shadows of earth-life, yet in another sense they are the sunbeams, and we would advise you to take no course whatever to prevent their legitimate action upon you, for if you should do so, under existing circumstances, I cannot see that it will be as well for you.

Q. Is it ever right to exercise revenge?

A. Yes, it is right to those who exercise it, but to those who see the dark, deformed side of revenge, it is not right. It surely is not the better way. The soul that exercises revenge does so because it is ignorant of the better way, always. I never knew an individual to exercise, or seek to exercise, revenge upon any of his fellows, when that individual was attended with wisdom upon the subject. The desire to be revenged is born of ignorance. When ignorance ceases to give birth to such monstrosities, then they will be no more.

By Abdal Hada, April 30, 1868.

Q. Is it true that both mental and physical sufferings are eventually beneficial to the development of the spirit?

A. The philosophy of mind reveals to us this fact: that intelligence can only become perfect through suffering, both mental and physical; as the earth can only reach a perfect state, or can only grow, through storms as well as sunshine, so the soul, or mentality of man or woman, can only reach a perfect state through the storms of sorrow and human despair.

Q. Have the inhabitants of the older planets, that were formed before our earth, arrived at such a degree of intelligence as to know how to keep in perfect health? and do they live in love and harmony?

A. Many of them do, particularly the inhabitants of Uranus and Jupiter. It is the destiny of the inhabitants of all planets to outlive these inharmonious conditions, which are a necessity of the earth's growth. The inhabitants of a planet grow as the planet grows. When there are no more poisonous reptiles, plants, or poisonous substances on the earth, no more tornadoes; when all these outward signs of violence — material, earthly signs of violence — have passed away, then the signs of violence that pertain more particularly to your human, physical life will also have passed away. This is the destiny, I believe, of human life.

Q. Have any of the inhabitants of any other planet ever visited this earth and made themselves known?

A. I think, if such a thing ever occurred, it certainly is something very rare. The inhabitants belonging to each separate planet, those who have passed beyond the material into the spiritual life, are, of necessity, more powerfully attracted to the planet of which they have been born than to any other. Indeed, it is almost impossible for the inhabitant of any other planet to visit the earth *in propria persona*, or *vice versa*. Everything is conducted in accordance with law and order throughout the universe, and no absolute law is ever violated by the spirit.

By Theodore Parker, May 5, 1868.

Q. If a person act as he is impressed, will he always do right?

A. There are an infinite number of degrees of right, each one being a discreet (?) degree. There are also an infinite number of sources from which an individual soul can gain impressions, and the soul is quite as liable to receive impressions from the lower as from the higher; therefore it is not always the highest wisdom to follow our impressions. I know it is so determined by very many souls, but I cannot so understand it. If we are sure that we are harmonious at the time with the highest good of which we can conceive, then we may be very sure that whatever impressions we receive at the time will be such as are not calculated to lead us astray; but if we are ourselves in the shadow, in an inharmonious condition towards the higher, we shall be very likely to draw corresponding impressions, and be liable to be led astray. In order to understand when our impressions are of the right character, and when they are not, and when they are likely to lead us up or to lead us down, we must understand always when we are in harmony with the great good that is beyond us. We must learn to measure ourselves by this great outside good, this eternal God, never forgetting that the balances are within. The only balance wherein we can weigh our own individual condition of being is within ourselves, and we call it reason, the highest of all the attributes that the great Father has seen fit to endow the human with.

By T. Starr King, May 7, 1868.

Q. Do the dwellers in the spirit-spheres construct habitations, gardens, &c., according to their individual tastes? and by what process, and of what materials?

A. There are, indeed, gardens in the spirit-world so much more beautiful than what you have here, that you can form no just estimate of them. Indeed, everything that finds expression here is more fully represented with us. All the beauty of life, all the power of life, everything that is expressed in art, in science, in nature, all find a counterpart in the spirit-world. It would be absolutely impossible for us to give you so close an analysis concerning the material of which all their beauty and power are constructed, because you are bound about by the law of your human senses. Your eyes cannot see, your ears cannot hear, neither can it enter into your hearts to conceive all the glories that pertain particularly to the spirit-world. You may catch faint glimpses of its reality, but the clear noon-tide glory of the reality you cannot behold, you cannot understand, until you too shall become disrobed of the flesh, and shall stand gazing upon it through spiritual senses.

Q. Some creeds would teach us that kindred ties

which exist in this life are no more when we enter the spirit-world. Is this true in any manner?

A. All ties that belong to the soul, the soul carries with it when it is resurrected from the body of flesh. The loves which we had are ours still; and all the conditions of our mental being we carry with us to the spirit-world, because we shall have need of them there. Our friends do not forsake us there, neither do we forsake them. All true attraction is most clearly represented in the spirit-world. There is no breaking of law; there is no sundering of ties, not by any possibility; and the soul finds that its hopes will be so fully, so absolutely realized in the spirit-world that there is no room left for doubt. The mother that loves her child finds the child beyond the tomb, and *vice versa;* and all our friends that we held so dear by those ties that God gave us, are clustered around us again in our spirit-home. No, no; do not believe in those creeds which teach of the sundering of ties that are so dear, so close unto the soul.

Q. I would like to ask if sufficient individuality lingers about the earthly remains of a departed spirit to enable it to recognize those particles and feel attracted to them when ascended and sublimated?

A. The summer-land, or spirit-world, is composed of particles that once inhabited material forms, because the ethereal spirit finds expression through all grades of matter. It comes up from the lower, growing into the higher, forever and forever leaving the lower and entering the higher. In this sense the summer-land is constructed of atoms that were once in natural crude forms. There is a certain attractive power by which the disembodied spirit returns to the earth, and is attracted to its cast-off earthly garments. There are some in whom the attraction is very strong, and it continues to act with potent power upon them until the magnetic and electric life becomes thoroughly changed in the body it has left; in other words, till all the particles become more or less decomposed; till it has thrown off all its magnetic and electric exhalations.

Chairman. — I think the questioner wishes to know if the spirit is attracted to those particles that have ascended or become sublimated.

A. Yes, certainly; that would be a natural consequence. Allow me to illustrate further. You have been taught that you build your spiritual dwelling-places day by day ere you enter them, and you do in this sense: by your earthly deeds, by your earthly thoughts, you exhale spiritual particles that find their appropriate place in your own spirit-home. If they are bright and beautiful, your spirit-home will be correspondingly bright and beautiful, and you must, of necessity, gravitate to your home at death. You can go nowhere else. It is the law of your being. You cannot find a resting-place in the home of a Socrates or a Franklin, but your own home is yours, and there you must go. Every spirit has its own locality, and it will gravitate there because of a law by which it is surrounded, and in which it lives. That law acts upon the home with attractive power; it acts also with the individual, — plays between the two, — and you go there by virtue of absolute necessity.

Q. Do spirits now living in the body pass from their body to mediums, and control them in the same way that spirits do that have laid aside the body?

A. Not very often. There are rare exceptional instances of this kind. But they are the exception, not the rule. Generally, the spirit who has not thrown off the external body, who desires to control another spirit, does so by virtue of a psychological power, through the medium of magnetism. They throw their will upon the negative subject, and it becomes their subject to all intents and purposes.

By William E. Channing, May 11, 1868.

The chairman read the following letter: —

"EDITORS OF BANNER OF LIGHT: I am a regular reader of your paper, and especially enjoy the message department, and am weekly watching for a communication from a dear friend who has lately passed away. But I fear that nothing he could write would favorably affect his sceptical friends if preceded by or published in connection with such a message as comes from Cornelius Winne.

"Freddy Harmon, in a communication in the same paper, says Mr. Parker would like to have his (Freddy's) mother *prepared* to receive the truth. I cannot see the propriety of publishing messages which are in their nature repulsive to people of intelligence and refinement, and calculated to make them feel that devils are "let loose upon the earth." Do such minds as Theodore Parker and William E. Channing approve such publications? I do not object to such communication in a private circle, if any good can come of it to spirit or mortals.

"I sometimes think there are spirits on a low plane who influence and pervert the minds of mediums not sufficiently guarded against false teaching; I cannot otherwise account for the folly and fanaticism that too often passes under the name of Spiritualism. Spiritualists claim to be governed by reason and science, and there is even more impropriety in their following blindly *all* that comes from the spirit-world, than for Christians who take the Bible as an infallible guide.

"There never has been anything more disastrous in its effects on mankind than religion without reason. Every kind of crime and persecution has been perpetrated under its name. And it is only when guided by science, reason, and wisdom, that we may expect Spiritualism to permanently bless mankind. That you may be guided by infinite wisdom in your efforts to enlighten the world is the earnest desire of the writer."

A. We are told that Christ came not to call the righteous, but sinners, to repentance. He came not to point the way to heaven to those who already knew it, but to those who had no knowledge of the way. He came not to lift up those who had no need of his strength, but he came to upraise the down-trodden; those who had fallen in the way of life; those who, in consequence of their ignorance, had made disastrous mistakes in life. To such Jesus came, and in behalf of such we are here to-day. Our platform is free to all, even unto the fabled Lucifer himself. The dusky-browed Indian and African, with all their ignorance, are welcome here; those who have been down-trodden in earthly life, who, in consequence of ignorance, of false teaching, of all those unhappy conditions that often cluster around the soul while here; those who have been under such conditions, and have entered the spirit-world with all that mental darkness that makes the hell that the soul is sometimes plunged into, *they* even are welcome here with all their darkness, with all their sin, and with all their stained garments; they are welcome here. Your correspondent asks if a Channing and a Parker countenance such communications. Most assuredly they do. I speak for myself, and I know my good brother Parker would say even more than I say upon the subject. If the founder of the Christian religion — that spirit who has been held up as a pattern of goodness, of morality, of all the Christian virtues, for many centuries — did not think it amiss to walk and talk and commune with publicans and sinners of the lowest class, shall we do less? The spirit of truth calls all to its standard, the high and the low, the bond and the free, the wise and the ignorant, and your correspondent makes a lamentable mistake in supposing that caste divides souls in this free spirit-land. It is not so. Such folly belongs to earth. It has no place in the glorious spirit-land — none whatever. The dusky-browed African and Indian are as precious in the sight of the great God as the fair Anglo-Saxon. The soul that is bowed down with ignorance and crime is equally dear to the Great Father. No darkness, however moral, however mental, no kind of darkness, is so dense that the spirit of truth and infinite love and wisdom cannot enter there. Your correspondent fears that the mother may not receive a communication from her departed one if appearing side by side with one of the lowly ones of earth. It is time your correspondent came out of that darkness into better light, and rose above these mists and fogs, and put on a garment that could not be contaminated by any of the conditions of human life.

Q. I would like to ask if the controlling influence recognizes as a fact that the power controlling the universe is of itself conscious of human consciousness.

A. I do not so believe. I believe that the great universal consciousness is expressed through forms, human consciousness, and perhaps nowhere else so perfectly. There is a kind of consciousness that belongs to certain lower spheres of animal existence, but when it rises into the human it becomes more perfect, more beautiful, more elaborate. I cannot conceive of a consciousness apart from form, from that which we perceive around us through our fellows. I do not believe in a God apart from his works. Such a God would be so far beyond my comprehension that I could not worship him. I believe that

God acts through his works, and manifests consciousness wherever there are organs adapted to such an expression.

Q. Do you recognize life anywhere, in any condition, without a consciousness to correspond with that condition?

A. I do. Yes, I believe there are an infinite variety, or number of kinds of life that possess no distinctive conscious condition. Still, life is there.

Q. Then consciousness must have a beginning.

A. Not necessarily. At all events, it would be very hard to determine where consciousness began. We have no knowledge of its ever having had a beginning. So far as forms are concerned, as a matter of course, it has had a beginning there. Consciousness had a beginning upon this planet, but had existed somewhere else millions of years before this planet came into life, no doubt.

Q. It is generally conceded that whatever had a beginning, necessarily has an end; and if consciousness is not found wherever life is found, it seems to me that it must have a beginning somewhere, and necessarily would have an end.

A. So far as form is concerned, it does have an end. The consciousness that belongs to your physical form will have an end, so far as that form is concerned. But the consciousness will live. It is dependent for expression upon form, and it changes according to form; but I do not believe that it is created by form, or that it ends with the decay of the form. It is possible that there may have been a time when consciousness was born, when it was created; but we know of no such time. Were we able to go back in our own conscious lives millions of years in the past, we should still find, I think, millions of years more where consciousness had life.

Q. It has been said that Christians seldom manifest here. Can you throw any light upon the subject?

A. That is false. We will venture to say, that at least seven out of every ten who manifest here have been in some way attached to some Christian church when on the earth. Those persons who think otherwise have only to peruse the back numbers of our paper; they can satisfy themselves. I am quite sure that those who have belonged to different churches when here, who have communicated at this place, are far in the majority.

By Edgar C. Dayton, May 14, 1868.

Q. If memory ever lives with us, may not it make the future life unpleasant or intolerable?

A. Yes, it certainly will, in many instances, make it exceedingly unpleasant. The man who has defrauded his neighbor in any sense, who has practised the various kinds of injustice that are exhibited on the earth, who has committed errors against his own conscience — such a one cannot but expect to receive condemnation in consequence of remembering those acts in the spirit-world. We carry with us all the lights and shades of our being here to the spirit-world, and if the shade preponderates, why, certainly, we cannot but be unhappy. Now, then, see to it that you do not carry those things to the spirit-world that, when you remember, will cause you regret. For if you do, you will carry your hell with you. Be sure of that.

Q. Do we not gain a heavenly condition by our own efforts and aspirations, or are we aided by divine influences?

A. We gain it by both. Aside from our own aspirations, from our own desire to obtain the best that God has in store for us, we also have the aid of all the good there is in earth, because all good is inseparably bound together. We make our own heaven and our own hell, but we find the law is augmented by outside conditions.

Q. Is there a distinction in the soul's future between sins of intention and of ignorance?

A. Certainly there is, so far as the individual is concerned. If you commit an error, and you know at the time you commit it that it is an error, — that it is not the best way, when remorse for the commission of that error comes, it will be very much more keen than if you had committed the error in ignorance.

By Thomas Paine, May 19, 1868.

Q. Does the human mind ever become impaired?

A. Certainly it does; for the mind is only the mirror that is placed between the external organism and the soul or spirit, through which the spirit reflects itself upon external things. As it is a result of external life, it acts under the law of external life, and is subject to the varying conditions of that life. If the body is sick, so is the mind. If the body is weak, the mind is correspondingly weak; but you are very apt to confound the mind with the soul, when the truth is they are two distinct bodies or entities of being, just as distinct from each other as soul is distinct from the external body.

Q. Can you describe the soul?

A. No, certainly not; any more than I could describe God. It describes itself. It writes its own history. It figures itself upon all things in being. The soul is expressed by the artist upon his canvas, by the muse when he gives forth harmonious sounds. The soul is expressed through mechanics and all the various arts and sciences of life.

Q. With regard to the first question, do you mean to say that there is a distinction between the mind and the soul in the lower animals, or that they have no immortal part?

A. I believe that all things, in a certain sense, are immortal. I believe, also, that that which is instinct in animals is the same as mind is to the higher animal, man. It is but the mirror through which the inner part expresses itself, — reflects itself upon the external world.

Q. The other branch of the question — are they immortal?

A. In a certain sense, they are. But so far as their individuality in *form* is concerned, I do not think that they are. I have no evidence that they are.

Q. Are educated and uneducated minds together in the other world?

A. Certainly they are, just the same as here. If they were not, I should have very small hope for the uneducated.

Q. Do the uneducated progress in the other world?

A. Certainly; just the same as here, only the facilities for their education are far better than here.

Q. Will not spiritual telegraphy one day supersede our present system of physical telegraphy?

A. It is by no means an impossibility. On the contrary, it is highly probable. There is a class of minds who believe that the time is not far distant when this phase of spiritual science will be brought to earth and successfully used. It is unconsciously in action amongst you all the time. Mind is perpetually telegraphing to mind, all over the world, and surely it is very reasonable to suppose that the time will come when you will have a thorough understanding of the science, and will make it applicable to the external world, — will make it of use. For thousands of years, ay, for millions, for aught I know, the lightning was of no possible known service to man. He did not know that he could make use of it. In his savage state he feared it, and there were many who worshipped it, but none who understood its power, and how to make it of use to human life. By and by a Franklin arose, and the lightning became a toy in his hands. And in later years it is your most humble servant. Now, considering that the soul is marching through all conditions of being, analyzing all, and making all subservient to itself, it is very reasonable to suppose it will not overlook this.

Q. Do men ever deteriorate in the other world?

A. I do not believe that they ever do; neither here nor there.

Q. Are not some going higher and some lower, there as here?

A. I have seen nothing to cause me to believe that the soul ever falls from its high estate. It may seem to, to senses that do not understand the *modus operandi* of life, but I cannot believe that it ever does. There are mountains and valleys in our experience. It is just as essential for us to descend into the valleys as it is to ascend the mountains; but because there are mountains and valleys, I cannot believe that the soul does lose anything of its high estate, its first pure life, by descending into the valley. On the contrary, I believe it is always in the ascendant, ever nearing its great source. You call that source God. Perhaps it is as good a name as you could give it.

By William E. Channing, May 26, 1868.

Q. In this question I am going to use the words wife and husband, first in their conventional sense, and then in what I call their spiritual sense. We know, as a matter of fact, that in this world a man will sometimes marry three or four wives, a woman three or four husbands; but, spiritually speaking, can a man have more than one wife, or a woman more than one husband?

A. No, I do not think they can, because I think the positive and negative form the whole. The one man and the one woman form the whole — the rounded being. One is imperfect without the other. The time is coming, but it is in the distance, when you will understand that that marriage which is not of the soul is no marriage at all; that that which is brought about by external conditions is altogether unlawful. That which God has joined together none can put asunder, but that which is joined together by the conditions of human life, almost any one can put asunder; and it is lawful that they should, because the parties are unlawfully bound together. The time is coming when you will understand this subject, when it will be more simplified, when it will enter as a part of all human education, and become, to a certain extent, the basis of human education.

Q. Considering the present condition of society, and how very little the moral sense is cultivated to what it will be in the future, is it not expedient that for the present there should be what we call a marriage form, and that persons entering the marriage state should give certain pledges to society, and receive the sanction of society to live in that condition?

A. Most certainly they should. "Render unto

Cæsar the things that are Cæsar's, and unto God the things that are God's." Society, in its present condition, demands certain things, which it is right to accord.

Q. Can you throw any light upon the psychological nature of what we call madness? To me it is a problem less relieved by light than almost any other, and as circumstances have brought me in connection with several persons suffering from it, I am particularly anxious to get some information in regard to this most wonderful and sorrowful phenomenon.

A. Madness is divided into a great many different phases, and is induced by as many different causes. Sometimes it is the child of antenatal conditions — very often it is. Sometimes it is the child of spiritual conditions — very often it is. Sometimes it is the child of human surroundings, begotten out of the ill-assorted conditions of human life. Now, in order to deal successfully with all kinds of madness, we must understand in each special case what the cause is, then deal with it according to the needs of the case, and by no means tamper with the effects. Then you will be sure of effecting a cure when it is possible to.

Q. I think I understand, so far as you have gone; but I would ask, What is madness in itself — in its own essence?

A. It is an unequal distribution of the nervous forces. The nervous forces, in all kinds of madness, from whatever cause, are unequally distributed. There is an inharmony between the forces, positive and negative, and whatever you can do to produce harmony or equilibrium there, will be sure to effect a cure. It lies in the imponderables of the system, nearly always; not in the solids.

Q. Will you allow me to make a statement personal to myself? For several years past I have had much experience in connection with this sad phenomenon of madness. I know a case of a person who now and then has severe attacks, and while they last she is in a most violent and unmanageable state. Now, if I go into the room while she is in this state, I have only to stand and look at her, and say, very quietly, "Sit down," and it is precisely as the waves dropped at the feet of Jesus when he said, "Peace, be still;" that woman is as perfectly calm and self-possessed as I am at this moment. Can you explain how this is effected?

A. By the most simple of all rules. You transmit through your thought, your desire, just that which is needed to produce this equilibrium of the nervous forces. You throw upon the subject a magnetic life which at once calms the mental waves.

Q. Is the power to throw this magnetism upon another a power independent of the individual who possesses it? I am not a relative of this woman. Ten years ago, I did not know such a person lived. No blood relation, no dearest friend she has, has the smallest power over her. They are sure to irritate her all the more. I calm her, as I say. How is it that I can do it, when no one in sympathy with her can?

A. Simply because you are in magnetic *rapport* with her, and they are not. She is receptive of your magnetic life, and is not of theirs. Yours is peculiarly adapted to calm this disturbance; theirs is not.

By Theodore Parker, May 28, 1868.

Q. I wish to ask with reference to testing spirits that come to us. We have sometimes been very sadly misled. When a spirit purports to be present, how can we know to a certainty that it is the spirit it professes to be? We have frequently tested them by asking if they were willing to say amen to the Lord's Prayer. This test was suggested to me by William Howitt, who said it had never failed him. Can you tell me of any test upon which we may always rely?

A. My dear, good friend, by no possibility can you, in mortal, under present circumstances, ever be thoroughly sure of the identity of any returning spirit, because the returning spirit is out of your sight, beyond the realm and sphere of your natural senses, and these senses alone are the powers by which you can weigh and measure all things with which you come in contact. Now, I may tell you I am the spirit of such an individual who lived at such a time, and I may tell you what is absolutely true. You may believe it, but you cannot know it. You have only my word for it. You cannot see me — I am behind the screen of another life. You only see that life, and as much of my own as I am able to give through that organic life. Now, I care not how many prayers you may repeat, or how many "amens" the spirit may add thereto. It will make not the slightest difference with regard to testing the identity of the spirit. You can only test it so far as your own reasoning faculties will carry you — no farther. "So far shalt thou go, and no farther," says the external life. Now, then, I will venture to say that seven at least — that is setting it low — out of every ten returning spirits come with an honest purpose. They give you just as much as is possible, under their conditions, and they have no intention whatever of deceiving. Those who do are the exception, not the rule. You find those who deceive, who love to deceive, here. They go to the spirit-world with the same tendencies; they return with the same, and they manifest the same till they have outlived it. It is a law of celestial life that the soul shall outlive all its imperfections. It shall pass beyond all its mental darkness. It shall come so near the Infinite that it shall part with all its grossness, with all that which fetters it, with all that which makes it in any sense morally deformed. Understand us to say, we know of no way by which you can, for an absolute certainty, test the identity of any returning spirit. We are honest in so telling you. You should measure all by your senses; receive all that comes within the test of your senses; all that you feel in your inner life to be good, to be true, to be what it purports to be, receive and appropriate to your own use, so far as you are able. But all that you cannot thus weigh, lay it one side till you can; but by no means cast out as worthless that which you cannot test or cannot understand, for by so doing you may shut the doors on the brightest angel that ever visited human life.

Q. I am much obliged to you for your explicit answer, though it is not what I expected. But I would like to mention a case in point. A spirit comes and tells me it is my duty to take a certain step involving an important change in my life, influencing for good or evil myself, my family, and my future prospects. There is nothing in the message itself that seems unreasonable. It may appear a perfectly proper thing to do. Would it be right to trust the spirit, and follow its direction? To make the case clearer, suppose the spirit to say, "You should leave your present sphere of labor; the climate is prejudicial to your health, and by going to another place you will do a large amount of good." Now, I am unable to say whether the climate is injurious, or whether by removing I should do more good; but, if certain of these facts, I should, of course, at once follow the spirit's advice. What would be my duty under the circumstances?

A. Well, my dear friend, from the experience I have gathered in such matters during my life as a disembodied spirit, I can give you only one answer, and that is, it would be absolutely wrong for you to be led in any direction by any spirit or spirits, however high, at the expense of the yielding up of your own reason. If you cannot see that it would be right for you to make any such move, it would be absolutely wrong to make it. Any spirit who returns asking you to lay down the brightest ornament of your manhood at their behest, you may be very sure is mistaken with regard to your highest and best good. I can only answer from my own stand-point of experience; but I have looked this matter fairly in the face, and have made it a subject of earnest investigation, and I can come to only this conclusion: that the reason which we have in human life is the oracle that stands between our God and ourselves, always pointing the way. We should heed it, and however much we may receive the advice of others, we should never appropriate it except it is in accordance with our highest reason. Do you understand?

Q. I quite understand what you say, though it has failed to remove my difficulty. In this case, I see no particular reasons either for or against. But if perfectly certain the spirit was advising me to do what it knew to be right, I should follow it. I have no other evidence to guide me.

A. Then I should say, by all means, remain just where you are till your evidence is sufficient to lead you.

By Joshual Beri, a Jew Rabbi, June 2, 1868.

Q. Can you tell us what has become of the ancient seers and sages? Can they communicate with us, or are they so far away that they cannot return here?

A. The ancient seers and sages are often in your midst, communicating the thoughts which they have gathered during their experience in spirit-life. They have by no means passed beyond the boundary that divides them from their old, earthly home; on the contrary, they are within earth's sphere, and are constantly lending their intellectual life for the benefit of those who remain on the earth.

Q. Then it is possible that they can come directly and speak to us, personally, is it?

A. They certainly can, and certainly do.

Q. Have you ever communicated personally with the spirit of Jesus?

A. I certainly have. Not with the idol of the Christian church, but with the meek and lowly Nazarene, who came out from the darkness of the church and sought to give a new light to the people then dwelling on the earth. He shed his light, and religious darkness crucified him. He was humble in his circumstances, in his human aspirations. He was not at all what the Christian world suppose him to be, and he returns to earth to-day, just as much a stranger unto those who profess to know him best, as he was in the days in which he lived in the body.

Q. Is not this the second coming of Christ, in a spiritual signification?

A. It certainly is.

Q. Not in a literal, but in a spiritual sense, I mean.

A. In both a literal and spiritual sense. That which

is literal is so unlike what you suppose, that you cannot recognize it. Your church declares that its saviour shall appear in the clouds of heaven with power and great glory; with many attendant angels; with more than the glory that an earthly king could command; with all the pomp that attends earthly sovereigns. O shame! shame! The truth of itself is grand enough without outward show. Wisdom needeth not to be exalted of her children. She will exalt herself.

Q. Who ordered Moses to go out against the Midianites and avenge the children of Israel?

A. Not the Infinite Jehovah, whose love is equal to his wisdom, but the darkness of the times, the superstition of the age.

Q. Did not some ancient spirit represent himself as the one God, accommodating himself to the superstition of the people?

A. The ancient church was in the habit of consulting with the spirits of the dead, and in their ignorance they believed, or the common people did, that these familiar spirits were none other than the Lord, the Jehovah. When Moses consulted with departed spirits, he returned to the people with a "Thus saith the Lord." But he should have returned with a "Thus saith the spirit with whom I have been communicating." It is very possible that the spirit might have been lower in morality than Moses, far beneath him intellectually, but death, to an unenlightened mind, clothes intelligence with superior wisdom; but to an enlightened mind, death takes nothing from the soul and adds nothing to it.

Q. Then are the ancients very much in advance of the moderns in development?

A. By no means.

Q. They have had the benefit of development in the spirit-world, and we in the material?

A. Yes; and the two generally keep pace together.

Q. May not this age be very properly considered the dawn of the millennium?

A. It certainly is.

Q. Is it not already inaugurated?

A. To me it is.

Q. And within a very short time, too?

A. Yes.

By T. Starr King, June 8, 1868.

Q. Have spirits power to foresee events, and if so, whence do they gain that power?

A. That they have the power to foresee events has been perfectly demonstrated many, many times. The old adage that "coming events cast their shadows before," is very true. It is these shadows that the disembodied spirit perceives, and judges concerning the objective form which will take place in the earth-life. Every idea that is outwrought fully in the earth-life, gathers to itself a large, long train of circumstances which are unseen to you, but not so to disembodied intelligences, and whoso is able to add together all these unseen circumstances, is able to give you a correct answer concerning the issue upon all points, from the smallest to the very largest.

Q. Do not many attempt to prophesy who are not competent?

A. Certainly. Many persons suppose they have solved a problem correctly, but it is one thing to suppose you have done a thing just right, and quite another thing to do it just right. But the failure of one individual does not detract from the power of another. By no means.

Q. Whence comes the material that forms the spirit-hands so frequently seen in the presence of mediums?

A. From the atmosphere, or from what is contained in the atmosphere, focalized and condensed through mediumistic life.

Q. Is it made from elementary compounds?

A. It is. You are well aware, or you should be, that the atmosphere contains the elements of which all forms are made. Every conceivable form that finds expression on the earth may be found in the elements of the atmosphere peculiar to the earth.

Q. I have seen H. Melville Fay perform quite a number of tricks, if we may so term them, with the Davenport Brothers. He says he is exposing them. Do you think he is a medium?

A. I certainly do. Nay, more than that, I know that he is. I know also that he is given to trickery, and will bear a very large amount of criticism.

Q. Then you think that spirits would assist him in his trickery?

A. I certainly do.

Q. Then spirits do, at times, assist in deception?

A. Why should they not? There are spirits disembodied who are upon the same plane with himself, and from them you should expect similar mental conditions. They would do what he would do. They stand no higher, no lower. They are ready to assist him in all that is possible. Mediumship, or spirit manifestations, are by no means dependent upon any high moral law. They belong to Nature; and Nature sometimes gives very crude manifestations, while again she gives us very lovely ones.

Q. Were not the Davenport Brothers good mediums at first?

A. And so they are now.

Q. Do you think it is a benefit to Spiritualism to allow Fay to go on?

A. It certainly does not harm Spiritualism. It cannot.

Q. Does it not in the estimation of the people?

A. No; not even in the estimation of its opponents. Spiritualism, as a natural science, cannot be harmed by the trickery of one, two, or a thousand individuals. All these persons who practise trickery under the name of Spiritualism, do but excite the populace to investigate, to know what is true and what is false. That which they would use against Spiritualism the great God throws into the scale and uses for it.

Q. Are spirits in the other world subject to impressions of the elements as are we? Do they experience, night and day, the benefits of the sun, &c.?

A. They do; not in the same sense that you do, but in a similar sense. They have their seasons of rest and of intense activity.

Q. More so than in this world?

A. No; perhaps not.

Q. Do they read time as we do?

A. O, no. There is no time in the spirit-world, not such as is recognized by you.

Q. Do they not reckon by minutes and hours, as we do?

A. Nothing of the kind. Time, if it is measured at all, is measured by events.

Q. How do they regulate their hours of rest?

A. By their needs. The spirit rests when it has need of rest.

Q. Then there must be a limit to their power?

A. Certainly.

By Theodore Parker, June 10, 1868.

Q. Is there any one on the earth who can teach and truly explain the mystery of godliness? If so, I would thankfully ask the spirits to proclaim the name of the person, through the medium, that the world may be blessed.

A. They who teach and continually preach of the mystery of godliness may be found among the little children of earth. I know of nothing in all the forms of mind and matter that preaches so eloquently of God as the little child; and would you be godly, learn of them. They will never lead you astray.

Q. How, and for what purpose, are spirit-lights produced?

A. Through electrical effusions; and they are produced to satisfy inquiring minds concerning the power of disembodied spirits. They are focalized by means of the power that is drawn from the medium's body, and they are ignited by the same power. They are capable of burning in your atmosphere till that power is exhausted, and no longer.

By John Pierpont, June 23, 1868.

Q. Is there any property system in the spirit-world analogous to the one we have on earth, as respects landed, personal, or monetary property?

A. The law of mine and thine, so far as universal nature is concerned, has an existence only on the earth, and I, for one, thank God for it. Whatever the soul has absolute need of, in the spirit-land, that it has, and no more. It cannot hoard up treasures in that kingdom of the hereafter. It cannot gather to itself any more than it can make use of; but all that it can make use of, for its own good and the good of its fellows, that it will always find. Land-holders, such as we find on earth, will lose their occupation in the spirit-land. Those who find their heaven in the sphere of real estate will step out of heaven when death visits them. And I would advise all such to change their sphere while here, for so sure as they do not, terrible remorse and dissatisfaction of spirit will be sure to overtake them.

Q. Do not the laws of Nature, justice, and harmony, guarantee to every one a free use of all the natural elements, such as sunlight, atmosphere, water, and earth, in such quantities only as are needed for actual use? And do they not forbid all monopoly of the same?

A. Why, certainly. The gifts of God are free to all. The sun shines upon the criminal and the pious man alike. There is no difference. The water is just as pure to the sinner as to the saint. Flowers bloom in the bad man's garden as in the good man's.

Q. Why should the earth be monopolized by a few, at the expense of the many, when the water, air, and sunshine are free to all?

A. According to higher wisdom there should be no monopoly, and when the soul has entered the sphere of the higher wisdom there will be none. It is only because you dwell in darkness. You are ignorant of the better way, that you choose that one.

Q. Cannot mankind be taught a better system for the distribution of the soil, in equitable shares to all, so that each and all may have home and plenty, instead of, as now, the two vicious extremes of excessive wealth and extreme poverty?

A. Yes, they can be taught in this direction, but it

will be by slow degrees. They have been a long time learning to accumulate. The spirit of greed has been too long a household guest. It is one of the idols, and when it is demolished there will come weeping and wailing because of its death. But by slow degrees the soul will be taught to understand that all that it gathers to itself that it cannot use, will be a drug in heaven's market. Now, remember that, every one of you. If you have a dollar more than you know what to do with, get rid of it just as quick as you can.

Q. Could not human laws be brought up to harmonize with the natural or divine, in guaranteeing this equitable distribution of land, in shares proportioned to population? and would not this do more than any other thing to abolish poverty, degradation, and crime from society, and to establish justice, plenty, harmony, and happiness among men?

A. Yes, but as I before said, it can only be done by slow degrees. There can be no sudden overturn in this direction. It must be brought about by a slow, even process of development. It cannot by any possibility be brought about, to stand upon a firm basis, in any other way

By Joseph Lowenthall, June, 29, 1868.

Q. Have spirits the power to visit other planets?

A. They certainly have.

Q. And do they?

A. They do.

Q. And return to this planet?

A. They do.

Q. Are the intelligences there informed like those of this?

A. Many of them, we are told, are very well informed. Some are in advance, in many points, of the children of earth. Upon some planets the arts and sciences are many steps in advance of what you have here. It would be very egotistical to suppose, in the present state of intelligence, that this small earth were the only one of the celestial bodies that was peopled by beings who were intelligent, who had passed out of the babyhood of the race and entered the manhood and womanhood of it.

Q. In visiting other planets, have spirits the same ability to enter the external sphere of the planet as they have of the earth sphere?

A. I have been told that they meet with many difficulties in such expeditions, but that they are all successfully overcome by the persevering.

By Theodore Parker, June 30, 1868.

Q. When the spirit leaves the body — if very pure — does it not ascend to a high altitude above the atmosphere, and live in the element called electricity? If the spirit is gross or unprogressed, is it not obliged to remain on or near the earth until it has become purified?

A. It is not necessary that the soul should pass out of the atmosphere of the earth in order to dwell in the highest state of heaven. The atmosphere which belongs particularly to the soul may be found everywhere. There is no special place set apart for it. It has an existence wherever there is harmony. Whenever and wherever the soul is happy, when it rests in a state of contentment and peace, then it is in that rarefied atmosphere which you call by the term heaven. It is not necessary that the soul should rise, pass beyond the earthly atmosphere, to one more rarefied and electrical as belonging to human things. You are so apt to confound the conditions which belong to mind and those which belong to matter, that it is almost impossible to make you understand that heaven, or the atmosphere in which the soul lives, is not a locality. It can be here; it can be millions of miles away; it can be everywhere. It is a mistaken idea that there is a land where the soul gravitates after death, sixty, seventy, a hundred or more miles out of earth's atmosphere. This is reasoning from an entirely material stand-point, and the soul takes no part in it whatever.

Q. You say the soul has always existed as an individual entity — that is, it existed in embryo prior to conception. Is not that the case with all organizing life-germs, whether vegetable or animal?

A. Yes, I so believe.

Q. It has of late been asserted by the intelligence controlling that the motive power controlling the body acts outside of the body, and controls and guides it as the musician does his instrument. If that is the case, why have we been told differently — that the spirit existed within the body, and left it at death? Again, if the spirit exists outside of the body, where did it come from? Did it emanate from the body, or did it exist as an entity prior to the existence of the body?

A. Both statements are equally correct. Allow me to illustrate. There is a life-principle within the flower, and that life-principle exists beyond the externally seen boundaries of the flower. It is not confined entirely to the inner, but goes beyond the material boundaries of the flower, is attached to the form, belongs to the form. Some spirits exercise their power upon their machine, the human body, from the external to the internal, while others exercise their power from the internal to the external. Some work from within to the without, others the reverse. There are no two souls playing upon these human instruments exactly alike. Every one varies. It may seem to the outside observer that the musical performer always acts from the external to the internal, but that is a mistake. So far as your external senses are able to perceive, he does; but there are senses that go beyond them. I know of many musical performers who perform from the internal to the external, even in the crude things of this life. It is common, and you can do no other way than to measure all by your human senses, and whatever cannot be measured by them you cannot understand. The soul eludes this power. You cannot grasp it. You cannot throw it in the scales of your human senses, there to be weighed. You cannot brıng it within the scope of your analytical uuderstanding, there to be analyzed. You cannot kill it; it escapes death. It is a subtle intelligence that predominates over all things. I believe it has ever had an existence, and ever will. As a controlling spirit, I surround this subject, and I act from the external to the internal. I possess myself of all the faculties of her being, but I do so from the external. A certain part of my life becomes absorbed, but it is a very small part. There are other spirits who become largely absorbed, so much so that they are obliged to act from the internal to the external. That is because the law of the life of the subject has a stronger controlling power than the external foreign spirit has. I stand upon the outside and draw out the forces, while others are attracted to the inner and throw out the forces. The sun sheds his rays upon the earth, and calls out from her glorious storehouse, but a certain portion of the sun's rays are absorbed by the earth. Study from Nature's great volume. It is open; it is free; and whoso would make it his own must study earnestly for himself.

Q. Is the difference we see in the natural ability or minds of men to be attributed wholly to organization and circumstances, or is there more soul, spirit, or mind element in some than others from the beginning?

A. The soul, when expressing itself through earthly conditions, is obliged to conform to the law of earthly conditions, and as all earthly subjects, or human bodies, vary in character and in being, so the expression of no two souls can be precisely alike. And as all bodies are differently constituted, so are all souls. There is a law by which souls are aggregated, as there is a law by which bodies are aggregated. Certain spiritual atoms compose the soul, as certain material atoms compose the body. All souls are compounded differently. The component parts of my soul differ from yours. And so it is throughout the vast chain of eternal life. But the life-principle, the eternal all-pervading essence, I believe to be the same in the Bushman and the Hottentot as in the Anglo-Saxon.

Q. It is said by media that clairvoyance is to be attributed to the peculiar organization of the clairvoyant. Will you tell us how it differs from that of the non-clairvoyant? Anatomists do not seem to find any. And if the cause is not in the organization, what is it?

A. Some souls have the power, from time to time, to gain the ascendency over matter, overcoming its laws, overreaching its boundaries. These souls are able to perceive things beyond the boundaries of time or the present. They are able to extend their perception into the past and the future, as into the immediate present. These are called clairvoyants, seers, persons gifted with second or abnormal sight. I do not know that these persons possess a different material organization from all other persons. I believe that the faculty or power of clairvoyance rests more with the spirit than with the body. I believe it is a spiritual rather than a material gift.

By Theodore Parker, Sept. 2, 1868.

Controlling Spirit. — In answer to a question which has been propounded to us at this place, but has not been answered, a selection will be read by the author, who has been absent from the body of flesh some fourteen years, hoping that it will answer the needs of that sorrowing spirit, and assist her to think in the right direction. The question is this: "Is it right for me, or for any one, to seek to obtain a permanent home on earth?" She further adds, "I have all my life sought for it, but in vain, and I have come to think that it is not right for me to seek longer for a home on earth. Still I am in doubt. O angels, give me light."

THE BETTER LAND.

"For here have we no continuing city, but we seek one to come."
Heb. xiii. 14.

No city here, no constant habitation
  Wherein to lay our throbbing hearts and fears;
No city here, where sorrow and vexation
  Can enter not, and bring their weight of cares;
No home of rest, where change can enter never;
  No home which time can crumble not away;
No love-wrought ties that death can fail to sever;
  No spot where darkness follows not the day!

We trust in friendship — like the tossing ocean
 The waves of time can soon deface the spell;
We trust in love — a word, a look, or motion,
 Can bear away the dreams we love so well;
We trust in fame, and find it but a bubble,
 Whose tints, when grasped, fade silently away;
We trust in wealth — 'tis on a sea of trouble;
 It taketh wings and flieth in a day!

We have no home, no region free from sorrow —
 Poor, houseless wanderers in a desert drear —
No place to call our own, no sweet to-morrow,
 Where pleasure comes unsullied by a tear.
No home? no home? On drooping pinion weary,
 Like the lone dove that wandered from the ark,
Must we roam on, still sad, unblessed, and dreary,
 Without a hope, a day-beam in the dark?

Ah, no! ah, no! From heaven's own broad expansion
 A spirit whispers, through the shadowy blue,
"The Father has full many a spacious mansion;"
 There is a home, a happy home for you —
A home where death and time can never enter;
 It stands uncrumbled by the flight of years,
A stream of bliss is glittering in its centre;
 'Tis God's own city, unalloyed by tears.

There, in that home, no throb of deep dejection
 Can check the gladness of the joyful heart;
But sweetly bound in God's own true affection,
 Nothing can rend those clinging ties apart.
We have no home on earth, but sadly driven
 Adown time's stream, where sorrow leaves a trace,

Hope on, sad soul; there is a home in heaven —
  A constant, firm, and sure abiding-place.

Let us not mourn, though life may bring us sorrow;
  Soon can we cast aside the cumbrous clay.
We have a hope, a glorious hope to-morrow —
  A home in heaven, a home of constant day.
We have no home on earth; then let us sever
  Our thoughts from earth and its alluring love,
And list the angel's voice, that whispereth ever,
  There is a home of constancy above.

By Theodore Parker, Sept. 8, 1868.

Q. Andrew Jackson Davis says, "Never allow any soul to pass out of the physical body through the agony of feathers or cotton, either beneath or in folds about the sufferer." Why does it cause them agony?

A. Feathers possess a large amount of animal magnetism, and that magnetism sustains the relation between the spirit and the body, sometimes for hours after it would otherwise have taken its departure. With regard to cotton, we are told that the excess of vegetable magnetism produces similar results. Knowing this to be true, remove all such obstacles from those persons who are fluttering between the two worlds, whose anxious spirits are only kept in misery here by ignorance.

By Theodore Parker, Sept. 10, 1868.

Q. Why do coming events cast their shadows before? For instance, the writer lately met with a disaster, previous to which he kept telling his friends that something disastrous was going to happen; and it did. Can it be accounted for?

A. O yes, upon scientific principles. Everything that lives in forms, which your human senses can take cognizance of, lived in a form which the spirit senses are able to take cognizance of before it entered the merely external form. Everything lives in eternity, is governed by the eternal law, has existed in the past, lives in the present, and claims an existence in the future. To my mind, immortality is the gift of all things. The old adage that "coming events cast their shadows before," is eminently true, and those sensitive persons whose internal lives are in close communion with the other life, are able to behold these so-called phantoms, to recognize their presence. You call them apparitions, forewarnings, and you suppose, sometimes, that they are specialities, sent by God to inform you of danger. This is not so. It is simply the exercise of a scientific law, and as you come within the sphere of law, you recognize it. Millions of unseen, unrecognized worlds exist, beyond the reach of the eye or the telescope. When one after another is brought within the range of human vision, science does not think of saying, "This is a special interposition of divine providence." No. The time of such folly has gone by. Everything that has existence at all, even in the most phantom-like shape, exists by law. There is nothing like imagination, not as you define it. There is no unsystematized vagary in all God's realm. Everything that is, is by virtue of natural law, and in so far as you understand the law and can come into communion with it, so far you sense that which in the external you cannot see, cannot hear.

Q. Is it possible that an internal disease — curable — can be cured by simply laying on the hands externally?

A. Certainly, it is possible; for the magnetic currents or healing magnetism that is used in the laying on of hands, passes more than over the surface of the animal life — it permeates the inner being.

Q. Can infants, of a few weeks old, recently deceased, return and give an intelligible, oral message through a medium? If so, please give an explanation.

A. No, they cannot do so. That is one of the things that are impossible. If you are told that they can, do not believe it. The child of three weeks old enters the spirit-land as a babe, nothing more. Could it talk here? No. Could it manifest intelligence here? No. Then do not look for it, simply because it has passed through the change called death.

By William E. Channing, Sept. 17, 1868.

Q. Will the intelligence please explain the following paragraph: —

"Strange Hallucination. — A strange and surprising incident occurred last week in the country some miles north of Corinth. A Mr. Mangrum killed a young man during the war, and a few days since Mr. Mangrum was on a deer drive, and while at one of the stands he saw an object approaching him which so alarmed him that he raised his gun and fired at it. The object, which resembled a man covered with a sheet, continued to advance upon him, when he drew his pistols and emptied all the barrels at the ghost. None of the shots seeming to take effect, he climbed a tree to make his escape. By the time he was a short distance up the tree, the white object was standing under him with its eyes fixed upon him, and he declared that it was the spirit of the young man whom he had killed. Mangrum was so startled at the steady gaze of the eye that he had been the cause of laying cold in death, that he fainted and fell from the tree. His friends carried him home, the ghost following and standing before him constantly, the sight of which brought up the recollection of his guilt with such force to his mind, that he died in great agony after two or three days' suffering." — *Corinth (Miss.) Caucasian.*

A. The writer of the article seems to believe that this phenomenon is but a hallucination, a something unreal, a vagary of the brain. You Spiritualists know better — you, whose minds have been enlightened with regard to the science of life here and life hereafter, know better. You know very well that it is not only possible for the spirit to return, but it is altogether probable that, under such circumstances, it would return, and, if the murderer had any mediumistic powers, would make use of them. Now, if the spirit were kindly disposed, and retained no spirit of revenge towards the murderer, it would be impossible for the spirit to seek to do the murderer harm. But should the spirit of revenge linger with the disembodied spirit, it would be the most natural thing in the world that it should seek to find expression here, and, finding means through which to express itself, would use them. This is no miracle; it is one of the legitimate manifestations of your time; a child of law, perfect in itself, and amenable only to the great law of the universe. Ignorant minds may cavil at such manifestations, but when their ignorance has departed their cavilling will have departed also.

Q. Can spirits in the other world exercise their power to make people do wrong?

A. They certainly can, and do exercise that power very largely.

Q. Cannot good spirits also exercise their power to make them do right?

A. They certainly can; but if the propensity to do wrong exists in the subject used, that propensity will be very likely to attract to itself a similar evil. Therefore the battery would be complete, and the undeveloped spirit would gain perfect control.

Q. Would not the good influence have power to counteract the bad?

A. Not always. No good influence can break any law, nor infringe upon any law.

By William E. Channing, Sept. 22, 1868.

Q. Why is it that at public circles our friends do not come as often as strangers?

A. If by public circles you refer to this place, we can assure you that all the intimate friends of the persons who are gathered here from time to time are prohibited from communicating.

Q. I mean other circles.

A. Then ask your own individuality why it is. Would you be as likely to communicate private, that is, domestic intelligence, to your friends when any number of strangers were present? Certainly not. You would nine times out of ten feel a retiring delicacy that would overcome your desire to meet the friends and communicate with them. Now, all spirits who desire to communicate with their own dearly beloved ones who have passed beyond the vale, should remember that those friends are human still. They possess all the attributes of human nature. They would rather meet their friends in private than in public. Therefore, if you desire to be satisfied in the communications that may take place between your friends and yourself, meet them privately, and see to it that you select the very best instruments that you have any knowledge of, for the very best are none too good.

Q. Please define the Deity. In your invocation you seem to address an Eternal Spirit; I would like to hear that Spirit defined.

A. I can only define God to my own satisfaction, not to the satisfaction of any other individual in the universe. To me, God is the living, eternal power of good that I see everywhere. I see this power in the flowers, in the rocks, in the air, in everything that I behold. In all things with which I come in contact I recognize this power. To me it is good; it is God. There is something of good in all things to me. In this sense I am a materialist. I do not believe in a God apart from his works. I do not believe in a God outside of nature; but I believe in one that is in and around us, and in all with which we come in contact. To me this is God. You may call it Jehovah, or Brahma, or by any name you please, but it is the great, living spirit that permeates all things and controls all.

Q. Why do we not have better mediums, when it is so essential that we should?

A. Because you do not know how to take care of those you have. When these are properly cared for, and not pampered in the wrong way; when they are properly understood, and educated by you into the recognition of the divine life, then, doubtless, the spirit-world will exercise its power to develop more. Now you cannot well care for those you have. Therefore do not ask for more of the same sort, or of a better sort. You would not care for them any better. Were the Jesus of other days to return, exercising his power tangibly over humanity to-day, would humanity recognize that power? Does it recognize the power? No. Jesus says, "I come to my own, but my own receive me not."

Q. If Jesus is really a person, and here among us, why does he not come to these circles, and answer these questions? Are we not now intelligent enough to accept it, if he did?

A. Would it be any more satisfactory? I think not. Would the mere attachment of the name of Jesus the Christ to any truth make it more of a truth? Certainly not.

Q. Would he come, were he invited?

A. It is possible, and perhaps probable. You are not to understand that Jesus the Christ in person, as a distinct spirit, cannot return and manifest to mortals, for he certainly can. He who, through the guardianship of truth, had so clear an understanding of these things, so far in the past; he who could see through the darkness of that past, sees equally well through the brighter light of to-day; and the same power that was so potent in other days is not less so to-day. Jesus the Christ lives to-day, as he lived eighteen hundred years ago. He has the same gifts, the same love, the same wisdom; but should he come *in propria persona* as a spirit, announcing himself as the veritable Jesus the Christ of other days, would he make you understand him? Immediately the cry of blasphemy would be raised; hands would be lifted in holy horror everywhere; and yet this meek and lowly Nazarene walks in your midst every day. Rest assured of that.

By William E. Channing, Sept. 24, 1868.

Chairman. The following question was sent to us for publication, with the request that some Spiritualist should make it clear, if possible. I will present it here.

Q. Are the elements in the world beyond subjective

or objective? That is to say, communications purporting to come from the spirit-land state that trees, mountains, rivers, and flowers exist there. Do they exist simply in the imagination, subjective, or are they a reality, objective? If you step into my parlor, you, in common with others, agree that there are windows, chairs, and pictures in the room; take the entire community, rich and poor, educated and ignorant, the good and the bad — all will agree to the same general fact. If a spirit-world exists, and the occupants thereof do really communicate with us here on earth, why, the unbeliever questions, do not the spirits unanimously agree, as above, in regard to the tangible reality of things purporting to exist in their sphere?

A. All the phenomena of nature, and all the forms in nature that have an existence with you, have also an *objective* existence in the spirit-world proper. There are things, places in the spirit-world, as well as thoughts. The peach and the pear, the glorious forest tree, the mountain and the ocean, do not exist alone in the imagination of the spirit, or in the memory of what has been. But they are living, tangible, present realities. Your correspondent asks why the spirits do not all agree upon this subject. It is very clear why they do not. The western prairie is by no means an eastern city. That you will admit. A wild man of your western prairie, when told of the swarms of intelligent beings that fill your eastern cities, doubts you, cannot believe you. And were he to pass to the spirit-world having no knowledge of these eastern cities, he would return telling you that his spirit-world was a prairie or a hunting-ground. You should not forget that the spirit-world is only a condition of being, just as your world is here. There are places where there are no trees, no flowers, no vegetables, none of the beauties of nature, nothing that would be beautiful to you, and there are intelligent spirits dwelling in such places. If they have the power to return, they come back reporting that there are no natural beauties in the spirit-world, no natural scenery. They have heard of it, but they have not seen it. It is all imagination. So it is to them. But to those who have been more fortunate, it is not imagination. The happy child that returns from the spirit-land will tell you of the flowers, the birds, the glorious spiritual prospects, everything that goes to gladden the soul. Perhaps at the next breath one will return, saying, "There are no flowers, no fruits; I see nothing of the kind. My spirit-home furnishes nothing of the kind." Has one been false? No; both have told you the truth. Your spirit-home is by no means the spirit-home of any other spirit. Your surroundings are dependent upon yourself. You are attracted by a spiritual law of gravitation that you cannot thwart to your proper places in the spirit-world. That place has its natural spiritual scenery, or it is devoid of it. Perhaps there are trees and flowers, grasses and rivers; perhaps not. The great scroll of spiritual revealments is fast being unrolled, and slowly the mists and fogs of your former superstition will pass away. You have believed in a personal Deity, seated upon a great white throne. You will by and by lay that false idea under your feet, and embrace one more rational. Just so fast as the light of God's wisdom and truth shines into your souls, just so fast you can perceive the truth in all its simplicity. We tell you again and again, there are beautiful things in the spirit-world — trees, flowers, grasses, fruits; all that you have here are faithfully represented there; you may be sure of that.

By William E. Channing, Sept. 29, 1868.

Q. Are all that were most pure in life and character here, and consequently most exalted in spirit-life, agreed with you in seeking to propagate the spiritual philosophy? and if not, why not?

A. Jesus has said, "Blessed are the pure in heart, for they shall see God." It is my belief that they who are truly pure in their inner lives cannot fail to see God everywhere. As the soul advances in purity and perfection, it perceives more and more of God's truths, those which he had heretofore called hidden, mysterious. It becomes more and more fully acquainted with the science of life, not only the life that is, but that has been, and is to come. Purity, goodness, perfection, are to me one and the same. They are only terms used to express God's attributes through humanity. Those intelligences that passed from this earth with pure thoughts, with holy desires, with their inner being elevated above the darkness of human life, cannot fail to perceive this angel, Spiritualism, in its true light; and seeing and understanding it to be the voice of God to the children of earth, if they are loyal to their purity of soul, they will do all in their power to roll on the car of Progress, so far as Spiritualism is concerned. The ranks are well filled in the spirit-world. That vast army who seek to benefit earth's people know that Spiritualism is to be the Saviour of this age. They know it to be the light by which the soul shall understand something concerning the mysteries of godliness, and knowing this, they will labor zealously in the cause.

Q. Are the opponents of this theory — viz., the churches and preachers of Christendom — ministered to by spirits?

A. They are. No one is left outside of Spiritualism and disembodied spirits.

Q. We are told that man's spirit has always existed in an individualized state; that whatever has a beginning must have an ending; but man, as an immortal being, has always existed. If I have rightly understood, then, I would ask, Did man, in any prior state of existence, know more than he did at his birth into this world?

A. The soul, in essence, is of God; ever has been, is, and I believe ever will be. But that external individuality through which the essence is expressed, is perpetually changing. It is subject to the law of change, and from all past eternity has been passing through an infinite number of changes. I believe in the eternity of the soul, past, present, and future, but not in the eternity of the individuality that belongs to the present. No soul can claim to possess an eternal individuality. Our immortality, that which belongs to our inner lives, is of God, changeless, perfect.

Q. What is progression? Could man's spirit have been progressing through all the infinite ages of past eternity, and still understand so little at its entrance into our world?

A. Progression, to me, is simply another term for change. The soul progresses in cycles, as does all life. It repeats itself again and again, ever revolving around its centre, God, and at each revolution takes on newer life, exhibits some more perfect attributes, stretches out further into infinity, becomes wiser, becomes, in the external, holier.

Q. I would like to have you give your idea of a power, that has been with some persons for years, by which, if they say to another person that a table is heavier than its usual weight, that person will, in most cases, acknowledge that an unseen power is upon the table, making it quite heavy, the one speaking not coming in contact with the table, or using his will-power knowingly.

A. Disembodied spirits have the power to add to the laws of natural gravitation, and to take therefrom. For instance, certain spirits have the power to make this article of furniture (the table) very light or very heavy, but the power can be used only through certain physical organisms. In all probability, the individual you speak of possessed the requisite power.

Q. Can this power be applied successfully in removing disease at a distance by sending a letter?

A. It certainly can.

By Rev. Henry Ware.

Q. Some one states that spirits have to prepare a person who is to become a medium, by spiritualizing his forces before they can manifest through him. Is this a fact? and what is the substance used in his training?

A. I am not aware that mediumship is a thing of art. To me, it belongs to life and to nature, and any kind of training cannot change its quality. Disembodied spirits do often experiment with mediums, but it is not that they may change the mediumistic forces, but that they may understand them. It is not that they may make a person a medium, but that they may learn to use the powers already in existence. Mediums are such from conception. It is a power over which they had no control, and in which they had no voice whatever. It is a part of their nature, and a part of their life. The elements used by disembodied spirits are found pervading the nerves. This subtle force that brings the departed spirit into communion with those still in the body, is the life-principle of the nervous system. No kind of physical training can create it, or change its inherent properties. The power that is within may be brought to the exterior, but it is essentially the same. And they who tell you that they can develop mediums, or make or change them, tell you what is wholly unsound. It matters not where the teaching comes from. Nature and the science of life determine it to be unsound.

By Thomas Paine, Oct. 12, 1868.

Q. Is the formation of the National Association of Spiritualists sanctioned by the spirit-world? In other words, was the movement premature, or otherwise? A concise answer is solicited by many inquiring minds.

A. There is always more or less agitation preceding the birth of any new idea, subject, or condition, whether mental, physical, or spiritual. The movement in question is in itself partly premature and partly upon the threshold of its proper time. Spiritualists and Spiritualism are by no means, at the present time, one. They are as clearly separate from each other as the earth is separate and different from the stars; belonging to one great spiritual system, but having distinct individualities. Spiritualists have hardly the first true idea of what Spiritualism is, and what it demands of them. To be united to Spiritualism is a very great thing. It is to part with all one's old ideas with regard to things of the spirit. It is to stand upon a new and untried platform. How many Spiritualists, in the deepest, and truest, and divinest sense, do this? I know of none, because I know of none who understand Spiritualism as it is — the all-mighty science of life to-day and life that is to come.

This movement, concerning which you desire an answer, as I before remarked, is in part before its time, and in part it is upon the threshold of its appointed time. I do not believe in seeking to force anything into existence before its natural, appointed time. I do not believe in seeking to force a man or woman to believe what they are not ready to believe, to sign articles of faith of which they know very little. And as I believe that Spiritualists have not yet grown large enough to understand Spiritualism, I believe the time has not yet come for the entering in of the body of Spiritualists to the great temple that they desire to enter so earnestly. It is well to organize; but it is well, before organizing, to understand what organization means. It is well to understand ourselves, and the great body of thinkers to whom we seek to become united. I would not, for a moment, throw one pebble in the way of this great stream of progress; but I would check those minds that are seeking to override the little things that they may gain the great things. I would force every Spiritualist, so called, to study the principles of Spiritualism ere they seek to ally themselves to the great cause of Spiritualism, either spiritually or materially. I am well aware that in union there is strength, and that as Spiritualists need to be strengthened, they need to be united; but I am also well aware that there is a union more to be sought after than the external one. When Spiritualists are more united in spirit, then they will of necessity organize in the material. They will flow into that condition, of necessity. But while they are so disunited in spirit, they may seek permanent organization, but they will seek in vain. Let the organization, then, commence in the internal, and work to the external. How is it now? Why, even a casual observer need not be mistaken. While, throughout the length and breadth of the land, Spiritualists are united, perhaps, upon the one idea that spirits can return, and can communicate with their friends in mortal, having said this much with regard to their unity, we have said all that we can.

By Theodore Parker, Oct. 13, 1868.

Q. The intelligence purporting to be Thomas Paine said that Spiritualists are united in the belief that spirits can return. We have constant proofs that our friends *do* manifest, through favorable conditions. Will you tell us something about the indwelling life of Spiritualism, whereby we can rise a step higher in this sublime philosophy?

A. Spiritualism belongs to life, and is always with you; and just so fast as you grow in the knowledge of spiritual things, just so fast you come to understand what Spiritualism is. It is always well to seek for the highest gifts, for the very best places in Nature from which to view God and his works. The soul ever aspires towards the better — some in one way, and some in another — and although in the outward some souls seem to retrograde, yet they never do. They are all seeking for happiness, for a better state of being. Mr. Paine remarked that Spiritualists were thoroughly disunited, except upon one point. I believe that to be true; but I believe also that unity will come to the great body of Spiritualists as they grow in spiritual things. Just as fast as they put the letter under their feet, and accept the spirit, they will rise, and no faster; they will come into possession of those diviner beauties that belong to Spiritualism; they will understand it better, enjoy it more fully, and be more nearly allied to it. Now, as Mr. Paine says, they are widely apart. Spiritualists and their belief are not married as yet, notwithstanding many suppose, no doubt, that their belief is very dear to them. So it is; but it has not yet become a part of their inner lives. All things in Nature grow by slow and distinct degrees, and as Spiritualism is of Nature, all that belongs to it unfolds by slow degrees. Nature makes no marked and distinct overriding steps. No. Slowly and surely she moves on through eternity; and so it will be with regard to Spiritualism and Spiritualists. In the years that are to come, those persons who recognize the truths of Spiritualism will enjoy those truths — they will be wedded to their inner lives, for those persons will have grown large enough to put on the beautiful clothing that belongs to Spiritualism; but you Spiritualists of to-day are not large enough. But do not mourn because you are not. You are in the alphabet of this great science of life, and you must learn that well, ere you can take the next step.

By Father Henry Fitz James, Oct. 15, 1868.

Q. What is the occupation of spirits in the spirit-world?

A. Each spirit is occupied somewhat differently from all other spirits. All the various occupations that are known to earth are also known and are in action in the spirit-world. The artist finds employment with us, the mechanic — all the arts and sciences are fully represented with us as with you, only on a larger and grander scale. Do not suppose that when you lay off your earthly bodies you will cease to be active as spirits, for I tell you you will not. There are no drones in the great hive of the spirit-world. All are exceedingly active. Yes, the mechanic finds occupation there. All that the soul enjoys to be occupied upon, it will find ample means to reach in the spirit-world.

Q. Are those who were teachers here, teachers there, or do they change their occupation?

A. That depends upon whether the teacher here was a teacher in spirit or only in the external. Many are teachers here simply from the force of circumstances. Such abandon the occupation when this life is done, and take up some other that is more congenial. But if such from natural inclination, you may be very sure they continue it beyond this life.

Q. Are all who profess to be clairvoyant really so?

A. Every soul is, to a certain extent, clairvoyant. Clairvoyance is an attribute of the soul, of all souls — some are more largely gifted than others in this respect.

Q. Is there as much evil existing in the spirit-world as there is here?

A. There is evil existing in the spirit; you may be sure of that. But I define evil simply as the lesser good. There is not that class of evil existing there that you find here, but there is an outgrowth of the same evil circumstances in the spirit-world as here. For instance, the drunkard enters the spirit-world as a drunkard. Death does not change him, only it takes away his external shell. It leaves the man precisely the same; and so it is with regard to all the evils or mistakes of life. The spirit-world finds you precisely where this lays you down. You do not become a saint upon entering the spirit-world when you have left this as a sinner — by no means.

Q. What means are taken to correct evil in the spirit-world?

A. All the various means that human or divine reason can devise. There are no prisons in the spirit-world; there are no gibbets. The soul is not forced into the better way through fear, but always through love; and love is always attended by wisdom and justice. With these three angels no soul can, for any great length of time, remain in evil, or in spiritual darkness. The soul who is prone to what you call evil, is slowly and distinctly shown the better. All the consequences of evil are distinctly portrayed to the soul in all their power, and, at the same time, the consequences of a pure and holy life are portrayed to the soul. It instinctively chooses the better way then, and if it is weak, there are plenty who are strong to give the helping hand. There are no Levites in the spirit-world. Good Samaritans meet you at every turn.

Q. Is ignorance universal on the earth?

A. It certainly is. It goes hand in hand with wisdom. You may be wise upon certain points, and exceedingly ignorant upon certain other points. Every soul possesses a certain amount — and that amount depends upon the capacities and characteristics of the soul — of wisdom and of ignorance. A Daniel Webster may be very wise so far as Coke and Blackstone are concerned, but very ignorant of the moral law.

Q. Several spirits have returned to me and reported that they had been lying in a trance state, or sleep, during their stay in the spirit-world, some four, some eight, ten, or twelve years. Can you explain that?

A. The soul sometimes remains in a mystified, befogged condition after death. The length of it depends upon the inner power of the spirit to burst the chains of darkness and set itself free. The excessive use of certain stimulants here on the earth will so mystify and befog the spirit that it will remain for days, perhaps weeks or years, in that clouded, uncertain state — neither conscious of their own condition nor of their surroundings. They cannot tell you whether they are on earth or in the spirit-world. But when their inner power asserts itself, the mists and fogs begin to disappear.

By Theodore Parker, Oct. 19, 1868.

Q. Does every person upon entering spirit-life become united to a conjugal companion *forever*, or is the companion changed as his or her condition changes?

A. Spirits grow and live in accordance with the law of necessity. If a companion is an absolute soul-necessity in the spirit-land to any individual, you may rest assured the companion can be found and obtained. Some souls grow better alone for a time, while others reach out for that close communion and companionship which is found alone with the male and the female. There is a marriage which belongs to the soul. The soul utters its own ceremonial, makes its own bonds, and breaks them whenever the law shall so determine. Now do not suppose that any condition of being, whatever it may be, whether marriage or the contrary, is eternal, everlasting; for you are all creatures of change. You pass from one condition to another by virtue of the law of necessity that governs you as individuals. Some rise by one process, and some by another. Some, in order to rise, go down into the valleys of despair, and thus gain power to rise, while others have no need of going there. No two souls unfold by exactly the same process. Every soul has its own inherent process of unfoldment, its own inherent law, and it obeys that law to the letter. There is no trespassing upon it, no setting it aside, no breaking it. All must succumb to the law of their being. If the law says a companion is a necessity, the law will provide it. Now you may be very sure of that. Here in this life you are cramped and confined by conventionalities that are not known in the spirit-world. They belong to the things of time, and when you are done with time, so far as this, your human life, is concerned, you are done with these crude conventionalities. You pass into a clearer mental atmosphere ; you enjoy purer perceptions ; you can see farther into the future, and your present is better understood by you. You know better how to choose from your surroundings that which will make you happy.

By Theodore Parker, Oct. 20, 1868.

Q. To whom should we pray?

A. The power, the spirit which giveth birth to prayer, will teach us all, individually, how we should pray. As our prayers are born of divine will, they will reach the source we designed them to reach. The soul prays ever to that which it conceives to be better than itself. It lifts up its sphere of ignorance to the sphere of wisdom. In its weakness, it prays to the source of strength. In its imperfectness, it prays to the perfect source. In its finite perceptions, it prays to the great infinite whole. As the little stream going down the mountain side finds the ocean, so our individual prayers will find the great ocean of infinite good, the eternal presence, the spirit of all good, of all wisdom. It matters not by what name we designate it. Names are of small account, only so far as they are used to represent ideas. We pray to Jehovah as the past, present, and future spirit of all things. The

Brahmin prays to Brahma as the Great Spirit that he understands. The Indian prays to the Great Spirit that whispers to him in the winds; that he hears in the laughing waters; that he sees in the falling leaf and in the tempest. And so on through all the catalogue of life; every soul prays to Deity in accordance with its conceptions of Deity, and all the prayers of the soul never fail to reach the infinite, the all-wise, the perfect father and mother of every soul.

By Theodore Parker, Oct. 27, 1868.

Q. Why do mediums have to suffer so much in allowing spirits out of the form to manifest? In some cases they become living martyrs.

A. All that which transcends the usual order of human life must of necessity produce suffering. Those persons who are called mediums are possessed of an extremely sensitive organism. It must be so, because they are sensitive to things beyond human senses, and this exaltation of the nervous system produces, under the slightest inharmonious conditions, pain, distress. If the mental and moral atmosphere surrounding your mediums were perfectly well adapted to the mediumistic life, they would suffer much less; but you are yet in the infancy of Spiritualism, the science of life; you do not know as yet what you should do for your subjects, and what you should not do. In your ignorance, you surround them by that which they should not be surrounded by, you take away that which they should have. We do not blame you, because you do not know what is best. And yet the very misery through which they pass is turned to good again by the great overruling power of life. These dark experiences are made use of by the angel-world for good, and some of the brightest of their mediumistic gifts are unfolded in the darkest seasons of human sorrow. These fair blossoms of the soil (alluding to flowers on the table) germinate in darkness, in the crude soil of the earth's crust. By and by the plant comes forth into sunlight, and what is the result? The fair blossom, the tender petals, beauty and fragrance. Use and beauty are there combined, and so it is with your mediums. For instance, look you at a Pierpont. Some of the brightest gems of his intellectual life were born into objective being in his darkest hour of trial. Then remember that hell and heaven are very near to each other; for it is only by the darkness of the one that we are made to perceive and enjoy the other; and again, only by the glory of the one can we know concerning the darkness of the other. There is a power governing all human things, which doeth all things well; and however much our sympathies may be excited because of the many Gethsemanes and Calvaries through which our mediums pass, still, as soon as we are enabled to peer beyond the present and behold the glory of the future, our sympathy and sorrow for their sorrow is in a degree mitigated.

By Theodore Parker, Nov. 10, 1868.

Q. Do spirits have streams of colored light emanating from the eyes, and other nerve-centres? If so, what are their colors?

A. They certainly do. Every nerve-centre has its own peculiar light, and that light has its own peculiar color, and the brain combines all the colors of all the different nerve-centres. You are physically and spiritually, so far as form is concerned, electrical machines; and because you are, you are constantly exhaling electricity, under all its forms, shadowing forth all its different degrees.

Q. Please give some plain understanding to the circle of the nature of spirit-artist control?

A. There are so many kinds of spirit-artist control that I am at a loss to know which kind your correspondent refers to.

Chairman. — Perhaps you can explain the method in which the drawings of Mr. Milson are given.

A. In that special case, where the mind of the earthly artist is not used, of course the control is mechanical. The thinking power is outside and beyond the earthly artist, while the hand only is used. But sometimes the brain of the earthly artist is largely used, sometimes to a very small extent; just as the controlling influence can best adapt itself to your external conditions. Sometimes it can be done better by controlling the brain, sometimes by cutting off the connection between the brain and arm, and using the arm mechanically. There are so many means by which spirits make themselves manifest, either in an artistic way or otherwise, that it would be impossible to enumerate them all in the short space allotted us.

By Theodore Parker, Nov. 16, 1868.

Chairman. — The following question is addressed to Theodore Parker in spirit-life: —

During the latter part of your earthly life, prayer was instituted throughout the churches of a certain sectarian denomination that God would either convert you or take you out of the world. Is it true that this concentration of many minds acting in unison for a special purpose did produce the desired effect? Was your health affected, or your death hastened, by these unhallowed prayers?

A. It is a well-known scientific fact that the human body is, to a very great extent, a psychological machine, because it is itself capable of being acted upon, either for good or ill, by all other minds. If a Dr. Newton or a Jesus of Nazareth could restore a diseased body, giving health through the influence of a psychological law, it is reasonable to suppose that a counter influence could as well be exerted, and with as much potency. During the last few months of my earthly life I clearly recognized the baneful psychological influence that had been exerted upon me from the source of which your question treats. As I neared the boundaries of the spirit-world it became more and more clear to me. I did not recognize it in the light of a wrong, but I recognized it as a power used in accordance with infinite law. As I was under the domain of law — not at any time exempt from it — I must bow before its decree. The forest tree falls before the storm. Who shall say it is not well? The lightning shivers the giant oak, and I believe it to be God's decree. Since I have become an inhabitant of the world where law is more understood than here, I have become clearly satisfied that my mortal life was shortened, perhaps many months, in consequence of this psychological influence. Their prayers were heard and answered. It was well. But as the great controlling influence of life makes use of all conditions for good, he made use of this. Every single phase of life, whether greater or lesser good, I believe to be in the hands, or under the guidance, of the great all-wise power of the universe — of all universes — and that what men act upon for seeming evil is always changed to good. The time is coming when these same persons who acted through their darkness will behold precisely where they stood, and how nearly they were related to justice, and how nearly I was related to justice; in what religious light we both stood. The scales will fall from every eye in due season, and every soul will be made to understand its relations to every other soul, and to the great God from whence we have all come.

By Professor Hare, Nov. 17, 1868.

Q. If two children should be born into earth-life, possessing equally good physical, moral, and mental organizations, and one should be favored with all the advantages civilization could bestow, while the other should pass into the hands of the wild savage, and both remain on earth threescore and ten years, and then pass into the spirit-world, what would be their relative conditions in the summer-land?

A. They would both be pure, but of different degrees of purity; both be wise, but of different degrees of wisdom. It should be known that the external world, the world of form in which you dwell as humans, is perpetually calling out from your spirits their treasures. The external acts upon the internal, and calls out of its beauty. You might be endowed with ever so perfect a physical organism, and ever so perfect an indwelling spirit, but if circumstances and surroundings were not adapted to call out the life within, it would remain within. You may be sure of that. Now, then, while dwelling here, the soul is dependent upon external action, external life, external circumstances for its unfoldment, just as the rose is dependent upon the raindrops, the sunlight, the air, for strength, for power to unfold its inner life to the external. Do you suppose the rose would bloom beautifully in a dungeon? No, it would not. The flowers need sunlight, shade, rain, a dry atmosphere, all the varied conditions of Nature, to bring from their inner lives that beauty which they contain. So it is with regard to the spirit.

The child placed among savages would give savage manifestations. The soul might be identical in the two, and so far as it was possible for the physical life to be identical, the bodies might be the same. The same physical life-line — their twin life — might run through the body, but it is the external difference, the external action upon the internal, that determines the degree, the cast of manifestation of the soul. Now, herein rests a great moral and intellectual lesson. It is this: ye fathers and ye mothers, it is a lesson for you; ye guardians of young minds, you should not pass it by, but know you that just as you call out the beauty of the child's inner life, it will come out. Do not undertake to force any beauty from the external to the internal. There is enough there; call it out. Give the child proper external circumstances, just the very best you can. Call out of the divine that is shrouded in the human, and you will make a most beautiful, spiritual, moral, and intellectual picture, I assure you. Ye who would be artists of the soul, pencil well here, that you may present a beautiful picture of life in the hereafter.

Q. Can spirits while in the human *form* control mediums and communicate to friends at a distance? If so, will the spirit please explain how it is done?

A. I am very glad that question has been propounded, for it is one that has staggered many minds; but they have failed to understand the truth that they faintly perceive. As I before remarked, spirit governs matter. It is superior to matter, and though it renders to the law of matter, or form, all that is due, it does no more. It should be understood that the spirit, as such, can leave the body at will, and return again at will. If it can do this, it can just as easily communicate through a sensitive organism as can a disembodied spirit. It is nothing unnatural; it is in perfect accordance with natural law, as you will hereafter see, if you cannot to-day. You go to visit your friends in dreams; you commune with them; you remember, though in broken snatches, that dream. It comes into your external consciousness, to be sure, often as a vagary, yet you generally remember some portions of it. The spirit generally transmits to the external consciousness some remnants, fragments of what it has been passing through in the dream. Now, was the spirit in the body at the time, or was it away with the absent friend? I answer most emphatically, it was away with the absent friend. It may be thousands and tens of thousands of miles away; it may be in the spirit-land; it may commune with its dear departed. Know you not that you, as spirits, can enter the soul-world and return again? I tell you you can. And this gift is not bestowed upon a few, but upon every one of you. The smiling infant in its dream meets with the inhabitants of the spirit-world ofttimes. Does it go away from the body to hold commune with others? Surely it does. Spirits are acted upon by the law of attraction and repulsion. Suppose, for instance, you have a friend in London to whom you are tenderly attached. That friend may be thinking intently of you. You lie down to rest. The thought of the friend reaches your spirit, and with lightning speed you are there, just as much a spiritual presence as you ever can be. It may be asked, Do you take your spirit-body with you? Surely you do; you could not go without it; could not make a single impression without it. Now, this will account for the many mysterious messages that have been supposed to come from a departed spirit, when it was afterwards ascertained that the spirit was in the body. There are exceptions, to be sure, to this, as to all other rules. It is by no means impossible for some disembodied spirits to assume to be whom they are not, and thus to impose upon the credulity of human life. I only tell you that this is not only possible to be done, but it is an exceedingly simple and natural process, and quite as easy to be performed as that I speak to you through this sensitive subject.

Q. You speak of spirit being superior to matter. What is your opinion of the theory that spirit is itself refined or sublimated matter?

A. I so believe; but I speak of it in contradistinction to matter, because you have been so educated. You have been educated to divide the two, but, to my own mind, spirit and matter are one and the same, spirit being only a refined degree of matter. Now, you well know that the finer, the more subtle an element is, the more powerful it is. Therefore, if spirit be, as I believe, refined matter, that does not destroy my theory at all, but renders it, if possible, more sure, more perfect. Matter is ever ascending in the scale, and the higher it ascends the more powerful it becomes. It has been said by some that spirit is ever ascending through matter. Very well; call it that. I call it the purer, the subtler part of matter, ever ascending, and the farther it ascends the more it unfolds, the more powerful it is, and the more it can exert great influence over all lower forms.

By Theodore Parker, Dec. 3, 1868.

Q. Supposing the doctrine of pre-existence true, is it at the option of the spirit that it returns and clothes itself in another earthly form? Spirit-life is described as being far better adapted to progression in holiness and purity, and, consequently, happiness, then earth-life; then why return?

A. No; it is not optional with the spirit to determine concerning the conditions of being through which it shall pass, and by which it shall progress. Since we have no knowledge of ever having had any voice concerning pre-existence, or so far as we, as spirits, are concerned as relating to the present, it is not at all unreasonable to suppose that the same law will continue with us through the future. It has been asserted that the spirit-world proper, or the condition of being that is beyond human senses, is better adapted to the unfoldment of the spirit than the conditions to which it is attached in human life. Considered in a certain light, this is true; but in another light, it is untrue. For since we know that we can only gain strength by action, and retain it by action, we know it is best that we be always active, it matters not whether it be in a physical, moral, intellectual, or spiritual sense. If there were no lesser good for the soul to war against, its powers would soon dwindle into insignificance. You may be sure of that. I believe that the experiences through which the soul passes during its journey through human life, are absolutely necessary for the welfare of the soul. I believe that certain powers of the soul are brought out better through the hard experiences of human life than in any other way. I believe that the sorrow incident to the earthly life is absolutely necessary to bring out and brighten and glorify the joys of heaven. Talk as much as you may of the better condition, the soul revolves in the spirit-world proper, I well know; and thousands, ay, millions of spirits attest to the truth of this assertion, that the soul has need of the darkness of earth-life; and as it revolves again and again, as round and round the circle runs, we gain at each revolution something higher, something better. We may pass through all stages of our being, but we part with something of our lesser good by so doing, and we gain some greater good.

By Joy H. Fairchild, Dec. 7, 1868.

Q. Will you give an opinion with regard to the following extract from Swedenborg's writings? "When spirits begin to speak with man, he must beware that he believe nothing that they say; for nearly everything they say is fabricated by them, and they lie; for, if they are permitted to narrate anything, as what heaven is, and how things in the heavens are to be understood, they would tell so many lies that a man would be astonished."

A. The experience which you, as Spiritualists, have passed through during the last twenty years should answer the question. If that cannot, I am in serious doubt as to whether I shall be able to answer it to the satisfaction of even one individual soul. To say that spirits return always telling what is absolutely true to all, would be uttering what is untrue. But to say that they return always bearing falsehood, would be equally untrue. If death finds a man a liar, it does not change him. He enters the spirit-world the same liar. He carries with him all that belongs to his spiritual nature. He leaves nothing behind. Death robs him only of the external members through which he manifested. But there are many different ways of defining a lie. Many people decide very unwisely concerning truth and falsehood. We are very apt to say that a thing is untrue which we know nothing about, which has not been brought to our senses so near that we could recognize it as a truth. We are very apt to stamp "lie" upon that which seemeth so to be to us. It is a fault of our human nature, and one which we can only outgrow by experience — by being brought in contact with all the different states of life, and being able to view them all with impartial perception. Swedenborg was a very excellent seer in his day. He was permitted to behold many things that pertain to the spirit-life, but he was by no means a perfect seer, for there never was one. He was by no means an infallible clairvoyant, for there never was one. If there was, or if it could be, then the function of seership would cease. Clairvoyance would have reached a state of infinite perfection, which I do not believe it ever can, or ever will. Since round and round the circle of human experience runs, there can be no such thing as absolute perfection in any one sphere of life. We attain wisdom by discreet degrees, says Swedenborg. I believe it. But I also believe that we never can attain the highest wisdom. There will always be something beyond, a state of beatitude that we have not reached, something that we did not know about, something that has not been brought to our comprehension. If every spirit returned giving precisely the same information with reference to facts pertaining to the spirit-world, would you be any better off, as Spiritualists? I think not. You would say at once, "They always tell us the truth; we can always depend upon them. We need not exercise our powers of observation. They are always on the right side. Let them lead us." Now they come with all the imperfection of human life resting upon their spirits, and by their acts, by all they say to you, and all they do with reference to you, you know that they are still human and fallible. What is the result? Why, you are kept in constant activity with regard to your spiritual belief. All the powers of your better nature are perpetually being taxed to know what is the best way, what is the truth. Instead of allowing any other spirit or spirits to decide for you, since you cannot place implicit faith upon them, you fall back upon yourself. You measure them by your own ideas of justice. You throw them into the balances of your own being, and you weigh them there, and if they are found wanting, your reason decides. Your reason can very easily detect whether or no they are wanting in all that makes up a perfect spiritual being. It would not be well for you, as Spiritualists or Christians, to be shown the better way at once. Life is a struggle, and not only a struggle for the angel-world, but a struggle for you who dwell here in time; and through these hard struggles you attain knowledge; you become wise for yourselves. You do not gather that wisdom which belongs to any other spirit and appropriate it to yourselves, but you gather that which belongs to you as individuals. You bring out all the powers of your inner life, and make them strong by action.

By Father Henry Fitz James, Dec. 8, 1868.

Q. Is there growth in the spirit-realm, and are the processes of assimilation and education the same as we find here in this material condition? And are the chemical changes at all analogous?

A. There is indeed growth in the spirit-world, and the various processes through which the spirit passes are indeed analogous to those of earth. Each spirit receives from all its surroundings, and gives, in turn, to all. The process of give and take is by no means entirely of earth. It belongs to the spirit. It exists through the sphere of mind as of matter. All the various chemical changes through which the body — the physical body — passes during its pilgrimage in earth-life, have their counterpart in the spirit-world. The chemistry belonging to earth is divinely and spiritually represented in the spirit-world. It is carried far beyond that of which your human senses can take cognizance. There is that change which is in itself analogous to the change called death. There is a gradual waste of spiritual forces, a gradual accumulation of newer forces. There is no such thing as rest, in the absolute, anywhere in the universe.

Q. You closed your invocation with the term "Father, Son, and Holy Ghost." How are we to understand that?

A. The term is used simply to convey the idea of the past, present, and future — an all-sustaining life that ever has been, that is, and ever will be.

Q. Is the life-principle manifested in the vegetable and animal kingdom, and in man, the same in essence?

A. In essence I believe it to be the same, but marked by distinct degrees through form. The indwelling life, the essence, the all-pervading principle that changes the forms of matter and changes your thoughts, I believe to be the same.

Q. Does it attain its highest possibilities when it culminates in man?

A. By no means; for man, as such, is only a few steps higher than his brethren of the field. We are apt to place too high an estimate upon self.

Q. Are we then to understand that there are races of beings in the universe higher than man?

A. O, yes; because there are conditions of mind far superior to those with which you come in contact, far superior to any that have an existence on this earth, or any other, at the present time. Life is a school, and we are all pupils therein. We never abandon the school. The master is ever beyond us, ever ready to teach us something that we have not yet known; consequently we are ever being drawn out. When we attain one glorious height, lo! there are more beyond us.

Q. by a clergyman. Are there any beings superior to Jesus Christ?

A. O, yes, very many.

Q. by clergyman. What kind of beings are they?

A. Beings like himself, who have had larger experience. It is the experience one gains in the world of mind and the world of matter that makes the human and divine glory.

Q. by clergyman. Have these superior beings passed through humanity? Have they been men?

A. Yes, I so believe.

Q. by clergyman. Jesus Christ was not, then, born of the Father, as he declared himself, when he said, "I and my Father are one."

A. O, yes, he was. And you and I may assert the same with as much truth; since we cannot live apart from the Father, since we have no existence apart from his — the great existence called life — we and that are one. It cannot be otherwise.

Q. by clergyman. Why did he deny that the Jews were the children of God? as where he said, "Because ye do not the works of God, ye are of your father the devil."

A. And by that statement he showed very clearly that he had not attained the highest wisdom; that he was human, as he was divine. For, had he attained the highest wisdom, surely he would have known that the Jew and the Gentile were alike precious in the eyes of the great All-Father.

Q. by clergyman. Who was the more inspired, Moses or Christ?

A. It would be very hard to determine; but it is not hard to determine concerning the order of inspiration. Certainly Moses did not have as high an order of inspiration as Jesus the Christ. He ranked very far below him.

Q. by clergyman. Then Jesus was not the light of the world, if he had human imperfections and follies in him?

A. O, yes, he was a light of the world, and a very great light too.

Q. by clergyman. Yet you acknowledge he lacked wisdom?

A. Certainly, he did not possess all wisdom, and yet he shed abroad those divine truths that he had gathered from all his surroundings, as none had ever done before him. And the light of those truths comes down to you of to-day; you fall down and worship them; and it is well. But in worshipping the spirit of truth, the glorious truths that were given through Jesus, you are very apt to also worship the form, the name. This you should not do. We are very apt to do it, because it is very hard for us to separate the life from the form. We are more apt to worship the Church than to worship the spirit of the Church.

Q. by clergyman. Is death inevitable, or is it the consequence of sin? Can it be avoided?

A. Death comes as the inevitable consequence of natural law, not as the result of sin. Science has proven that to be true. Ignorance determines otherwise. We are told of a fall, away back in past ages, and, in consequence of that, came sin and death into the world. But as the light of a newer and diviner dispensation dawns upon us, we see the folly of such a belief. Science tells us that death is the inevitable result of law. Change must come to these forms. They cannot exist in their present state but a certain length of time; then they must be resolved back again to their primal elements. It is not, by any means, the result of the sin of one pair or a thousand pairs.

Q. by clergyman. Is there any such thing as being translated, as is recorded of Elijah — that he never tasted death?

A. No; I do not so understand it. The ignorance that surrounded the common people of that day gave rise to such a story. The priests, the heads of the Church, knew better, even then.

Q. by clergyman. Then that is a false story?

A. Absolutely; falsely rendered in your record.

Q. by clergyman. Is Jesus risen with that body which was nailed to the cross? or where is that body?

A. Gone back to its primal elements; lived again and again in a thousand times ten thousand forms, for aught I know; but never resurrected from the dead, as your record affirms.

Q. by clergyman. Then the apostles were false witnesses?

A. By no means. They so believed because Jesus had the power to make himself an objective reality to those minds and those human senses. He took upon himself material conditions, and was, to all intents and purposes, living and acting through the material form. They saw it, they felt it; it walked with them and talked with them. But was it the literal body of Jesus? O, no.

Q. by clergyman. Did he not declare unto Thomas that "a spirit hath not flesh and bones as ye see me have"?

A. Certainly he did — so the record says; and he invited one of his friends to thrust his finger into his side. But we do not affirm that this body — this objective body — was a spirit. O, no; it was a material body which he had gathered from the elements, precisely as spirits do, under certain conditions, from your media to-day. It is being done to-day. Jesus had the same power.

Q. by clergyman. Then the angel that told them, "He is not here; he is risen," told a lie?

A. No; he was not there; he had risen. The body was not the man.

Q. by clergyman. What became of the body?

A. We are told that it was taken away by the nearest and dearest friends of Jesus. They, like you of to-day, loved the body, and were not willing it should fall into the hands of their enemies.

Q. by clergyman. Then the Jews were right in saying the disciples had stolen the body?

A. They were right, certainly.

Q. by clergyman. Then the apostles were all liars, and the Jews were right?

A. No, they were not liars; but the Jews were right.

Q. by clergyman. But the Jews declared that the disciples had stolen the body, and you confirm the same from the spirit-world.

A. Yes, but they were not liars, because they did not say the body has risen, but he has risen, meaning Jesus —

the spirit, not the body. Nowhere in your record can you find anything that will determine concerning the resurrection of the body. The disciples did not say, "We have not stolen the body of Jesus;" they simply said, "He is not here; he has risen." So he had.

Q. by clergyman. But it was the Jesus that was laid in the tomb that was meant; of course we all understand that it was the very same body that was nailed to the cross.

A. O, yes, you understand it so, because you are apt to deal more with the body than with the spirit. Was the man the body? You will say yes. I say no. It was the thinking spirit, not the body. What had Jesus to do with the dead body? Nothing at all. So the disciples declared that the living spirit had risen; they said nothing about the body.

Q. by clergyman. But these declarations don't hang together. Either all Christianity is a humbug, or these declarations are false.

A. So far as the Christian Church understands Christ there is very much of error mixed up with their understanding of him, because they have worshipped the body; they have talked of the body; they have prayed to the body. That has been their ideal. I was a believer in the literal resurrection of the body of Jesus Christ before my death. But I know better now. The whole Christian world has indeed been imposed upon, but by its own ignorance — by nothing else.

Q. by clergyman. But what assurance have we that we are not imposed upon here?

A. None whatever — nothing that you can absolutely rely upon.

Q. by clergyman. Then we may declare that we are

now imposed upon, as well as the Christian world has been?

A. Certainly, you have the right so to do. It is incumbent upon you all to weigh and measure everything by your own senses. Never believe a Paul, or a Moses, or a Jesus because they are such. Do not believe me because I declare myself to be a departed spirit returned here to communicate with you. But believe whatever seems to be true to you, and ignore all the rest.

Q. by clergyman. But what is the good of having communications from departed spirits, if we cannot depend upon them? If we must take their instructions on our own judgment, I don't see any use in them.

A. So you may say with regard to all kinds of instruction, whether through the Church or the spirit-world.

Q. by clergyman. There is a great difference. We give authority for ours.

A. Ah, you have a very poor understanding concerning those of the spirit-world. You, like thousands of others, have placed the seal of divine authority where that of humanity alone belongs. When you shall learn that the spirit after death is human, as before, then you will cease to expect so much of them. They are fallible, like ourselves. It is only their opinions and the experience they have gained in the spirit-world that they bring you. Nothing more.

Q. by clergyman. Does a spirit come by divine authority to teach us this?

A. All things that are taught at all are taught by divine authority.

Q. by clergyman. I don't believe it.

A. You have the right to disbelieve.

Q. by clergyman. Lies are not of divine authority.

A. Since I believe in one God overruling all things for good, of course I recognize the divine authority running through all. Therefore, to me all teaching is of divine authority. It may not be so to you.

Q. by clergyman. Are the most infernal lies by divine authority?

A. All that do not agree with our best judgment are lies to us. It matters not what they are to anybody else. That which we cannot conceive to be true is not so to us. The Jews believed Christ to be a liar. Not so with the Christian world. But were not the Jews honest? Surely they were.

Q. by clergyman. Then there is no such thing as absolute truth?

A. No, there is no such thing as absolute truth. Rest assured of that.

Q. by clergyman. Then I say you are of the devil; for God is absolute truth.

A. But since we cannot measure God, we cannot bring that absolute truth down to our comprehension and make use of it. Therefore, we have no absolute truth, because, if we had, we should have all of God, which we have not.

Our time has expired. We must leave you to your own opinions, trusting you will in time grow out of the darkness around you as an individual. You have the right to your opinion, as we to ours. We are all marching towards the same great light of truth. We are all under the benediction of the same great Father. It matters not what we believe.

By Theodore Parker, Dec. 10, 1868.

Q. Cannot a person standing by the side of another benefit him spiritually?

A. Certainly. I believe that the mission of Christ on earth was not alone for diseased bodies, though he healed the sick and restored to the blind their sight. He did many so-called wonders in the material line, but he did many more in the spiritual line. He was capable of healing the spirit, of restoring it to the normal or happy state; and what is true of him is equally true of every other healing medium.

Q. Jesus said, "Lo, for eighteen years has Satan bound this woman." Are all diseases the bindings of Satan?

A. Yes, you may as well call them that as anything else. The bindings of ignorance, or of the lesser good, may as well be called Satan, or Lucifer. Whatever name you give it, it is still ignorance. It is still the lesser good.

Q. Swedenborg says that all disease is communicated by evil spirits. Is he right?

A. He is right, only he is misunderstood. Disease is spirit, and because it makes you unhappy it is evil. Therefore it is the action of an evil spirit. The potato rots in the ground. It is acted upon by an evil spirit. This evil spirit runs through all the vegetable creation, through the mineral, the animal, the spiritual. But it has ever been, and is to the present day, largely misunderstood. Of course, you are aware of that.

By Father Henry Fitz James, Dec. 17, 1868.

Q. Is the Deity a being, or is he a principle pervading all Nature? If the latter, why do you address him as a being, in the invocation?

A. That our God is a personal, and also an impersonal God, is equally true. Since the God-power or God-life is everywhere, he, it, or she is of course personified everywhere. I believe in the worship of all that is worthy of worship. If it is the flower, let us worship there. If it is the human soul, let us worship there. If it is a lofty thought, let us worship there. Wherever we see anything, or perceive any state, either of mind or matter, that is worthy of worship, there we should worship. All Spiritualists, I believe, consider God to be an infinite principle pervading all forms, occupying all space. I believe this. I have seen nothing during my life in the spirit-world to cause me to believe otherwise. I did not believe it when here. But the Book of Life hath been so widely opened to me since death, that I can come to no other conclusion than that God is a principle pervading all forms, and occupying all space. God is in the atmosphere, and is the atmosphere. God is in the sunlight, and is the sunlight. God is the sun and the shadow. He is everything, and is in all places. It is absolutely useless to endeavor to confine God to any particular place or state of being, for could we do that, we should rob God of the God-power. We should at once chain this great eternal principle, this infinite life, to finite space. We should at once bring it down within the scope of human analysis. And I, for one, am glad we cannot. But we have been so in the habit of addressing this Deity, this Power of Life, as though it were a man or woman, a personality like ourselves, that it is very hard to change our course; and indeed it would not be well for us so to do, because, as I before remarked, our God is a personal God, and therefore it is proper that we should thus address him.

By William E. Channing, Dec. 21, 1868.

Q. Will there not soon be more distinct communion between the spirit-life and the earth-life?

A. If your correspondent means to ask if there will not be very soon a more general and direct communication between this life and that which is to come, I shall answer, just so fast as you are fit to receive communications of an emphatic kind from the spirit-world, you will receive them. You seem to suppose that that world is situated far from you, when it is really in your midst, and the communications coming therefrom are as closely allied to your own souls as they can by any possibility be. Every soul seeks for light from the spirit-world, for new revealments concerning this modern faith; is constantly expecting something greater, something more clearly defined, something that shall answer the call of human nature more definitely, something that shall appeal emphatically to the senses. This is well. And will their expectations be realized? I think they will. The spirit-world is constantly making great efforts in your behalf. Societies are being formed all over our spirit-world for your good, for the good of all those minds that are bounded about by clods of clay. One set of minds can be reached in one way, and another set in another way; one demand the alphabet of the science of life; another group demands something higher, and so on. All are calling for certain degrees of these spirit-revealments.

Every soul will be answered, I believe, in due season.

Q. If Spiritualism were proved false, what effect would it have upon the history of the Bible?

A. To my mind it would have a very serious effect, because by and through the life of Spiritualism — ancient Spiritualism — the Bible has its existence. It lives through that, if it lives at all. So to prove that Spiritualism were false, would be to prove that all the circumstances recorded in the Bible were equally false; for they every one of them stand upon the spiritual platform and exist by spiritual life, if they exist at all.

By Theodore Parker, Dec. 22, 1868.

Q. Why cannot mediums give full names as well as parts of a name?

A. There are various reasons why this cannot always be successfully done. In the first place there are very few mediums through which the full tide of spiritual, personal information, or inspiration — call it by what term you please — can be received. Mark me: there are very few through which the full tide — it may come in ripples, it may bubble upon the shore and break — but the full wave can come only through a very few, compared with the great whole. Now suppose, for instance, I were writing a communication through the hand of a medium. I may have what I call magnetic control; that is to say, I may have been successful in cutting off the electric and magnetic current running through the arm and thence to the brain, thus conveying impressions. So I might have a hand and arm to use as I would a pencil. Well, what then? Why, the medium is looking on, sees what is written, and knows, nine times out of ten, when the power is diminishing, because of the tremor that passes through the arm. The outside spirit is losing control, and the indwelling spirit is resuming control. The medium can tell that, and so he says, "This message is almost finished. Now, I wonder what name will be attached to this." There comes the obstacle which interferes very much with the giving of the name. The positive brain is exercised, consequently it cannot be given. When mediums learn the philosophy of this they will do differently. They will see to it that their wills are abstracted from the work of the spirit. If they do this, it will be very much easier for the spirit to finish up what it began. It is hard to give a name, because, at that point, the spirit of the medium becomes positive. The forces of the spirit have grown less. They have about exhausted their power with the medium, and just as they are going to finish up and sign their name, as I before remarked, the positive power of the medium comes in and interferes; so you don't get your name. Now, do not say there is some fraud because we have got no name. Rather say, It is something we do not understand. Let us look into it, analyze it, weigh and measure it, bring all the powers we have at command to ferret out the cause of this deficient communication. If you took half as much pains to do this as to find fault, it would be very much better for you and for us. Pardon me; I am a plain-spoken individual, used to telling the truth in very plain terms.

Q. How is it that some spirits can control so soon after they leave the form?

A. Some spirits happen to be very fortunate in having spirit-friends who know how to return, who understand the *modus operandi*. Consequently they bring their friends to some media, who, they know, will assimilate with their magnetic life. What is the result? Why, they are forced right back through mediumistic life, whether they will or no. [Forced, you say?] Yes, that is the word I intended to use.

Q. I asked because it has seemed to me as if some spirits *were* forced into possession of this medium.

A. They *are* absolutely forced. They come within the magnetic attracting power of the media, and it absolutely forces them to come into bodily control, and then they may as well speak as do anything else. It is easier to speak than not to.

Q. Some who have passed from this life return and tell us that they have no remembrance of any other existence previous to that commenced on this earth. If, as has lately been maintained on this platform, "*the soul ever has been, is, and ever will be,*" in what respect does this lack of continuity of memory differ, as regards the individual's identity, from total annihilation? Of what avail is it to the thinking part we call I, *if the essence of man is immortal,* if that essence is not eternally connected with his individual being? and how can this be otherwise done than through the memory?

A. Memory is subject to the call of external circumstances. Now, always remember that. Memory is subject to the call of external circumstances, and may slumber in some of her parts for thousands of years if external circumstances do not resurrect her. Do not forget that, for you will have need to use that simple knowledge, all of you, by and by. Some spirits are fortunate, but very few are, in being resurrected in memory, concerning a past existence, by external circumstances. A Pythagoras would tell you, did he speak with you, that he remembers three distinct earthly lives. Mark me: three distinct earthly lives he remembers clearly. Not all their circumstances, to be sure, but enough to show that they are three distinct earthly lives. He has been fortunate in having external circumstances to call up, to resurrect this past memory, that belongs to the past, that slumbers with thousands of souls, because there is no morning peal of the present, no chime that might call up the past. Now, let me illustrate, to make my position more simple. Suppose, for instance, a friend of your childhood might come into this room, either a disembodied spirit, or one in the body, and should address you by name. You look into his face and say, "I do not know you." "You do not?" "No." "Do you remember," he says, "such a person that you used to play with in your boyhood days, who lived in such a place, occupied such a position in life?" You think a minute. The external words of the man are called up to your memory from the past. You say, "O, yes, I remember it: O, yes, now I know you;" and you go over and over your boyhood days with him. All the green fields are present in your memory; all your little boyish acts are called up and lived over again. You know the man for an absolute certainty. It is precisely the same with regard to a past existence. Thousands and tens of thousands of souls are waiting for some resurrecting circumstance, that they may remember, that they may see, that they may live again, in thought, in the past, and know that they have lived there. Do you understand? [Yes.]

By Theodore Parker, Dec. 28, 1868.

Q. Is Spiritualism, as a religion, to supplant Christianity?

A. Spiritualism, as a religion, I believe, is to supplant Christianity. The era of the Christian religion is passing away, changing. It will lose nothing of its life, nothing of that that the world of mind has need of; but it will part with its dross, and become absorbed in the newer and more perfect.

Q. Have you ever seen a person, while inhabiting the body, in spirit-life?

A. Yes, very many times; times without number.

Q. Are there any spirits of the present day that have seen Christ?

A. Yes; I have seen him myself.

Q. What is his mission in the world?

A. A mission of love, as it was when here; a moral teacher.

Q. Does he profess to be one with God?

A. Yes; he professes to be one with God, but as I profess to be one with God; in no different sense. Not according to the Christian idea of his oneness with God. O, no, by no means.

Q. Does this same Christ visit the earth as other spirits do, for the purpose of inaugurating this new dispensation!

A. Yes; he is in the work, and he does visit the earth.

Q. Has he visited Boston, to your knowledge?

A. Yes; many thousand times.

Q. Will you not invite him to speak to us here at this circle?

A. No; certainly not. He needs no invitation. He comes unbidden, and partakes of the feast of wisdom prepared by every individual soul; does not need any special invitation to be your guest.

Q. Does the spirit, while inhabiting the physical body, ever manifest like one that has laid off the form?

A. Yes; that is quite a common occurrence.

Q. Then we are living in both worlds?

A. You are. The senses of the body take cognizance of the things of this world, the objective and material life. The senses of the spirit take cognizance of both worlds, live in the inner life, and understand what is being done in the external life.

By Theodore Parker, Dec. 29, 1868.

Q. Is the individualized human spirit a result of acting natural and spiritual forces incident to the human physical form, and in and through the same elaborated, unitized, affinitized, and perfected to an individual conscious existence, beyond the reach of decomposition and decay? or is the human physical form a result of a pre-existent spirit-entity which descends into the germ of being, allying itself with earliest infancy or life, and which unfolds and develops its stature to maturity, lingers with it till death, then returns to the God who gave it?

A. I believe that the spirit claims a life anterior to the body. I do not believe that the spirit is an outgrowth of the body. On the contrary, I believe that the body is an outgrowth of the spirit. The spirit is distinct, and comes up through an infinite number of degrees of material life. It passes through the different degrees, and manifests itself according to the degree in which it lives. Human life manifests as human life, vegetable life as vegetable life, mineral life as mineral life, and so on through an almost infinite number of degrees. I believe it is one great spirit, after all, one infinite ocean of life, acting through all forms, and manifesting according to the nature of the form in which it exists.

Q. It is your opinion that the spirit has power to choose the form through which it shall manifest?

A. I do not so think. Indeed, all past experiences prove to the contrary.

Q. Then there is a law still surrounding the spirit which causes it to take the form through which it manifests?

A. The spirit, as a whole, is a law unto itself. But each one of the individualized particles composing the Great Spirit, is amenable to the law of all the rest. It can go so far, but no farther.

Q. Will each individual soul come to a knowledge of a prior existence, as did Pythagoras?

A. There are thousands, ay, millions of souls in the spirit-world who have no knowledge of having had an existence prior to the one they passed through in earthly life. These seem to be the rule, but there seem to be very many exceptions to the rule. I am not prepared to say, for I have formed no definite opinion upon the subject, whether all souls will finally become possessed of this knowledge or remembrance of a former life. I believe, ay, I know, that there are circumstances which, if they act upon the soul, will call up that memory; but whether they will ever act or no, I cannot say.

Q. I learn by experience that a certain class of spirits return and communicate often directly after they have left the form, but soon cease to come, and do not again manifest their presence for months or years. Please explain why this is so.

A. In all probability they are so far absorbed in the scenes of their new life that they have not a sufficient desire to return to enable them to overcome the obstacles in the way. There must be a straightforward, positive will on the part of the returning spirit who would be successful.

Q. How do spirits employ their time in the spirit-world?

A. There are an infinite number of ways by which the spirits employ their time, or are occupied in the spirit-world. They who are artists, because they have a love in that direction, employ their time in that way. The mechanic — for we have mechanics in the spirit-world — who is such from the love of it, pursues the same avocation in the spirit-world. Each one pursues the course that is best adapted to him, but none are forced into the pursuance of any course. There is no compulsion in these things in the spirit-world. Each one acts in accordance with his wishes. There is no poverty to interfere here. There are no railroads demanding a fee for transportation; there are no hotels charging exorbitant prices; no dealers to fee; nothing of the sort; but each one pursues the avocation which he is best adapted to, and for the love of it. There are no drones in the spirit-world. All are active.

Q. How do mechanics exercise their powers? Have they building material with which to work?

A. You forget that these buildings which you inhabit are in the spirit-world, every one of them. They have an inner as well as an external life. Every one of these works of art has a soul; and the external appearance of that soul has need of an external architect — somebody to fashion it, somebody to take care of it, somebody to embellish it. Can you do it? No. You can perform that part which belongs to material life, but no more. You overlook the soul of things in your march through the body. It is quite natural; I did the same while here.

By Theodore Parker, Jan. 4, 1869.

Chairman. A week ago last Wednesday I left here, at three o'clock P. M., to visit a child who was very sick in Newark, N. J., and arrived there at one o'clock the next morning. My wife, who was here at home, said that at three o'clock of the same morning she saw me at her bedside so distinctly that she spoke to me, asking, "How is it that you are here? I thought you were in New Jersey." I was at that time standing by the bedside of the child in Newark. I would like to ask if it was my spirit proper, or whether it was my thought of her that took this visible shape.

A. You seem to forget that your thought is, in fact, your spirit — nothing more, nothing less. And you also seem to forget that the spirit has power to overcome time and space. It occupies no sensible time — not according to human senses — in passing from one point to another. It can travel faster than light. It is here, and instautly it is there. A spirit dwelling in the body obeys, to a certain extent, the physical laws pertaining to the body, and, to a very large extent, it is free even then. It goes whithersoever it will. It traverses the universe and other universes. It holds communion with the inhabitants of the most distant star, and as perfectly, as a spirit, as it can hold communion with its fellows here. Now, then, this being true, it would not be at all strange — nothing out of the natural course — to suppose that your spirit did indeed visit your earthly home, and in such a tangible way as to be recognized by the senses of your companion. I say it would not be strange, and, from your statement, I am inclined to think that this is the case. Had I been present, I should have known to a positive certainty. As it is, I can only form an opinion from what I have known of other similar cases.

Chairman. My wife said that she was, at the time, perfectly wide awake, and recognized me just as clearly as she ever did in her life. I remember of thinking of her several times, but had no idea of reaching her in any tangible way.

A. I have been informed that you are specially gifted in this respect — that you have the gift of retiring from the body, leaving that in one locality, and making yourself spiritually apparent, thoroughly recognized, at another place.

Chairman. This is not the only instance of the kind. My spirit has been recognized by others in distant places, but I never knew it to come so near home before.

Q. Are we to understand that the spirit is absent from the body while at some distant place, or that there is a double consciousness — the same spirit occupying two places at the same time?

A. All spirits have the power to project themselves into external life, and become recognized by the external consciousness, to a certain extent. You are indeed possessed, under all circumstances, of a double consciousness — that which is present with the external form, and that which is absent by virtue of the action of the distant law. For instance, you may have a friend in London, while you in physical form are in Boston. You think of the friend in London. He thinks of you at the same time. There is a direct vehicle over which the spirit passes, communicates, but at the same time it is conscious within the physical life in Boston. There is a consciousness which belongs especially to the physical human life, is governed by that life — can express itself in no other way than through that life.

Then there is a consciousness that belongs to the spirit-body, and it can express itself at any distant point, wherever it chooses, however far distant from the physical body, at any time when the attraction is sufficient to cause it to leave the body. These indwelling spirits elude human senses. The scalpel cannot detect the spirit. It is beyond it. It cannot be weighed and measured by your human senses, and yet it acts upon those human senses as best pleases itself. We have always told you that you were living, here in this world, three distinct lives — the life which belongs to the animal world, that which belongs to the spiritual world, and that which belongs to the higher, the soul or divine life — three in one. There is a great truth underlying the doctrine of the trinity which is yet to be revealed.

Q. Does any change of temperature occur in the spirit-world?

A. Yes, there is an infinite number of degrees of change — all the various gradations that are necessary to spirit-life.

Q. Extreme cold and extreme heat, with all the gradations?

A. Not such cold or heat as you experience here, but that which is equivalent to it.

Q. Are those living there made uncomfortable by these changes?

A. No, not necessarily, because the spirit has the power more perfectly than here to adapt itself to conditions. The law of adaptation is better understood there than here. If you understood it here, the fire would not burn you, the water would not drown you; when the air was at a very low temperature it would not freeze you.

Q. Do you mean to say that if we understood the

law we could resist these changes with our physical bodies?

A. Yes, I do mean that you shall understand me precisely thus.

Q. Will that knowledge ever be possessed by men on earth?

A. I think not. At all events, it is so far in the future, if it ever comes, that it would be folly to hope for it.

By Theodore Parker, Jan. 7, 1868.

Q. How are the blood letters placed upon the arm of the medium? and how are communications written in a room without any one being present?

A. The phenomenon of writing upon the arm and other parts of the human body by processes which of course are unseen by and unknown to you, is in itself exceedingly simple. The communicating spirits have but to draw an almost imperceptible point of electricity towards the part that they desire to affect in that way, and at the same time to use this point of electricity as one would use a pencil. The little child can perform the operation as well as an adult can. It is one of the simple things belonging to Nature.

You ask how communications can be written when there is no one present. Well, that could not be. There is some one present, although that some one is invisible to mortal eyes. Spirits have hands, and can use them, and the atmosphere contains all that is necessary to the formation of all things which you have here in use on the earth, and thousands and tens of thousands that you have not here — that you know nothing about. Therefore, you have what is equivalent to a pencil, or pen and ink.

Everything, from the mineral kingdom up to the highest spiritual, can be formed out of the atmosphere you breathe. It is the great repository of the life of this planet. It contains your gold, your silver, your precious stones. It contains all the elements of every form that is brought before your notice; every form that takes an objective life, the power is in the atmosphere with which to create it. You should remember this, and instead of talking about the atmosphere being a void, talk of it as being a great repository of life — all kinds of life.

Q. Will those formations made by spirits out of the atmosphere retain their form permanently?

A. O, no, not at all. That must come by and through a process natural to the planet, not by art. All these spirit-forms, from the form of the flower to the form of the human body, are works of art, and therefore perishable.

Q. Why is darkness necessary?

A. Because darkness is more negative than light. Light is positive, therefore overcomes, eats up the conditions requisite to these manifestations. Why don't you see the lightning as well in the glare of the sunlight as you do after the sun has gone down?

Q. Will the time ever arrive when these things will be done in the light?

A. Yes; when the spirit-world, or those spirits who are engaged in making these manifestations, are more acquainted with the laws that are in activity in the positive force, when they become better acquainted with them, and can master them, these manifestations can be performed in the light; but at present they cannot.

Q. On a certain occasion at a spiritual circle an oyster supper was furnished to the guests by the spirits. I would like to ask whether the oysters were made by the power of the spirits.

A. I was not present on that occasion, and therefore could not say. I presume they had the power to furnish the oysters from your mundane sphere precisely as they have the power to furnish you flowers. They bring their mediums flowers, and various things. If they can do that, they can bring them oysters as well.

Q. Then the eighth commandment has no power in the spirit-world?

A. The eighth commandment has no power in the spirit-world. It is a nonentity. Every spirit there has the right to whatever it has need of. You may be very sure you will never be taken up for stealing in the spirit-world.

Q. The flowers, then, are not formed from the atmosphere, but are taken from some neighbor's garden, and belong to the owner of the garden?

A. They have the power to form them out of the atmosphere. But such flowers soon fade away; that is to say, they are absorbed again by the atmosphere, perhaps while you are looking at them; but those that are a natural outgrowth of the earth of course render obedience to the law of the earth. You pluck them from the parent stalk, and they live a certain time, and then droop and fade away. Yes, they do take them from the gardens of their neighbors.

Q. How are spirit-shapes made apparent to our natural senses?

A. As I before said, the necessary power is taken from the atmosphere, and carried to the medium, and condensed or rendered objective there, and of course when it is once objective, it is apparent to your physical senses. You can use it, you can handle it. It is, to all intents and purposes, an objective form. It is a chemical process. There are many chemists in the spirit-world.

Q. Then the form is not their own?

A. No, not absolutely. In one sense it is, and in another it is not. It is not their spirit-form, for that you could not see, but it is a clothing for that form, that they have gathered from the atmosphere.

By John Pierpont, Jan. 12, 1869.

Q. We frequently hear persons express a desire to rest for a long period of time upon entering the spirit-world. Does this result from absolute weariness of their earth-life?

A. All the experiences of your earth-life cast their shadow upon the spirit. It matters not what they are, whether they are those of joy or of sorrow, of weariness or the opposite; and a certain amount of time is required for the spirit to outlive it, pass beyond the shadows that are attached to it in consequence of its earth-life. There is a mantle of remorse, an uncomfortable atmosphere surrounding the drunkard, surrounding the miser, surrounding all those persons that have not made the very best use of their time here. There is also an uncomfortable atmosphere surrounding those that have been encumbered with unhealthy physical bodies. The atmosphere is oppressive. It rests upon the spirit like a heavy weight, and as the spirit during such an experience in earth-life has been in conflict, in hard conflict, with those rude experiences, rest, quiet, a condition wherein it can recuperate its wasted forces, is absolutely necessary in spirit-life. I know it was so with me, and I am sure it is equally true of all others.

Q. Is that rest of long duration?

A. The period of the time consumed in that way depends upon the necessity. If there is need for a long rest, you may be sure that the need will be supplied; the long rest will come.

Q. Does this intense desire for rest induce this state of absolute repose?

A. Yes; for none will desire this rest unless they have need of it. The desire is child of the need.

Q. Are they conscious of any lapse of time during that rest?

A. Yes.

Q. Are we, then, to understand that there is time there?

A. Not the time that is understood here with you, but a lapse of conditions, experiences, periods. Of course we do not reckon time by the revolution of the planets, as you do, or by the passing of day and night. It is not divided into years, months, weeks, days, hours, minutes, &c.

Q. Still it is capable of measurement?

A. O, yes.

Q. Do not spirits understand our time here? Can they not reckon it as well as we do?

A. Certainly they do. It is called the earth time.

By Theodore Parker, Jan. 14, 1869.

Q. Can spirits injure each other by striking and wounding?

A. O, yes; but not with physical force, for the physical body it parts with at death. But there is a force far more potent than that which belongs exclusively to this earth.

Q. Are spirits subject to bodily accidents?

A. Yes, they are; but not in the same degree that they are when here inhabiting these physical forms. There are no physical accidents, no physical pain, but whatever tends to render the spirit unhappy mars its spirit-body, and produces a stain upon its external garments.

Q. Some spirits, it is said, after the lapse of years in spirit-life, still insist that they are in earth-life. What can be the cause?

A. They insist that they are, simply because they are here. Your friend having passed through death, he does not of necessity pass out of the earth's atmosphere, or away even from the earthly dwelling, the congenial ties that bound him to friends here. It is unwise to determine that your spirit-friends are absent from you because your external senses cannot take cognizance of them.

Q. Is it true that the superior races of humanity have developed from the gorilla tribe?

A. It is true, an absolute fact, well attested in Nature. We are very apt to turn a cold shoulder on our inferior relatives as we rise in the scale of human life. It is not at all unnatural thus to assume a superiority which does not belong to us.

Q. Will individuals of the gorilla tribe, now on the earth, develop in the spirit-world?

A. They will develop through natural and spiritual processes. Spirit and matter are inseparable. Spirit always rises through matter, or develops, as you understand it, through matter, and at the same time develops matter. Spirit is always dependent upon matter for expression, and the kind of expression depends upon the kind of organic matter through which the spirit expresses.

The gorilla, as such, cannot be the finely developed Anglo-Saxon, yet the same spirit runs through both.

Q. How far down through animal life does this relationship of ours extend?

A. Farther than you or I could by any possibility reach. We are not only allied, related, and intimately, too, to the animal creation, but we are to the vegetable and the mineral. And the best and most absolute proof of this we find in the blood circulating in the veins and arteries of the human system. There we find represented all the animal, vegetable, and mineral kingdoms, each positive and distinct. That the human species have come up through all these lower strata of life there is no denying, for it is absolute.

Q. You mean to say there are no discreet degrees, no well-marked lines of distinction?

A. Contrary to the Swedenborgian idea, there is to me no discreet degree between the human life and the life of the rose, save that which we see in the external. We are just as much related to the rose as to each other. As I before remarked, the blood circulating in our veins and arteries determines that — shows us there what will make the rose. How came we to have it if we were not related to the rose? If there were these discreet degrees in physical life, how is it that we are microcosms of all that is beneath us, standing as the crowning point of the animal, vegetable, and mineral kingdoms? This is a question that science will answer for us, and most emphatically, too.

By Theodore Parker, April 29, 1869.

Controlling Spirit. As we are in the constant receipt of inquiries from friends at a distance — questions propounded to the controlling spirit of the séance — it may not be amiss to make a few plain statements with regard to the case in question. In the first place, it should be understood that these séances are not controlled at all times by the same spirit, but for each occasion an intelligence is selected best adapted to that occasion. Persons sending their inquiries from a distance do not seem to understand this, and they often inquire in regard to the difference of opinion that seems to find expression through the said controlling spirit of the circle. It should be understood that each distinct intelligence, or human spirit, retains its own special intellectual integrity after death as before. All are entitled to their own opinions and the expression of the same, if they express themselves at all. All questions relating to well-developed scientific facts will, without doubt, be answered, by all intelligences coming here, in a similar manner. The idea will be one and the same, though the expression or clothing of the idea may be different in all. But with regard to all questions of theology, you must expect that each spirit will preserve his or her own opinions, and if questioned will give them according to their best ability so to do. Theology is but a vagary at best. It is founded upon speculation. It lives by speculation. It cannot by any possibility be demonstrated by science. As theology it has no part with science. Science and it have never been married, and never will be, because theology, as understood in human life, is thoroughly at variance with science; therefore all questions propounded with regard to theology, of whatever caste or color, will be answered by the spirit controlling on the occasion as he understands it. The Catholic answers in his own way, the Protestant in his, the Mahometan in his — each in accordance with the theological light they have received. You make a very great mistake, oftentimes, in supposing the departed spirit to be possessed of an almost infinite amount of knowledge regarding all subjects. You forget that they are still human, bounded about by the conditions of human life. They are not infinite. They are finite still. And though their clairvoyance is largely unfolded in spirit-life, yet it does not extend to infinity. It only reaches a very small degree into the future. It does not perceive all the past, neither does it all the future. It can take cognizance of events as they come within its sphere of action, but no farther. Now, then, consider the friends who come to you from the other life as human, fallible, and entitled, each one, to their own opinions. You gave them that liberty while they were in the mortal form, and if you are wise and just you will give them no less now.

Q. What is the medium of exchange in the spirit-world? or what is used there as our money is here?

A. Merit; that which belongs to the inner life. Whatever you merit you will have. There is no special medium of exchange that is equivalent to gold, silver, and greenbacks, in our life. You may be very sure of that. But there is a medium of exchange. If I have what I do not need, and my neighbor has need of it, I pass it to him. If he has what he does not need, and what I need, he passes it to me. There is a perpetual interchange of the good things of spirit-life. None can retain any more than they have need of. A very hard place for misers to come to, particularly before they get rid of their miserly propensities, I assure you. So if you have any such, better get rid of them here.

By Rev. Joseph Lowenthall, May 4, 1869.

Q. What is the cause of those ways of feeling that sometimes sweep over the soul, which can only find their appropriate expression in prayer — those intense, often unutterable desires for greater light, holiness, purity, closer communion, and more perfect assimilation with the spirit of all goodness? In other words, what is the spirit that prompts us to prayer?

A. I believe that we are acted upon constantly by the great infinite spirit of Nature, and when we feel in our souls that rising up, that spirit of prayer which would cause us to leave our darkness and enter light, then it is, I believe, that the spirit of infinite goodness sheds holy dews upon us. We rise by temptation. We are tempted to leave the past perpetually. The soul feels that there is a better state of existence, and that it is an heir to that better state. It reaches out clairvoyantly and perceives the future, and being dissatisfied with the present because of the future, it holds up its hands in prayer to the great infinite spirit, and thus comes nearer to that spirit, comes into *rapport* with the higher good, leaves its present state of mentality, and rises, for the time being at least, to a higher state. It is, as one writer hath said, "the key to heaven." Another hath said, "Prayer is the wings of the angels." And another hath said, "It is the voice of God speaking to human hearts," and I believe it is.

Q. When we thus pray, do we receive the things for which we ask? And may our friends be blessed with these same promptings and desires in answer to our prayers?

A. It is a self-evident fact that we do not always receive the things for which we pray, but it is a self-evident fact, also, that we are made better by prayer. No one can ever give birth to a high and holy aspiration — which is prayer, to me — but is made better for it. They rise in the scale of mind. They shed something of their darkness, and take on something of light.

Q. What is the secret of the different degrees of faith we feel at different times, in regard to the bestowal of the blessings we seek?

A. We are constantly being acted upon by all our surroundings, and because we are, we are perpetually changing. Our mental state is constantly changing. We are sometimes full of faith, and sometimes where faith should be there is a vacuum. We act upon all other intelligences, and all other things, all other intelligences, act upon us. We are motes in the sunbeams of God's infinite power. We are sometimes here, and sometimes there. Sometimes the rays strike us perpendicularly, and sometimes aslant. We cannot always think alike. We cannot always act alike. Variety seems to be the order of change. No two expressions of a soul are exactly alike. No two things are exactly alike.

Q. Does spirit-power manifest itself by intense pain in the arms, and what is its object?

A. Sometimes the action of a foreign spirit is manifested in that way. When spirits desire to come into *rapport* with media by writing, they sometimes seek to cut off the electrical flow that passes between the brain and the fore-arm, in order that they may use that limb without using the brain. When this is done it is very apt to produce a heavy, dull pain; at other times, when a spirit acts upon the arm in connection with the brain, there is a sharp, quick pain. And it is produced by a foreign electrical force passing through the nerves coming in contact with that which is legitimate to the individual. Do you understand? [I do.]

By John Pierpont, May 6, 1868.

Q. What is the peculiar principle, or attribute, in the human soul, as distinguished from lower organization, upon which we predicate immortal existence?

A. Divine aspiration and divine inspiration. We do not find the brute creation aspiring to anything higher. We do not find that they can be inspired with divine things. They live in the sphere of their brute life. They do not ask to go beyond it. But the human soul is never satisfied. When it has attained one heaven, it asks for another still better.

By Theodore Parker, May 10, 1869.

Q. I once heard a Swedenborgian preacher say that there were in the spirit-world mountains, hills, rivers, bones, blood, digestion, nerves, brain, hands, feet, &c., and that the ground, in the spirit-world, is just as solid to the tread of spirit-feet, as the ground in earth-life is to us. Is the above true?

A. It certainly is absolutely, positively true.

Q. You mean the blood and bones?

A. I certainly mean just that.

Q. Are those who are slaves to circumstances in this life, likewise fettered in spirit-life?

A. To a certain extent they are. You are not ushered into a state of perfect happiness at death. The other life finds you precisely where this life leaves you. You are surrounded ofttimes in the spirit-world by conditions that seem to be adverse to your happiness. You struggle against them, and in struggling you grow strong.

For my own part, I would not wish to live in a world where there was nothing but ease and quiet comfort. I should lose my strength. I should take on weakness. We only know of the better good by comparing it with the lesser good. If we had no mental storms, no dark hours, wherein our spirits were bathed with dews of unhappiness, we should hardly know how to appreciate an opposite condition. Supposing we had all peace and joy; would we be satisfied with that forever? I think not. We are so constituted spiritually, as well as physically, that we have need to meet with opposites. We cannot exist only as we exist between two opposites. They play upon us alternately, and in consequence of that alternate play, we live and move and have our being. We have need of the shadow; we have need of the joy; and for my part I thank God that we have them both.

Q. Are we tormented in spirit-life by persecution and slander?

A. Not precisely as you are, because society is differently organized in the spirit-world from what it is here. To a certain extent it may resemble it, but it is much superior to society here. A man or woman in the spirit-world is known for precisely what they are, nothing more. The slanderer wears the garb of the slanderer; the peace-maker wears the garb of the peace-maker. The fashions, so far as external adornment is concerned, originate in the inner life. That is the grand Paris of the spirit-world. You may be assured that you will all get your annual fashion-plates. You won't have to purchase them. They come to you.

Q. Are not those who are wealthy and at their ease in this life, and thereby possess the means of improving their social, moral, and intellectual faculties and relations, much more advanced in spirit-life than the poor, who through poverty and adverse surroundings lead the life of deprivation and unhappiness?

A. No, by no means. Jesus, the sage and philosopher, was poor. He went about with poor raiment, and without scrip, not even the poor kind that you have to-day. And if we are to take his condition as an example, surely we cannot reckon much upon happiness as accruing to us as spirits from riches, the riches of this world. Why, I have seen the richest spirit being resurrected from a form that had not enough of this world's goods to hold it and the spirit in unison; therefore the separation came. And again, I have seen poor spirits coming from robes of purple and fine linen. They had no garment to cover their nakedness in the spirit-world. O, you must not measure happiness by riches. If you do, you will make a very great mistake.

By William E. Channing, May 31, 1869.

Q. Is it wise for mortals here to consult with spirits on questions of a purely business nature? Is their advice likely to be valuable? and can we trust it more than the advice of mortals on the earth?

A. There are a large class of spirits freed from the mortal form who are intensely interested in the business of this physical life. They find their heaven here, and are never more happy than when acting out the desires or peculiar conditions in which they find themselves placed. They are attracted to your business sphere. They have never been cut loose from it. They revolve in it as motes revolve in the sunshine, and under favorable conditions they may be good advisers to those who dwell in mortal, because they can see farther than mortals can. They can reach the thoughts of your friends, of your enemies, can see their secret motives, can understand what they intend to do, what moves they intend to make in life; while you, with your human senses shrouded by mortality, might not be able to determine concerning the thoughts that might be revolving in the brain of your neighbor, they might be able to determine concerning all. And yet it would be poor counsel to advise that you lay down your own powers of perception at the feet of any spirit, in or out of the body. Advice is most excellent, but it is not always well to appropriate to our own use all the advice that may be given us, whether it comes from the world of spirits out of the body or in the body. There are some minds who consider it very impious to call upon spirits to aid them in the things of this life. That is a mistake. Since they move in that sphere yet, it is not at all unright to call upon them to act for you. But again I say, have a care how you lay down your own power, how you fail to use your talents when you have them, but are ready to use those that belong to another.

By Rev. Phineas Stowe, June 1, 1869.

Q. Can mankind be spiritualized much in advance of material surroundings? If not, ought not those surroundings to be improved, as a first step towards enlightened spiritual revelations?

A. Spirit, even while it struggles in the womb of matter, causes that matter to grow, to unfold, to become more perfect. It is no use to deny that we are influenced for good, or for what men call evil, by our surroundings. Place the criminal in beautiful and harmonious conditions; give unto that spirit that which will satisfy it; take it away from its haunts of vice; surround it with beauty; make all things that the eye rests upon appeal to its sense of beauty, and what will be the result? Why, in my opinion, the criminal will be such no longer. It is only the hard conditions of unfortunate human experience that make your criminals. Take them away from these, and the divinity of their spirits shows itself, even through the crudity of human life.

Q. According to the doctrine of the church of which I am a member, if a family in this world do not live rightly, if certain members go astray here, when they go into the spirit-world they will be separated. Is this true?

A. There is a spiritual affinity binding soul to soul that cannot be infringed upon. If the members composing your family are spiritually attracted to each other, no power in all the universe can prevent them from meeting and associating with each other after death. They will as naturally gravitate together as a ball will fall to the earth, if dropped from the hand of the holder. Nature — Nature's God — hath made wise provision for us all. Sin, or the mistakes which we may make in life, will have nothing to do with our being kept apart, or attracted together. If there is a soul-affinity, drawing soul to soul, that is blessed by God, which no power can separate. There are many mothers in the soul-world who are not attracted to their offspring. They give birth only to the body, and not to the soul. This may seem a strange assertion, but it is true. And again, there are souls that never met in this life, that are attracted together by a subtle law that binds them, whether they will or no. This is the power of God, working through intelligence. Those families that are grouped together in spiritual life here, will be grouped together in spiritual life in the hereafter. But if the reverse, they will be as widely separated as the planets are widely separated from each other.

By Theodore Parker, June 3, 1869.

Q. Is life, or that principle of vital activity which is manifested through the human organism, spirit? If not, what is it leaves the body at death?

A. Spirit I define as something undiscernible by human sense; something which no living soul can measure or analyze. I define life to be, so far as we understand it, a manifestation of spirit. Those things which our senses perceive, recognize, are the things of life, all *living* things, every one of them — not one dead; and they are all manifestations of spirit. That subtle power that defies the scalpel, and passes out of the body at the change called death, I believe to be spirit, co-eternal with the God-spirit, and part and portion of the divine life, — such a part as that divine life saw fit to exercise over humanity. You call it the spirit of man, the soul of man or woman. It matters not by what term it is recognized. It is the one spirit, the infinite, all-pervading — a something indestructible, without creation and without end.

Q. You consider all spirit immortal?

A. I do, most certainly. And I have most ample proofs that it is all immortal.

Q. Then animals are not at death swept into a grand chaos — the great mass of spirit — to be again worked over into some other form?

A. By no means. Here is the rock — the rock of form — upon which all classes of theological scientists split, and many of them founder; the rock of form, supposing that the form we have or behold to-day will exist forever; that the immortality rests with that, is dependent upon that. By no means is it. Forms are constantly changing, as spirit has need of higher instruments through which to express itself. The instrument is made better. How is it with regard to the flowers? They are not to-day what they were years ago. And why not? Because the God that was within them called upon the God that was within the human intellect, and said, "Come, intelligence, shed your dews upon me, act upon me, bring me into a higher form of good." What was the result? Why, the husbandman went to work to make more beautiful flowers, to add new hues to their fair faces, to make more beautiful their forms, to change for the better the rose and lily, not at all infringing upon Nature or Nature's God. Immortality does not call upon the form for its power. By no means. Forms must change. You have evidence of that every day of your lives. But the immortality that belongs to the form is immortal forever and forever. There is no sudden change of those forms, but a gradual growth. If the change was sudden it would produce too great a shock in the realm of intelligence; therefore it is very slow, comes as you are prepared for it. The years throw their snows upon your brows as you are prepared to receive them — just so fast, and no faster.

Q. If spirit is not matter, is all spirit the same — that is, equally advanced or perfect? If so, what benefit is derived from its manifestation through matter?

A. That spirit is not matter, matter is every day proving. But that spirit is inseparably connected with matter, matter is also every day proving. Matter is the expression of spirit, not the spirit; the outer bark, the foliage, the branches, not the inner, invisible life. What the advantage? Why, all intelligence can answer that question as well as we can. Of what advantage is it to you of this age that you have greater light than they who lived ages before you did? Since you require greater light, certainly it is for your advantage to have it. All the expressions of spirit through matter are not only an advantage to matter, but is also to intelligence, to that subtle force that expresses itself through the human brain, and says, "Behold, this is very beautiful or very grand." The world of matter was made for the world of intelligence. When you keep this in your mind, you will hardly wonder that matter changes its form.

Q. Is the spirit of the infant an emanation from that of the parent? and, if so, is the spirit of the parent less an individualized entity, or does it suffer any diminution or disarrangement in its powers?

A. The infant is physically a physiological result of the parents' life, but spiritually it is not. It is a spirit independent of either father or mother; you may be sure of this. It is from God, the Great Spirit, the Father and Mother, the Whole, the Universal Life.

Q. If the spirit of the infant is not an emanation from that of the parent, whence does it originate? At what period during the incubation does it take possession of the human organism?

A. At conception.

By Theodore Parker, June 7, 1869.

Q. Can you describe the separation termed death from your side?

A. At death, the law of attraction begins to cease between the particles composing the physical body.

They grow less and less active. Their power passes off, and takes on a purely electrical form. All the forces of the body slowly pass out when this disintegration commences. Clairvoyance can behold them, and describes them as a mist, sometimes as a halo, sometimes as a smoke floating out of the form, generally forming the most dense cloud from the brain. Nature seems to gather all her forces together in the brain at the last extremity, and the last magnetic vital force that exists in the body exists in the heart and brain. When this is no more, then the whole body is pervaded with the electrical force. There is an entire absence of the magnetic, and the spirit cannot hold connection with the body after all the magnetic force has retired. The spirit passes out of the body. When the last particle of magnetic force goes, the spirit goes with it, and not till then. Sometimes when you call a person dead, when you say the body has parted from the spirit, it is not always so. There may be an appearance of death, when the spirit may be strongly attached to the body still. But after the last magnetic life is gone, then the electrical force is predominant, and the work of change commences at once. It is, under natural circumstances, not at all painful. It is quite unlike what you have supposed it to be. But when the change comes in consequence of violence to any part, or in consequence of violent disease which is not in the order of nature, then there is pain attendant upon the disease. But when death comes naturally, as it should did you all live in accordance with Nature's laws, there would be no pain. The passage would be easy and pleasant, attended with no fear, but with a certain joy that freedom only can bestow upon the spirit.

Q. How long does the separation take?

A. That depends upon the natural magnetic vitality of the individual, or, in other words, upon their tenacity to physical life.

By Father Henry Fitz James, June 8, 1869.

Q. I have been searching and investigating this spiritual philosophy for nearly twenty years; have taken the "Banner of Light" at various times and places, obtained subscribers for the same, feeling that in due time I would get some message from a departed friend. I have lost many and very dear friends, one of whom passed away two years ago, with a promise to me that, if it was possible, he would return and give me some test by which I could recognize him; and as he knew Mrs. Conant personally, the test might possibly come through her mediumship; but I get nothing, either from him or any other friend. Now, the question is — and it is asked by thousands; I only ask to have it answered philosophically — why I get no message, while every paper is replete with messages that we know nothing of?

A. Christ came to save that which had need of salvation, or, as the record hath it, he came to seek and to save that which was lost. The object of these séances is not to convince those who are already convinced; is not to bring proof to those who have already more than they can well digest. The object is to bring it to those who might remain in spiritual darkness for a long time, did the light not come to them from this source. Seven out of every ten of all the messages that are received at this place go to those who have little knowledge of the spiritual phenomena. Consequently they are silent upon the subject when they receive their messages. But the work is accomplished, the seed is sown, and the harvest is just as sure to come as is the harvest to the husbandman here in vegetative life. The spirit-world is constantly in receipt of urgent desires on the part of friends here, for their friends in spirit to return through this avenue. But since, should their call be considered and spiritually attended to, others who have greater need would be shut out for a time, it is deemed the better course to let those who are not hungry remain without the loaf. Those whose spiritual gardens are already blooming with flowers and green with leaves — the angel passes over them with a silent blessing, and stops only upon those desert places where the earth is ready for seed, and where none has been sown. It would be well for your correspondent to address a note to the spirit in question, seal it satisfactorily, and send it to this place, and see what will come of it. In all probability, some answer will be given.

Q. If the Indian is hereafter to enjoy his hunting-grounds, will there not be something for him to hunt? and does not this involve suffering, and even death? The idea of suffering and death, in such a sense, and in such a condition or state, is revolting to my mind. Are these statements to be taken literally or figuratively? Will you enlighten?

A. They are not figurative expressions. By no means. We mean that they shall be literally understood. When the Indian tells you that he has hunting-grounds in the spirit-land, he tells you what is true. If he has hunting-grounds, that presupposes that he has something to hunt. That, also, is true. That there is death in the spirit-land is equally true. But what is death? It is only change. Flowers change their forms for better ones. The morning sun and the evening shade, though coming from the same source, differ, and no two rays of light issue from the same central source exactly alike. There is a difference in the form and in the action of all things at all times. Nature never makes two precisely alike. Death is vested in sable garments with you. But not so with the disembodied spirit; standing apart from death, and viewing it from the philosophical stand-point, we find it bereft of all shades, and clothed with light. Forms change; old things pass away. All things are perpetually being resurrected. Not only is it here with you in this life, but it continues so to be in the future life, and I doubt not it will so continue throughout the endless future.

By Father Henry Fitz James, June 15, 1869.

Q. Do disembodied spirits ever cause mortals to commit suicide? Is the act justified under any circumstances?

A. Disembodied spirits do often influence mortals in this direction, as in all others. Every act is justified by its parents — by those propelling powers that force it into objective life. This is no exception. All the mistakes that the soul makes in its passage through time must be dearly paid for. No one can atone for them except those who commit them. You call them sins; so they are, because they stand out in the light of evil to your sense. You understand them to be such. All that which does not appeal to your sense as right is in that degree evil — a sin. But we call your mistakes results of ignorance. No one will commit suicide if they are, at the time the act is committed, in the possession of a proper amount of knowledge concerning the fate of the suicide. But there are a variety of circumstances that force the weak one to take this choice. Poverty sometimes forces in that direction. Pain, disease, indeed, all the ills that human life is heir to, may become levers, forcing the intellect in this channel. And the act is of necessity justified by the propelling power of which it was born. But wisdom never justifies any act that is not in harmony with our highest light. When the soul becomes wise — above ignorance — stands apart from it, and beholds the mistakes it has made, in all their deformity, then it is that remorse comes, and the soul receives its due amount of chastisement.

Q. As I understand it, the physical form is for the purpose of individualizing spirit. If so, will the time arrive when all unindividualized spirit will thus have become individualized, and consequently there be no necessity for an earthly existence?

A. Every individual possesses a double individuality, one belonging to the inner and one to the outer life. The latter is the result of physique, education; the former of divine inspiration. They are separate and distinct from each other; although while in the body they hold the closest relationship to each other, yet there is a distinct dividing line ever running between them. Since you are both divine and human, you have need of not only a divine but of a human individuality. One pays allegiance to the things of this human life, and the other pays allegiance to the divine life. And they are perpetually at war with each other, because they are two opposites, and in chemistry when two opposites are brought together there is violent action, opposition. But be it understood that all opposition, in the end, in the *finale*, results in good, in great good. The very friction that is produced by this opposition is that which elevates the soul and gives it a certain amount of knowledge that it would otherwise be without. Soul, as purely soul, could never be understood. It must come in contact with form in order to express itself. Music would forever remain unheard were there no instruments through which its mystic power could play. Music is in the air, in all things, but it requires proper instruments under the law of music in order that it may demonstrate its presence. So it is with spirit, the soul. There is also a spiritual body through which the inner life can express itself. It holds the same relationship to the soul or the spirit that the body holds to the spirit-form. A triune nature have you all, and when one form is laid aside as useless to the spirit, as having fulfilled its mission, done its work, you are not to suppose that the spirit passes out in an unindividualized state, so far as form is concerned, that it has no longer need of form, for this is not so. Nor are you to suppose that your individuality that belonged to the form earthly is carried intact to the spirit-world and has form there, for it has not.

Q. The last part of the question is, will the time ever arrive when all unindividualized spirit will have become individualized, &c.?

A. No time has been revealed to us wherein such a state of things exists. So long as the earth is capable of producing physical forms, temples through which intelligence can unfold, can come into communication with outer objects in nature, so long they will be produced, in my opinion.

Q. Is it not possible that in succeeding ages, both matter and spirit having passed through a refining process, they will again unite and repeat the circle in a greater developed condition?

A. It is not only possible or probable, but according to the law of chemistry in nature it is a something that must take place.

Q. Do you mean to say that these spirits that now occupy forms may at some future stage of life come back and take another, perhaps finer form?

A. Judging from the experience of others, predicating our faith upon their experience, we are as sure of it as we are of our immortality.

Q. I have felt myself that I once inhabited this earth in another form, that I lived far in the East, in India; whether it is true I cannot say.

A. It is not at all improbable. In all probability your spirit projects faint glimpses of a prior existence through your present physical senses. But they are so faint, and come to you in such broken fragments, that you can scarcely understand them.

Q. I do not understand. I only have a sense of something far off and indistinct that has been in the past.

One of the Audience. I wish to state that some forty years ago, in this city, I was conversing with a brother-in-law of mine on this subject, and he said he was positive that he had had an existence prior to this. He is not now living, but if he would come and corroborate that statement it would be very satisfactory to me.

A. We meet with those who have a similar experience. That which was vague and shadowy in that respect in earthly life, becomes clearer and clearer as they pass out of the mists and shadows of the earthly life.

Q. Is this common to all humanity?

A. It is. It belongs alike to every one.

By Rev. Joseph Lowenthall, June 23, 1869.

Q. As all things in Nature, whether of the mineral, vegetable, or animal kingdom, have a point of commencement, of completeness, and of decay, as regards their individualized forms, will there not also come a time in the far ages of the future, when this our planet, earth, having brought her productions to their highest possible development, will gradually pass into decay and cease to exist in its present form, its elements being absorbed into other and newer planets? and is not the same true of all systems of worlds in the universe?

A. Forms are constantly changing their place; and that is not all — they are constantly becoming disintegrated and as constantly taking on new particles, absorbing and giving out. Planets are no exception. The grains of sand under your feet are constantly passing through a variety of changes. Form loses its identity, but the spirit of form does not lose its identity, save that which is allied to form and dependent upon form. Every special kind of life has a distinct mission of its own to perform, and having performed that mission it changes its place, steps out of its orbit, and gives place to something higher. The earth, like all other planets, has a destiny to fulfil, a certain mission, so far as its earthly career is concerned. Having fulfilled that, it will pass out of its present orbit, enter a spiritual orbit, and will become more etherealized, more spiritualized, than at present, and incapable of sustaining the same kind of life that it sustains at present.

Q. Is the use of table stimulants, as tea, coffee, &c., a positive hinderance to the development of mediumship, and especially of clairvoyance? and in what way can a person desiring such development aid its progress?

A. All such stimulants do not hinder the progress of mediumship, not in the least, but they do sometimes change the character of mediumship. They affect in that way, but they do not hinder the progress of mediumship. Some of the rarest exhibitions of clairvoyance, of spiritual vision, have been given when the clairvoyant was under the influence of some powerful narcotic. It is a well-known fact that the seers and seeresses of olden times were in the habit of visiting certain places where the air, by its peculiar electric condition, would contribute to clairvoyance, to second sight, to the trance, to the changing of speech, and all the various manifestations incident to mediumship. These table stimulants are but children of the same parent. They are but those conditions which under proper states produce those exalted states called mediumship. Used to excess, of course they produce unhappy conditions; and again, as I before remarked, they sometimes change the character of mediumship, but they do not cause the wheels of the car of progress to stand still.

Q. In the transition to spirit-life does the spirit enter at once into a healthy, manly condition, or must it go through a process of development before coming to its full stature?

A. As death, or the change so called, leaves you, so the spirit-world takes you up. Some spirits may become possessed of that entire vigor of manhood or womanhood that is so desirable to mentality, immediately after entering the spirit-world; others remain in a dormant state, incapable of action to any great extent for a long time.

Q. Is there any condition in this present life where people can live free from sin?

A. That depends upon how you define the term sin. All growth involves mistakes. So long as individualities grow, so long they are liable to make mistakes. Those mistakes you call sins. Perfection, if such a state can ever be attained, shuts out all sin. But I know of no one who has ever attained that state of perfection that church people so earnestly pray for. Not in this life can it be found, and I have not found it as yet in the spirit-life.

Q. Is there any standard of right and wrong in the spirit-life?

A. No, none whatever, save those standards that are erected in every living soul. Each one has a standard for themselves, and no one can borrow of another.

Q. Are clairvoyants always controlled by individual spirits?

A. No, certainly not. There is what is termed independent clairvoyance — a state wherein the clairvoyant becomes suddenly thrown into a condition whereby the past is revealed, and the future, together with the present, without the intervention of any second intelligence.

Q. By what power are they drawn into it?

A. By the action of natural law — that law that is found in the physical form, and that finds a correspondence in all its surroundings. Clairvoyance is dependent for agents upon all that by which it is surrounded, even that that is called independent clairvoyance, which does not need the aid of any foreign intelligence. You sometimes wander apart from the body in sleep without the aid of any foreign spirit. You are clairvoyant then. You take cognizance of things passing perhaps in other lands, perhaps in the spirit-world. You receive visions of the to come; you receive pictures of that which is past, and the living reality of that which is present, all through independent clairvoyance. But this same independent clairvoyance is dependent upon the soil, upon the electrical and magnetic currents by which the subject is surrounded, and by these conditions, but not by the intervention of any outside spirit.

By Cardinal Cheverus, June 22, 1869.

Q. It is said that the spiritual body possesses all the organs of the physical body, and that there is nothing without use. If this be the case, of what use to the spirit are the teeth and stomach? Do spirits eat food, masticating and digesting it, and passing it out of the system in the spirit-world as we do in this? If not, of what use are the internal organs?

A. The spirit-body possesses all the organs known to the natural body, and all the attributes, all the functions, known to the natural body, and more also; for at each successive step in progress the spirit has need of new functions, new attributes, and the Divine Providence provides for all it hath need of. Yes, the spirit has a stomach, has teeth, and uses them. Spirits have need to eat, as you have. They do not subsist upon nothing. Here you are in the rudimental state of spirit-life, and here you eat. There spirits dwell in a more refined state, but there they eat also. Receive and give is in the order of nature, divine and human. Therefore, all the processes by which progress is carried on here, are known also and made use of in the spirit-world.

Q. Is the spirit-body a perfect type of the natural physical body? When the latter is deformed, will the deformity appear in the spiritual body after death?

A. Those deformities that are the result of accident, so called by you, will not appear upon the spirit-body, for it can suffer no accident. That deformity that appears upon the body that is outwrought from the inner forces will appear also upon the spirit-body.

Q. Can the spirit detach itself from the spiritual body?

A. Yes; but as spirit is always dependent upon form as a mode of expression, it can only detach itself from one spirit-body to become attached to another.

Q. Can we change these forms at will?

A. Yes, under proper circumstances, but under circumstances requisite to the case. You can commit suicide here if you are only furnished with proper conditions, and it is the same yonder.

Q. In reference to the previous question I would ask, suppose a person is born with native deformities; are these seen in the spirit?

A. They are seen upon the spirit-form, and remain there till that form passes beyond them in growth.

Q. Then the spirit will of necessity make itself apparent in that form in returning to earth through mediums? It might be recognized clairvoyantly by those deformities?

A. Yes, certainly, as by the color of the hair, the eyes, the skin, the size, the temperament. All these are results of the projecting power of spirit through matter; therefore they appear upon the spirit-body as upon the natural body. But if by accident, by violence, a limb of the natural body is lost or disfigured, or any portion of the body is disfigured, that is not seen upon the spirit-body, for it comes from the external, and belongs to the external. The negro is the negro still in the spirit-world;

the Indian is the Indian still. And why? Because he has been made such by the action of the inner or spiritual forces upon the outer or natural forces.

Q. Is spirit-power communicated to physical bodies through electricity as a medium? or by what means are they enabled to move chairs, tables, or other material bodies?

A. Electricity is the most powerful agent we know, under the direction of spirit. It is by that power that all tangible bodies are moved — all the so-called miracles are performed.

Q. Does this account for the power of healing by electricity?

A. Yes, I believe the terms magnetism and electricity are synonymous. They are only different terms of one power. It is a subtle force, in the hands of intelligence and under the direction of intelligence, that becomes all-powerful everywhere.

Q. Is the medium of necessity gifted with more of the positive force than of the negative or recipient?

A. No. Sometimes the more negative the medium or subject, the greater the power that can be exercised through them; for it so happens that nearly all your cures performed by your healers, either modern or ancient, are performed by the intervention of spirit — perhaps many spirits. The material form is but the tunnel through which the power is poured. It is that instrument that causes the forces to come to a focus, that thereby they may be centred upon the one to be healed. Sometimes there are persons found who are so largely gifted in their own natural bodies that they can perform very strange and wonderful cures aside from the intervention of any other spirit.

By Cardinal Cheverus, June 24, 1869.

Q. If, upon leaving the body, the spirit gravitates to a congenial sphere, how can it be unhappy? or, in other words, how can you reconcile congeniality with unhappiness?

A. I do not understand that spirits at death are ushered immediately into a congenial sphere. I do understand that they may gravitate, each one to their own proper sphere, whatever or wherever it may be. No one can occupy the sphere belonging to another. It is congenial to their needs, to their state, but not to their desires; therefore it does not provoke happiness. The second state of existence, or that which is so understood to be by you, is a very natural state, devoid of all the lines of castes and creeds and conventionalities of this state. Here, people, by virtue of the needs of this life, dwell in states that do not belong to them spiritually. It is not so in the other life. Gold cannot buy place or position. Wealth, that wealth that is recognized to be such by the soul, purchases only for the soul that that the soul is ready to receive, nothing more.

By Cardinal Cheverus, June 28, 1869.

Q. How do spirits obtain the *food* they use? What equivalent do they give for it? Do they work for it as we do here? and, if so, are they subject to the terrible reverses humanity experiences upon this earth on that account?

A. It is said that it is the order of Nature, in physical life, to obtain bread by the sweat of the brow, by toil, by exertion; and we may add further that to obtain anything that ministers either to our pleasures or our needs, we must exert ourselves, we must toil, we must labor. There is a kind of labor that belongs especially to the physical body, the physical, organic life, and there is another kind of labor which belongs to spiritual life. This kind is desire — ardent, earnest desire. You know very well what the kind that belongs to physical life is. You are not unacquainted with the toil of the hands, of the feet, the exerting of the members of the body to obtain what is necessary to sustain the body. But you are not so well acquainted with that which belongs more especially to the spirit; although you have sat, many, perhaps all of you, in the primary school of that spirit-labor, yet you have hardly crossed the threshold. Yes, spirits do labor to obtain what is necessary for them to have. They labor by earnest desire, but they do not meet with those terrible reverses that are met with here. The soul's needs in the soul-world stand out prominent and clear, and they demand a supply. And as the great Father Spirit has furnished an adequate supply for every want, no desire can have a fruitless birth. It must draw to itself that which the soul has need of. A very large class or group of spirits, who are as yet magnetically attached to the earth and earthly conditions, obtain much of their sustenance through the action of human life, through the magnetic conditions that belong partly to human life, or stand as agents between this world and the world of souls. This subtle element called magnetism is the agent in the hands of whoso can understand it; and a very powerful agent it is, too. Poverty is known to the spirit after death, but not that kind of poverty that is experienced here. The soul can possess itself at will of all that is necessary for its good, for its advancement, for its unfoldment. The law of mine and thine is done away with in the spirit-world. Let us thank the great Father for that. No soul can hug to its bosom any more of God's gifts than it has need of. No one can have more of the beauty of the spirit-world than it can well appropriate. Therefore you see there is enough for all.

Q. Am I right in believing that the body serves to develop the spirit or spirit-body, and, having answered its purpose, fades and dies? — the spirit-body, having attained its maturity, remains firm, not sharing in the slightest degree in the decay of the material body, and presenting the same appearance when the man dies at the age of ninety that it would if he had died at thirty-five or forty?

A. Your correspondent is very nearly correct. The spirit-body is indeed, to a very great extent, a production of the physical body and physical, magnetic life. And that spirit-body is not always matured here in this life. The infant possesses the spirit-body of the infant, and that spirit-body matures after death, perhaps just as well as before that change.

Q. Do the souls of men and women essentially differ, independently of the conditions that surround their bodies?

A. Not as souls; in essence they are one; but in the manifestation that accrues from the essence they are more than one.

Q. What is the difference between spirit and animal magnetism?

A. The difference is in degree. One is more refined than the other. Animal magnetism is that that is adapted to animal life; more crude, more dense than that adapted to spirit-life, In essence they are one. They differ only in degree.

Q. Is the power emanating from healers of the sick this spirit-power, or is it blended with physical power?

A. It is sometimes pure spirit-power; at other times it is pure animal power; at other times it is a blending of the two.

By Theodore Parker, June 29, 1869.

Q. It has been stated through the medium, on different occasions, by various parties, that a spirit is constantly developing, rising to higher life, and that the spiritual body is constantly putting on changes to correspond to this development. Now, in my mind, there is an antagonism between this statement and the statement that spirits do, or will in time to come, return to and reinhabit the earth, in mortal bodies. Viewed from my stand-point, the return of a spirit to and reinhabiting the earth in a mortal body, is retrogression, not progression. From the second statement it would seem as though a person, after toiling to the top round, or thereabouts, of the spiritual ladder, was compelled to go to the bottom and remount. Will you please explain the apparent antagonism between the two statements?

A. The antagonism consists in your ignorance of the law, and of the true definition of the term progression. It is not simply a straightforward, onward and upward course — by no means. But it implies change, and all change takes place in cycles or circles. This is the order of nature, both human and divine. The germ progresses spirally, and what is true of the germ is true of mature life, so called. You go up on the mountain-top; you descend into the valley that you may ascend upon the next mountain-top. You seem to think that progression is attended by an even, uninterrupted sphere of action.

It is not so. There are different tones in the great scale of human progression; some are low and some are high; because you have touched once upon the low notes, you are not to suppose you are never to touch them again — by no means. Because you have known what human misery is once, you are not to suppose you are never to know it again. Though you ascend into the highest heaven, you are not to suppose you may not descend again to the lowest hell. Take for example the man Christ, who was said to be the special son of God. All Christianity so believes. Some consider him equal with the Father. If this be true, and if the record concerning his life be true also, surely you are not to expect any more than he had during his natural and divine life. He descended into the valley and shadow of death with all his godliness and with all his divine life; and, more than this, he mingled with publicans and sinners. In the garden of Gethsemane he sweat great drops of blood in his agony, and cried in his human weakness, "If it be thy will, let the cup pass from me; nevertheless, let thy will, not mine, be done." And upon the cross he cried, "My God! why hast thou forsaken me?" This was progression in its divinest and truest sense. Jesus lost nothing of his godliness, nothing of his divinity, nothing that belonged to him as a superior being when he descended into these deep valleys of human misery. Shall we say that he ceased to progress then? That would be a libel upon God and upon human nature, for progression is unceasing, eternal, never stops. If Jesus, the pattern of the divine life — such to the Christian world at least — could go down into the valley to progress, you must not expect anything better. It is life ever the same. Study it in form, and from a superficial stand-point, or from the deep voice of your inner souls. Hear it. Study it down below the surface. Probe it clear to the bottom, if possible. See that he did not descend into valleys of human misery, and rise again uninterruptedly to the mount of transfiguration. You make a very great mistake in supposing that progression implies one constant, uninterrupted march onward.

Q. Is man anything more or less than the creature of birth and circumstances? If he is born with strong moral and mental characteristics, and the circumstances in which he is placed are congenial, he lives, as a matter of course, a moral and intellectual life. If, on the other hand, he is born with mental and moral qualities but moderately strong, and his surroundings are strongly adverse, he leads a depraved life. Now, taking this view of the subject, can man be considered a responsible being, or responsible in that manner and to that extent which the world, or a certain portion of it, considers him to be.

A. The poet says, —

> "'Tis education forms the common mind;
> Just as the twig is bent the tree's inclined."

And the poet tells here a great truth. Education does almost everything towards fashioning your human lives, towards determining concerning the course you shall take in all the various avenues of this life. If you are educated to consider this path the best, you will be very likely to take it. If you are educated to consider the opposite best, you will very naturally take it. Your human nature is moulded in this life by your education. But there is a divine judge placed in every reasoning individual that will call the individual to account for all deeds and all thoughts, and to that judge you are responsible, and to none outside of that. No one is there outside of that divine judge which belongs to you as an individual to call you to judgment. You may infringe upon the rights of another, but the judge within will call you to account. Be sure of that, if you have in reality infringed upon another's rights. You can make no mistake in this life that you will not be punished for; that you will not be held accountable for by the divine judge which belongs to you as an individual.

Q. You do not mean to say that this punishment falls at once upon the trespasser.

A. I mean to say that just as soon as you in your external nature come into *rapport* with the voice of the inner judge, you must respond, and you must come to judgment. It cannot be otherwise, and your sentence is quick and sure.

By Theodore Parker, July 1, 1869.

Q. Should the prayer be addressed directly to our departed friends, or to some other power or principle that may be enabled to assist?

A. It matters not whether you make an agent of the spirit you desire to commune with, or whether you pray to the great general Spirit, that which is within each one of us. It makes no difference.

Q. Is there any such thing as a special Providence that directs all the acts of life, to whom we can pray to ask for particular blessings?

A. All the special Providence that I know of is general law, such as pertains to general life. I do not know — indeed, I do not believe that we can change the law one jot or tittle by our prayers. We can place ourselves in harmony with our circumstances, with the conditions by which we are divinely and humanly surrounded, by prayer, which is all, in my opinion, that we can do. We might pray to all eternity for the sun to come down that we may examine it. Would it come? I think not. We may pray to all eternity that Mount Vesuvius may be removed and cast into the sea. It will not avail. I know the record says so, but I do not believe it. Prayer, in that case, without works, would fail; but we could go to work with shovel and spade, and perhaps do very much towards it. Prayer makes us in harmony with the law. It fits us to receive what we ask for, but it does by no means change the law itself.

Q. Was Christ a Spiritualist?

A. Yes, he was a Spiritualist in the largest sense, and he lives to-day in your spiritual movement just as much as he lived in the spiritual movement of his day.

By Cardinal Cheverus, July 6, 1869.

Q. We find recorded in heathen mythology the history of a prophet almost identical in name and acts with Jesus — his name Chrishna, or Chrisma — and the circumstance of women wiping his feet with their hair is such a remarkable coincidence, that while it shakes the faith of the Christian, it furnishes strong proof to the sceptic of the mythical character of Christ. Can you give us light on the subject?

A. Every nation has its idols — its gods and goddesses — peculiar shrines whereunto the people are called to worship. Neither Chrishna, nor Christ, were entirely beings of mythology, but so far as a certain portion of their lives are concerned, there is much of the mythic attached to them, and this is the case with all those beings that the nations worship. The aborigines of the country have their divinities, whose original is in real life, but that original is surrounded with so many mythical figures that the real is almost entirely lost to the human sight. While contemplating the mythic Christ, we are very apt to overlook the real personality, the spirit. We are very apt to see only the external paraphernalia that the real has been surrounded with. It is not at all strange. It is in accordance with our organization as human beings. We are growing up through a variety of conditions that determine for us, whether we will or no. These conditions determine concerning our religious worship, concerning our God even. It is these conditions that form the image of our God, and determine that we shall worship that God, and none other. And as intelligence marches on through the ages, as mind becomes more and more enlightened with regard to the history of past nations, and past religious histories, those images that have been invested with divinity begin to assume different shapes, begin to stand out in their real characters, begin to be seen for what they are. We understand them better as the light is shed upon them — the divine light, that which emanates from the past, which comes to us from the present, and that which is shed to us from the future. All things conspire to aid the spirit in its search for truth, all kinds of truth. The knowledge that such an individual as Chrishna lived, does not at all detract from the reality or divinity of the Christian's Christ. But it only shows, or should show, the Christian that one of the fundamentals of the Christian Church has been borrowed from ancient mythology. The Christ may be himself pure and intact. The truth is there, but the clothing has been borrowed. The rite of baptism is a borrowed rite. In fact, all the rites of the Christian Church, every one of them, are borrowed — some from Chrishna, some from Vishnu. In fact, all the gods that preceded the Christian God have loaned of their wardrobe, and the Christians have appropriated it that their Christ may be clothed. The present age offers great light, and whosoever refuses to see by it, and learn of it, will refuse to eat that bread which cometh down from heaven, which will nourish the soul for eternity.

By Ab-dal-Ha-da, July 12, 1869.

Q. Is there an element of life distinct from life-germs?

A. Life and form are one and inseparable. Spirit and matter ever act in concert. They are never separated. When you talk about spirit as divorced from matter, you enter a wide field of speculation, that will always be a field of speculation, and nothing more. Spirit and matter are one and inseparable. You can no more separate them than you can separate God from his works. Can you do this? I have never found the individual who could. I have seen very many who have attempted it, and who have worked very hard to do it, but I never saw one that was successful. Spirit and matter belong together, and we can only know of spirit or life as we know of matter. There is a subtle ether pervading space, entering all bodies, and assisting in all manifestations of life; but as subtle as that is, it is connected with matter. The unseen forces pervading all nature are connected with matter. We only know what the air is by the matter it is connected with. We can never know anything of life only as we know it through forms of matter. We only read the Scriptures of our God through matter. I am a materialist, in every sense, because I know from observation and earnest study in the spirit-world that matter and spirit always go together, and are never separate.

Q. What becomes of the life, the sensation, the instinct, the knowledge existing in the animal creation below man at their death.

A. All the instincts or reasons that belong to all the species of life below man and up to man are constantly changing places. The lower takes the qualities of the higher, passes through the higher, and goes on, forever on, changing its form and characteristics, but preserving its life intact. Nothing is lost, but everything is subject to the law of change. You are not to suppose that these human forms are precisely like those that the spirit manifests through after death. They are crowned with new attributes there, although they retain all that ever belonged to them. They are constantly gathering fresh ones, constantly changing place and changing form. The animal does not lose its identity at death, by any means — it is an animal still. It comes through death to a higher plane, and there waits for another change. When that comes it takes a higher stand. It passes ever onward and upward, but it does not lose its identity. The horse is the horse still; the dog is the dog still; and yet you know that all species of life, whether animal, vegetable, or mineral, are capable of improvement. You can improve them by your intelligence here; and if this is true, do you not suppose they go on improving to all eternity? The dog is a finer dog in the spirit-world than here; the horse is a finer horse; the tree is a more glorious tree; the flower is far more beautiful there than here; and yet they preserve all that belongs to them, but they take on new life at every change.

Q. The Christian world do not admit the tree nor the flower into the spirit-world.

A. O, no, of course not. The Christian world, as you well know, doubtless, has made a great many mistakes. Christianity has always bowed down to error, and to nothing else. Christianity has overlooked the real life, and bowed down to idols always. In my time I had not the slightest faith or sympathy with your Christianity, not that which is embodied in creeds or churches — not at all. I had faith in all that was good. I believed in the principle of goodness — in the one God superintending all things and guiding all according to his own will; but I had not the slightest faith in the soundness and genuineness or truthfulness of your Bible, your creeds, or your churches. They were to me false lights, leading us into ditches and pitfalls and miry places.

Q. We classify all existences into the ponderable and imponderable. Your existence is to us that of the imponderable. Can you take cognizance of the elements we term imponderable as plainly and palpably as we can that of the ponderable?

A. That which you cannot feel, or recognize with all of your human senses, is imponderable to you. The air is an imponderable substance — for it is a substance. To us the air contains images, forms of substance as tangible, as real as the solid earth to you. We take cognizance more clearly of those conditions of life that are imponderables to you than you do, because we have passed into nearer *rapport* with them. We stand face to face with them. But there are subtle elements in advance of us. There are elements still imponderable to us. Advance as far in life as we may, we shall still find an element that is imponderable to us. We approach one; we come into *rapport* with it; we analyze it; we find out what it is, and having disposed of that, lo! there is another presented. Our Father, God, does not mean that we shall be idle, that there shall ever come a time to our souls when we can say we have learned the whole, there is nothing more for us to learn or to do. God is wise. He knows that our spirits need to be active, and he gives us just one lesson at a time, and no more.

Q. Is there any truth in astrology?

A. Yes, the basis of astrology is eminently true. There are many features presented by astrology, modern and ancient, that are not true. But in the main the science is eminently true. We know that every form is connected with all other forms. There is a reciprocity of action throughout all Nature. The planets act upon us, and we upon them. They determine concerning certain characteristics of our being, and they, possessing the larger life and larger power over us, of course guide us to a very great extent. We cannot guide the planets, because we are inferior to them; but the planets can guide us, can determine concerning our physical lives, to a very great extent. The science of astrology, when considered from a spiritual stand-point, is sublime. It presents wonders to our spirits that no other science ever has. It holds within itself the glory of the past, the present, and the future, and it beckons us onward as no other science ever has, or, in my opinion, ever can.

By William E. Channing, July 13, 1869.

Q. Do not the teachings at these séances tend to educate us to reject a belief of the spriritual superiority of Jesus over all other men living, or who have lived? Speaking for myself, as a lover of Jesus, I know I have great consolation in that love, and would very much dislike to have it lessened. Even accepting that your teachings are true, does not my special love for Jesus result beneficially to myself and to my daily life, by bringing me more *en rapport* with the principles of which he was the embodiment? Take from us our love of and belief in Jesus, and even the best of us have nothing left but general moral sentiments. But leave Jesus to us, and we have friend, counsellor and example — in a word, God Incarnate. I do not ask (of course not) that truth be sacrificed to expediency; but cannot we justly believe that Jesus was more than man, and more than any man has been, or ever can be? Take your own teachings of what God is, cannot we safely believe that Jesus was more of this than men were or are? If this (to my view very important) string of queries be replied to, can the reply include some special reference to myself that shall convince me that it came from "over the river"?

A. If Spiritualism teaches any investigating soul to think less of the pure doctrines of Jesus of Nazareth, then such a soul had better abandon the investigation of Spiritualism. Spiritualism is but the voice of this same Jesus the Christ, speaking unto the people of this day; but how few there are who recognize this voice! Even those who pretend to know most about Jesus know the least generally. Your correspondent, Mr. Chairman, seems to be wedded to an idol. He seems to have more love for the personality of Jesus, than for the divine principles he taught. He seems to forget that there is a divine truth in Spiritualism, precisely analogous to that which was taught by Jesus. Christianity has ever tended to idolatry, and I suppose it ever will, because Christianity has bowed down before the form, and has not thought of worshipping the spirit that animated the form. Christianity has recognized only the form. It is to be deplored, but it is true. Your correspondent says he is a lover of Christ. It is well; but he had better be in love with the divine principles of truth that this man Jesus taught, than to be in love with the man; for he is nothing more than man — human, fallible, like ourselves. Behold him in his agony in the garden, praying that the cup might pass from him! If he were God, would he have thus prayed? Surely not. Again, behold him upon the cross! "Father, forgive them, for they know not what they do." If he had the power to forgive, would he have thus prayed? If he was God in the flesh, as a speciality, would he have thus petitioned the Father to forgive his enemies? No; surely not. All our reason rebels against that idea. He was our elder brother, preëminent in virtue, in all those glorious principles that shine so bright through every age, in the midst of all kinds of darkness. But there have been others than Jesus through whom these lights have shone. Every nation has been blessed with its divine teachers. Every tribe of men has been blessed with its prophets, its seers, its wise men and holy women; and shall we say that none of them were divinely inspired but Jesus? It would be hardly fair to so determine. I would that there were more devout worshippers at the shrine of the spirit of Christ, and less at the shrine of the personality. I would that men and women could worship more the divine principle, and less the image. But so it is. The crust of humanity at present is not thin enough for the spirit to look out and behold beyond the form of the spirit that animates the form. But since we are growing through the conditions of life, passing higher and still higher, we have a hope that the time will come when religion, pure and undefiled, will be known; that religion that worships God in spirit and in truth; that knows no form; that recognizes no altar save those the living God has erected everywhere; that expects no general jndgment, but knows that the judgment seat is within every living soul. Your correspondent has but to compare notes between modern Spiritualism and that Judean Spiritualism taught by Jesus, and he can but come to the conclusion, if he is a reasonable individual, that they are one and the same, and that if he worships the spirit of Christ as exhibited upon the plains of Judea, he worships the spirit of Spiritualism as it is seen to-day.

Q. Do spirits regard the misdeeds of their earth-friends in the same light they did while here in the physical form?

A. O, no; they regard them with sympathy, with charity, with pity; they regard them in the full light of truth; they are able to see behind the effect, and discern the cause; they know wherefore their friends take this or that course in life; they see the propelling forces, the levers that move their friends in this or that direction. And when they see them forced by circumstances to take that which is the lesser good, they mourn over the course they have taken, but not without hope; because they know that by the experience they will gain in travelling that way, they will attain strength to free themselves, and will avoid such a course in future by coming into harmony with better laws, by making themselves acquainted with their surroundings. When we are thoroughly acquainted with the laws that govern us, we shall, of course, place ourselves in harmony with those laws, and shall move on in concert with them. It is only because we are ignorant of ourselves and the law, and our relation to the law, that we kick so hard against law. If we were not ignorant, we should never do this, because we should know that the law is greater than ourselves, and would rend us more severely if we were not in harmony with it.

Q. Is there such a thing as that which we have been accustomed to term the vital principle or vital force, or is it a mere mode by which the elementary principles of life act?

A. Yes; there is such a thing as a vital force, a subtle principle that not only pervades the human form and keeps it in motion, but pervades all other forms. You call it sometimes electricity, sometimes magnetism. You divide it off into different degrees or states, and give it different names. It is an imponderable essence, that keeps these human machines in motion by playing upon the nerves, and the nerves in turn play upon the muscles. If it was not for the presence of this vital force in the system, decay would ensue. Wherever it is absent, decomposition begins to take place. If any part of the system is diseased, the vital force is not there. If it was, it would ward off disease; it would keep the parts in health. The absence of it lays us open to disease. The presence of it keeps off disease, and keeps us in harmony with Nature's laws. When the vital force is lacking in a plant it dies. Its leaves wither; its stalk becomes unable to transmit anything that will give new life from the roots. So it is with all kinds of animal life. When the vital force is lacking, the animal form begins to change, to decompose. The particles begin to separate. This vital force is found in the atmosphere, in the water, in the lightning, in the darkness. You find it everywhere. We may as well call it God as to call it anything else.

By Theodore Parker, July 15, 1869.

Q. Can there be such a thing as a new and original idea?

A. No, not absolutely, because we do not know how much of the idea that we think we originate belongs really to us. We cannot tell how far we are inspired by circumstances. We are never able to determine whether our thoughts are absolutely our own, the productions of our own being, or infused into our minds by some outside source.

Q. According to geological theory, there was a time when the matter composing our earth existed in a state of liquid fire. Now, if the organizing life-germs of all things are eternal as individualized entities, where, at that time, were the life-germs that in the far distant future were to clothe the earth with vegetation, and people it with animal life?

A. We may say, and truthfully, too, that the germs of all physical life, so far as planet-life is concerned, are contained within the primary elements. Fire constitutes the basis of this planet, and all others. An eminent French chemist once said, that, to him, it was a fact that the flame produced from any body that was in process of burning contained within itself the entire body; and more than that, if it was of a vegetable or mineral nature, the germ of that vegetable or mineral form. The flame held that germ intact, and a form representing the external form or thing that was burning. We know from positive knowledge, from observation, that if we burn a rose upon the surface of the water, a microscope will reveal the shape of the rose intact upon the water, provided the water is still. I believe that not only the inner life, but the outer form, possesses, to a high degree, immortality. I believe that Nature holds in memory and in her vast laboratory all the forms that have ever been, preserves them all, loses not a single one.

Q. Many persons believe that vegetation does sometimes spring from the earth under conditions which preclude the possibility that any seed with a material covering could have been there. Do you consider such a thing possible?

A. Yes; I do.

By Theodore Parker, July 19, 1869.

Q. Is the veil separating the spiritual and material worlds as much an obstacle to spirits as to mortals?

A. Yes, it is precisely the same, no difference.

Q. Mortals penetrate this veil by clairvoyance, or the quickening of the spiritual senses; but how are spirits cognizant of earth-scenes? Is it through their spiritual senses, or the corporeal senses of the medium?

A. It is done by materializing the spiritual senses. This process is performed by coming into material *rapport* with certain mediumistic bodies — bodies that are constantly throwing off through their magnetic and electric lives the aura that can be used by spirits. They make use of it to see, to hear, to feel, to come into *rapport* with all the objects that belong to this life.

Q. Please give the mode of birth into spirit-life. Is the newly-born spirit a spontaneous presence to his spirit-friends, or is it a gradual process?

A. When the last particle of magnetic life has been separated from the animal body, then the spirit-body is thoroughly and well formed. It is a distinct, objective intelligence to all other spirits.

Q. Do you, as a spirit, possess a more definite idea of your destiny, and the destiny of the human race, than you possessed while in the earth-form?

A. Yes, more definite, but not absolutely definite. We see a little farther into the future than we did when here; that is all.

Q. What is the use of feet and legs to the spirit, whose locomotion is accompanied by and with the rapidity of the will?

A. There is a use for all the limbs, all the parts and portions of the spirit-body. The rose possesses beauty of color and form. It is not conscious that it does possess that beauty. It is all unconscious of the homage paid it by admiring mortals. Nevertheless, it possesses the beauty. Its petals are delicately formed and delicately painted. The spirit has need of form through which to express itself. The life of the rose, the spirit of the rose, has need of the form through which to express itself. It is a mistaken idea that spirits do not use their limbs in the spirit-world. They do. They walk, they plan, they build, they have use for brains, for hands, for all the organs of the body, and as fast as the body has need of new unfoldment in form it has that new unfoldment. It does not remain always precisely what it was. If it did it would not grow. The infant spirit, as it passes into mature intellectual life, has need of a more mature form. Every peculiar atom of life generates within itself a peculiar kind of electric and magnetic being. So, then, as the spirit is dependent upon these agencies, electricity and magnetism, for expression, and as these agencies are dependent upon form for expression, therefore the spirit grows till the form matures.

Controlling Spirit. Our attention was called this morning, by the lady medium whose organism we use, to an article appearing over the letters "H. C.," in a Louisiana paper — I think bearing the name of the Livingstone Herald. It seems that the author of the article has been somewhat shocked by seeing a message given at this place, purporting, as he says, to come from a negro girl. To him that circumstance places the negro not only upon a level with the white creation, but a little above it; and he says the contemplation thereof is perfectly heart-sickening. He contends, if I understand him aright, that the negro has no distinct immortality. If he has any at all, it is only that that has been borrowed from the whites. All he knows of the arts and sciences, of religion, of politics, of anything pertaining to intellectual life, he has borrowed from his white brothers. Being an imitative race, parrot-like, he says only what he has been taught to say, nothing more. Well, how much are we, claiming to be intelligences under white skins, in advance of the negro in this respect? Do we originate a single thought? Hardly. Do we not copy from all the past through which we have come? Certainly we do. Do not we pattern after everything that we happen to fancy? We certainly do. If we hear a great thought expressed, we make use of it, no matter who expresses it, generally, unless prejudice forbids it.

Farther on, the article seems to express the idea that Spiritualists make a very great mistake in believing that the negro is an immortal soul, and ends up by making reference to a spirit-message which he tells us he has received from a reliable source. The spirit informs him that all caste and color and grade of development, &c., are preserved intact in the spirit-world. Caste is attracted to caste, color to color, form to form, race to race, and so on. We are not able to quote the precise language, but we give the idea.

Following that article there appears one from the editor, which in itself is rather ambiguous. He does not take any particular stand in it, that we are able to discover, but seems to carry the idea that if immortality means anything at all, it means a conscious individual existence after death. There seems to be a feeling thrown out in the entire article that the white race alone has the crowning gift of immortality; that we, God's favored, chosen ones, are alone endowed with eternal life; that we, and we alone, possess and hold our individuality intact after death. Now I wish to make here a very broad and unqualified statement, and it is this: according to the accepted definition of the terms individuality and immortality, we do not, any single one of us, possess immortality — not one of us. There never was an immortal spirit; there never will be one. Nature and Nature's God seem to have forbidden it. All intelligence seems to define individuality and immortality in one way — at least all that intelligence that is exhibited through physical life; and more than that, this intelligence seems to connect the two inseparably together. They seem to have woven bands around their immortality and individuality, and will not allow them to be separated, when they are in fact distinctly separated, just as much so as the musician is separate from the instrument upon which he performs. It is a well-known scientific fact that we are constantly changing our individualities, and if a man or woman was to be measured spiritually by their individualities and the characteristics which they possess, and immortality is allied to that individuality — inseparably so — then we cannot be immortal, because those individualities are constantly changing. We are not to-day what we were yesterday — not any one of us. The individuality that belonged to us yesterday is not ours to-day. We do not think precisely to-day as we did yesterday; we do not act precisely the same. We change constantly. Those who knew us in childhood only recognize us in mature age perhaps by our outward features, by our name, by those chisellings of physical life that may be recognized, but not by our thoughts, not by that which goes to make us intelligent beings. Paul says, "When I was a child I spake as a child, acted as a child, but when I became a man I put away childish things;" in other words, I changed my individuality. The mother who expects to meet her infant babe as a child in the spirit-world, after years have been added to it in that life, will be disappointed, for the child grows in form and in intellect. The old individuality it possessed with its baby life here has been added to again and again and again, till the little germ is entirely changed. Our immortality does not consist in form, or in the amount of intelligence we have, or in the particular kind of intelligence that we are endowed with. What does it consist in, then? Why, that we have the gift of life, under some condition, forever and forever.

By William E. Channing, July 20, 1869.

Q. Will you define the knowing principle, consciousness? Tell us where it begins in the scale of Nature. And is not the consciousness in man the same as that which we observe in the lower order of animals? And why should the consciousness of man have any more claim to immortality than that of the dog or horse?

A. The consciousness of the human has no more claim to immortality than that of the dog or horse, in my opinion. Each sphere of conscious life possesses its own distinctive kind of consciousness. We do not part with our consciousness when we sleep — neither does the dog or the horse. The evidences that prove to the contrary are numerous. We do not even enter a state where we part with all our consciousness — where we sleep, in the absolute. In our hours of deepest sleep, here in physical life, our spirits are conscious. There is an inner consciousness that never sleeps. The dog dreams, and demonstrates the fact. Those who watch him can realize it. The horse dreams. If this is true with regard to these two animals, why not with regard to all the rest? Scientists who have investigated in that direction tell us it is true. It is not possible to define consciousness, except by saying we are awake to our surroundings.

By Theodore Parker, Sept. 9, 1869.

Q. What is the actuating principle of the involuntary forces of the body? If you say "Life," we ask, "What is it?"

A. The body physical being possessed of two distinct sets of nerves, the voluntary and the involuntary, science tells us that the action of the subtle nervous aura, or force, when passing over the involuntary system, causes involuntary action. In its play upon the voluntary system, it acts upon the brain; its force is first applied there, and from thence it descends throughout all the voluntary nervous system. You may ask, "Is there any difference existing between the force that acts upon the voluntary and that which acts upon the involuntary nervous system?" I should answer, "No; I believe them to be one and the same power." We may give as many names as we please, but after all it is one force. You call magnetism and electricity two distinct forces. This is a mistake — they are one. Seen under certain circumstances, you call them magnetism — under others, electricity. These terms must be used by you so long as you have need of them; but as you go up in life, you will drop one after another, and come down to simplicity of expression. To-day you cannot understand it; so you must have your magnetism, your electricity, your psychological forces, and a thousand and one terms for one and the same thing.

Q. Are spirits enabled to behold the material universe independent of a medium through which to gain an entrance to our plane of action? If so, are they not often rendered miserable in beholding the many sufferings and violations of law in this life?

A. They are able to behold the material universe, but not in precisely the same sense that you behold it. You see that part of the universe that appeals to your bodily senses; we see that also, but very dimly, unless we are in clear *rapport* with some physical organism called a medium. But we behold distinctly and clearly that which you do not recognize at all; that is the tangible to us — it is the intangible to you. To us, in our pure spiritual state, aside from mediumistic control, all the objects in life that you can recognize with your human senses are intangible to us; they are shadowy; while that which you cannot see or feel, is the real life to us. "Are they not often rendered miserable," asks the questioner, "in beholding the many sufferings and violations of law in this life?" To a certain extent they are, but not without hope. It is not that kind of midnight gloom which sometimes settles over the spirit in the earthly life. It is a keen, sharp pain, which leaves the spirit better for having passed through it. When we sometimes see our friends here in sorrow, we mourn with them — we shed tears over their sufferings. When we see them walking in paths of vice, which lead straight to the furnace of affliction, we lament over them, but not without hope; for we know that the spirit will finally overcome its weakness, and these scourges and whips will but have done their duty for them. Were they our children, we might mourn to be called upon to chastise them, and yet we might feel that it was best that we should do so. We may scourge in love, that the spirit may, through discipline, attain to fairer forms, and rise to better things.

By Father Henry Fitz James, Sept. 21, 1869.

Q. Is it true that people are led into the wilderness by the spirit, as much as they were eighteen hundred years ago?

A. I do not know why it should not be true. If mortals could be led by spirits then, I do not know why they cannot be to-day.

Q. Do you not think we are led into the wilderness of doubt, and left therein by those in spirit-life?

A. Sometimes. Spirits have as large a variety of means by and through which to work upon mortals as the varying circumstances of the case demand. Every condition requires a different degree of action.

Q. Are spirits possessed of greater knowledge than we in this life?

A. Only by observation, research, and study. They have knowledge, because they have seen more, or heard more. You would have greater knowledge concerning London, if you had lived there fifteen years, than you now have.

Q. Yes, but not if I had just arrived there. Do spirits receive knowledge immediately on arriving in the spirit-world?

A. No; knowledge is not shed upon us without efforts on our own part. It becomes precious to us only as it is hard to obtain.

Q. Are spirits conversant with the affairs of this earth?

A. They are — some of them.

Q. Why should some be, and others not?

A. Because some are not interested in the affairs of this world. Some on earth are not interested in politics, and those who are are much better informed than they upon that subject. So in our life, those who are not interested in the affairs of earth do not know so much of them as those who are.

Q. Do spirits know of the future of affairs pertaining to this world?

A. Only by comparison. They know that certain effects will follow inevitably certain causes. And they, being able to see those causes, while you are not, can thus more readily perceive the future.

Q. Then they know more than we do?

A. Life is a mathematical problem; the past, present, and future are connected. They who understand the present clearly, and know the past, can judge very correctly concerning the future. Astronomers can predict with positive certainty the approach of certain changes in the heavenly bodies. How can they do this? By study and mathematical demonstration; by comparing the past with the present, and judging in connection with the future. Life, in the absolute, admits of no division; the past and future are, in the absolute, the whole — the present.

Q. Is not the information of one spirit available to all?

A. To all who desire.

Q. Then why cannot the whole history of the world, from its creation to the present time, be given to us?

A. Because there are no instruments fitted for the work? Why cannot you see the farthest star? Because there are no instruments by which your eye can secure the knowledge. Not because the eye is not capable of seeing, if it had a telescope of sufficient power to aid it. It is because you have not the instruments to-day.

Q. What do you mean by instruments?

A. I mean persons who can receive in your life this knowledge, and reflect it in the same light.

By Theodore Parker, Sept. 27, 1869.

Q. We are told every person has a spirit-guide. If this is so, by whom or by what law are they appointed?

A. It is to be supposed that every person dwelling here in physical life has some one spirit, if not more, who, in obedience to the law of want and supply, will be attracted to him or her. These spirits take a deep interest in them, and exercise a watchful care over the frailties of human life. Such would be considered guardian spirits. They are so by virtue of spiritual law; they come to you, if at all, by spiritual attraction. All souls, as well as the atoms of life, are repelled from or attracted to each other, as the case may be, by fixed law. If a soul is drawn to you, it is drawn by law, fixed law, and becomes your guardian spirit by law. Love is an attribute of law, divine, perfect, and holy, and it is the avenue by and through which your guardian spirits work.

They love you, hence they seek to do you good; they come to you and watch over you. Because you are told that each has a guardian spirit, you are not to suppose that they are always present, and never absent. They come when the law of their being and yours demands that they shall come. Are you sick? You desire to be well, and your interior life instinctively and naturally extends out for something higher, beyond you, to make you better. It matters not whether it be the great God, or some kind spirit; and this desire reaches out to these spirits, and they come to you because they love you. When the need is supplied, they leave you, and wait till the next occasion brings them to your side.

Q. Does not the idea of a spirit-guide interfere with the freedom of our actions, and our responsibility to God?

A. By no means; because these spirit-guides are not your leaders. You may as well say that you are not responsible beings, because you were not born such; because you had fathers and mothers who diligently cared for you till you were well able to care for yourselves. These guardian spirits do not take away our responsibility or our individuality; but they only aid us when we need aid. They are to us as supporters when we need them, but they are not our leaders.

By Cardinal Cheverus, Oct. 4, 1869.

Q. In this life some have good memories and more have poor memories. Can those of the latter class hope to be able in the future life to recall all that knowledge of history or science that they have once acquired, but seem to have totally lost?

A. Each spirit possesses a distinct recollection of all its thoughts and of all its acts. It has an account of all it has experienced in all its past life, and of all in its present life. Memory, with the spirit, is eternal. Those who have no large faculty or gift in that direction here, have it not because of physical deformity — physical want; the bodily organs through which memory makes itself known are perhaps in an inactive state, so much so that the indwelling spirit cannot use them with success. But it is not so in the after-life; every condition through which the spirit has passed is made a record of by the spirit, and that record is as eternal as the spirit is eternal.

Q. What is the reason that spirits find such great difficulty to correct their errors of judgment in religion and philosophy in the future life, although their capacities are enlarged, and other more enlightened spirits are presumed to stand ready and willing to instruct them? And are not our opportunities much better here than in spirit-life for acquiring knowledge of all kinds, as is to be inferred from the difficulty spirits seem to have in correcting their errors and changing their bad habits of thought and action?

A. "Presumed" — that word is well used. It is presumed, says your correspoudent, that enlightened spirits stand ready to assist the benighted who come from earth-life; but be it understood that although enlightened spirits, upon all subjects, stand ready to give light to others, they are only suffered to impart in accordance with the law which controls them. When the benighted spirit asks in all honesty of soul for more light, and seeks for it, is ready to receive it, and make good use of it, then are they ready to give it. But if it were forced upon the darkened spirit, the old maxim of earth would be applicable here: —

"The man convinced against his will
Is of the same opinion still."

Spirits do not find that difficulty in overcoming their erroneous opinions that you may suppose. You should not think that because they do not jump into immediate knowledge after death, they have a hard time to attain it. But it is the law of all spirits that they advance by slow and distinct degrees. There are no arches to span the gulfs over which spirits can march at will; they must move forward by regular gradation; they must ascend the ladder of human wisdom — no round being overlooked — ere they can pass out of darkness into light. The sun does not come immediately as the shades of night begin to disappear, and Nature moves in all her departments slowly and surely. Thus it is with the spirit.

By Rev. Joseph Lowenthall, Oct. 5, 1869.

Q. Has the Indian become more progressive than the white? and for that reason are they exterminating the red man?

A. Spiritually, in an absolute sense, the Indian is far in advance of the whites. I know well that the egotism of the white race will rise up and deny this assertion; but there will come a time when the religions of the two will be weighed in the balances of Justice, and we well know which will be the sufferer. The pure, unadulterated religion of the Indian will put his white brother and his religion to shame; and when in yonder sphere the soul of the white man shall stand unclothed of all false surroundings, it will see that the Indian's religion is far in advance of his own. The Indian has received his religion through the reasonings of his soul — that is the natural kind of religion; that is unadulterated, pure, intuitive, free from the world's uncomeliness. It has come to him intuitionally; he sees God in all things, hears him in the winds, perceives his attributes in all the workings of Nature, which is his Bible — the Bible of God. I would that you with white skins had a religion as pure before God as that of the Indian.

By Theodore Parker, Oct. 14, 1869.

Q. Is it true that in the spirit-land we may pursue and follow out any branch of knowledge, whatever it may be, that has claimed our attention here, but which we have not been able to continue on account of the shortness of our stay here?

A. Yes, it is true. The bud that is blasted here blooms there. That which really belongs to us by soul-right, we can pursue there as a pleasure or as an employment in the spirit-world. If the artist was such from his inner life — if he was such because he loved to be, not because external circumstances forced him to be — then he is an artist still, and all the circumstances that tended to cramp his efforts here are swept away there. He finds a larger range, greater liberty, more power. He finds that his artistic faculties unfold; he has those which he did not know he possessed here.

Q. Of what use will a knowledge of many languages be to me in a future life? I have a passion for and have labored hard to acquire them, and it would be a pleasure to me always to continue in the pursuit of that branch of knowledge; but I am often led to inquire, Will a knowledge of different tongues be of any use to me in a future state, since spirits of all nationalities can understand each other simply by the reciprocal reading of mind or thought?

A. Language belongs to earth. It is the vehicle

through which thought is expressed here in your life, but is not so in the spirit-world. Therefore the acquirement of all the languages known would avail the student but little in the future life.

Q. Are our every-day incidents and actions indicative of the future sphere to which our souls shall gravitate by the force of magnetic attraction?

A. Yes; we lay the foundation at least of our houses spiritual here in this life. All those croppings out of the spirit which we see in the characteristics of individuals, in their acts, in their words, in all that goes to make up their lives, moral and mental, is carried into the spirit-world, and becomes a part of their existence there.

Controlling Spirit. — Our attention has been called to an article appearing in the "Livingston Herald," in answer to one that appeared in the "Banner of Light" some few weeks since. This article is entitled, "Has the negro an immortal soul?" The article which appeared in the "Banner of Light," upon that question, a few weeks since, was a criticism upon one which appeared in the "Livingston Herald" some time prior. The author then took the ground that the negro had no immortality, or, if he had any, it was only that which was borrowed from his white brothers, and he lost it at death. He had no soul apart from the soul of the white man. It seems that the authority of the ideas in question, namely, that the negro has no immortal soul, is a disembodied spirit, who comes to this life, and through mediumistic life gives his views with regard to the negro. In a note, from the editor probably, we are charged with evading the subject of negro immortality in our article, and of being very careful not to say that he had an immortal soul; that he lived after death. He charges us with elaborating upon general ideas and avoiding the point at issue, and winds up by saying it is evidently a new subject to us, and has, no doubt, taken us by surprise. Well, certainly, the negro is no new subject to me; was not when I was here, and is not now. I do not propose to enter upon this subject at any length, because I have not time. I only propose this afternoon to make a statement, which, I trust, will be understood. Since I failed to make myself understood in the former article, I hope to be understood now.

First, then, I would plainly and distinctly declare that I *know* that the negro possesses as much immortality as as I do. I know that he has an existence in the spirit-world; that I meet him at every turn. I know that immortality does not depend upon black skins or white. How do I know it? As we know all things: by observation, by study, by what we see, hear, and feel. When I meet and talk with the negro in the spirit-world, he is as much a disembodied spirit as I am. I know he lives there; it is not a matter of speculation with me. If immortality were dependent upon the white race, or was the result, as "Hiskenean" says, of phrenological development, I should pity the God that made us, for he would have made a most egregious mistake. Immortality dependent upon phrenological development! Then we must go still farther. We must say our immortality, our soul-life, is dependent upon nature, upon form; that we grow up out of nature; and if we do, God does. If the soul in us is a result of natural development, then the God that protects us is a result of natural development.

Now, I contend that spirit is prior to matter; I contend that ere matter was, as such, spirit was; I contend, also, that spirit is dependent upon matter for expression, but not for being; I contend that immortality is dependent upon matter for expression, but not for being; I contend that immortality, soul-life, is not dependent upon a white skin or a black, upon the phrenological development of the negro or the white man or woman. Why, I should descend very far down the steps of human science, I should forget that which has brought me to my present standard, I should ignore my God and the God of science, if I believed that immortality was dependent upon anything human. If our correspondent defines immortality as individuality is defined, why, then, of course he is right. It changes itself, of course, in expression. The immortality that is ours in expression to-day — now, mark us — that is ours in expression to-day, may not be ours in expression to-morrow, because the organic life through which immortality expresses itself is constantly changing. Therefore the expression must constantly change. But immortality, as immortality, is not dependent upon any change, upon anything in this world, upon anything in our world. Now, we should be very much pleased if this spirit, whether he be in or out of the body human, would come out from under his mask, and tell us who he was when he lived here in this earth-life; tell us what his moral principles were; tell us what he was politically; tell us where he stood mentally; then we shall be able to measure him — to know what he is worth, what his opinion is worth. If he still keeps under his mask, we cannot know. I never did like anonymous articles when I was here; I do not like them now. I come out and declare myself to be Theodore Parker; nobody else. I answered the article in question. Everybody knows, that knows anything about me at all, what I believed when here. Everybody knows, that knows anything about me as a disembodied spirit, that I hold very closely to some of my ideas that were born here. I have abandoned some, and have gained newer ones. But, again, let me distinctly declare, for fear I should be misunderstood, should be charged with again going round the subject, and evading the point at issue, "Has the negro an immortal soul?" yes, he has, emphatically. I know it, because I see him here in my life. I know it, because I come into spiritual *rapport* with him at almost every step I take. I labored hard to benefit him here in this life, and I still continue my labors in that that you call the spirit-life. God grant that I may long labor in that vineyard, for there is need of it.

By Theodore Parker, Oct. 25, 1869.

Q. Is it not true that highly cultivated men and women, departed from earth-life, rarely find either pleasure or duty in returning to communicate with us? and when they do so, it is a kind of self-denying, missionary spirit that prompts them so to do; and by consequence, our communications through ordinary mediums seem ordinarily of a low intellectual order — sometimes low in morals and good taste?

A. No, it is not true, in any one sense. It is absolutely untrue. Those who have passed from this earthly life long ages ago, who stand high in the spheres, whose brows are crowned with wisdom, and love, and power, are they who find their highest heaven, it may be, in returning to earth and preaching to you spirits who are in darkness, to you souls who are still present in mortal, to you who can scarcely peer beyond the veil and believe even in the future life. They come to keep alive that belief, to inspire you with faith, to give you in your inner life, at least, faint glimpses of the promised land. If it was not for their coming, the doors of your inner spiritual life would be securely closed. You receive their light, if any light at all, concerning the future state. You would all be in doubt. They come to you when you know it not; they minister to your spiritual needs; they strengthen your faith. The old earth-home is still bright to them, and however great may be the difficulties they labor under in returning, they are glad to war against them; they are glad to find their feet pierced with thorns on returning; they are glad to mingle again with earthly scenes, that they may lead you up to the plane where you can at least have faith in another life, and a strong hope that that other life will be better than this.

Q. Have spirits the same name in heaven that they had on earth?

A. Not always. Sometimes it is so, but generally it is otherwise.

Q. How, then, can we know if they are the persons we inquire for?

A. On returning here it is expected that they give the names by which they were known on earth.

Q. Always?

A. Always.

Q. What should I believe if a child on coming back said she was my daughter, and still called herself by another name — one that I never heard?

A. If such a child had an earthly name, you should persevere in demanding that name. It is your right. In all probability, the child does not know it. In its experience as a spirit, it may have lost that earthly name, but there are others who can give it information. Persist in your efforts to obtain it, and, in all probability, you will at last succeed. It is your right to have it.

Q. Will other spirits call that child by the name it had here on earth?

A. No, not necessarily; but they know — some one doubtless does in the spirit-world — what name it had here — what name you will know it by.

Q. Do the evil deeds we commit here come to the memory in the spirit-life, and disturb our happiness?

A. They do, most assuredly; and that disturbance is more keen than it could by any possibility be here.

Q. Is there any limit to the continuance of their unhappiness?

A. There is, but no general limit. When the soul has outlived the conditions that produced the mistake here, then the remorse will pass away. Evil is transient, and must pass away, while goodness is permanent, and must ever remain.

By William E. Channing, Oct. 26, 1869.

Q. Does the use of tobacco injure the spirit, or spirit-body, in spirit-life; and does it prevent the development of medium powers?

A. There can come no permanent injury to the spirit. All such that may seem to be injuries inflicted upon the spirit are but shadows that transiently fall upon it. Tobacco is one of those subtle poisons that prevent the soul, or mind, from giving a natural expression through the body. It so paralyzes the senses or keys of mortal being upon which the spirit plays in expressing itself in outer life, that it is impossible to use them naturally and perfectly. But as I before remarked, all the injury that it can do to the spirit is but transient. It can leave no permanent scar there, though the effect will be carried with the spirit to its future home, to that other life which belongs to it as a spirit; but as the sun of the natural and divine love is shed upon it, these clouds will pass away, and you will see that the spirit is pure, untainted, and carries no scar. You ask, "Does it prevent the development of mediumship?" No, it does not; but it does affect mediumship. We have the case of a medium, Mr. Foster, in mind. Those who know him best, know that he is an inveterate smoker, makes large use of the poison, tobacco. And this, what may be called an evil, is permitted, excused, suffered to be, by his controlling foreign spirits, those who come to him from time to time, to bear messages to their loved ones here. You may ask why. I answer, because in a strictly normal state he would be very hard to use as a medium. The power would be there. His mediumship, as such, would be just as well developed and unfolded as it is now, but those spirits who come to him to use those powers could not so readily use them, and so they are willing to come, even through a cloud of tobacco smoke — which, I assure you, is very offensive to them — that they may come to those who remain here and are in need of good; those who are in the shadow and in need of light. They make sacrifices for you which, I am quite sure, you would be hardly willing to make for them. They lay aside all the loveliness and the pleasure of their beautiful homes beyond the river of death that they may serve you; they come; they are your most humble servants; they teach you, as best they may; they answer your calls; they cheer you in your sadness; they assure you of another life; they give you a hope beyond mortality, a solid reality that there is a better world than this, a condition of being where you will be freed from many of the oppressions that hang about you here in your mortal life.

Q. Are the privileges for acquiring the natural sciences as good in the spirit-life as here?

A. When they relate especially to the things which can be recognized and measured and analyzed by your physical, mortal senses, then it is harder to become acquainted with sciences; but when not especially related to the things of this life, but more intimately related to the spirit, then they have advantages far above you. Those who have made a certain branch of science their study here, who have mastered it, have laid for themselves an ample foundation to carry on or build a structure of beauty and power and strength in the other world. For instance, the geologist, who has mastered the science of geology, as relating to this life, goes to the spirit-world with the foundation well laid. He can go to work at once and rear a spiritual structure without any difficulty. There is not the impediment of poverty to hinder him; he has no sickness to contend with there. He can travel as he pleases. He finds teachers at every turn in life, those who know more about the subject than he does. He has but to ask, and he receives. There are schools of science in our life which are far beyond your conception. You are in the alphabet of science, even as it relates to the things of this life, as yet. You know very little concerning your surroundings. The geologist cannot go very far down into the earth. To a certain distance he can go; beyond that it is all speculation. When you consider that all that is in this life that you can recognize, everything that the earth contains upon its surface and under its surface, everything that the air contains, and all that is in the sea, all these have a spiritual existence as well as a material, and that the spiritual is capable of being analyzed, challenges the science of the spirit-world to analyze it, — when you consider that, you will not wonder that I tell you that the science of life in the spirit-world is far beyond your human conception.

By Theodore Parker, Oct. 28, 1869.

Q. Is it not a misfortune, and detrimental to one's happiness and harmonious progress, to be a Spiritualist, philanthropist, or reformer — if he be poor, without the means and influence to correct the many disorders of society, and when the current of popular follies are too strong, rendering his efforts vain, and often carrying the reformer with them against his will?

A. So far as the things of this life are concerned, it is a misfortune, and a terrible one, because the philanthropic soul is constantly warring against that which he cannot overcome, and the hard conditions of fate are continually beating upon the soul. But there is another life than this, and he who was a reformer here — a good man or woman here — will carry that goodness with them to that other life. Then it is that all these difficulties, poverty, sickness, various inabilities that present themselves from day to day, will disappear. The highway will be open, and there will be no bridges over which the soul must pass where there are fees charged. Everything will be free, and the benevolent soul can outlive his benevolent desires, and carry on that which he could not here. That which was a misfortune here will constitute his highest heaven there. So cherish it, though it bring you thorns here; hold it close to your hearts, and never let it go — carry it with you; it will be a passport that will admit you to a high heaven hereafter.

Q. Are we not endowed by our Creator with passions and appetites for legitimate and holy uses, and, therefore, is it not wrong to be constantly decrying and denying the animal propensities, instead of controlling and directing them in their uses, as God evidently designed?

A. All the lower functions of our human lives belong exclusively to the things of this world, to the needs of physical life, of body and sense; and therefore they should be kept under proper subjection to higher ends, in subjection, if you please, to the moral law, to those functions of our nature that are pre-eminent above these animal functions. The use of them is good, very good. That is rendering unto the things of this life what is due to them, but the abuse of them not only makes misery for you in this life, but so arrays your spirit in darkness in the other life, for a time at least, that it would hardly be well to allow them too much freedom. They were given each and all of us by the same power that gave us our moral faculties, our reason, and we should always allow reason, the highest light of our nature, the divinest wisdom we possess, to guide and direct in all the lower needs that pertain to our lives, ignoring nothing, but directing, guiding, and giving each its proper place, a proper use and proper time. It is a great thing to know how to govern one's lower self. It is a divine thing, and when we shall all know how to do it we shall become gods in wisdom, in morality, in all that constitutes gods.

By Theodore Parker, Nov. 1, 1869.

Q. In a recent number of the Banner the spirits say this is the most perilous period of the world's history. I ask, do they refer to volcanic action, or to the action of human governments, as they affect the welfare of man?

A. Their reference in that respect is general — refers to your spiritual and material — to the vital changes that you are passing through at this time. And as you are passing through changes, so is the earth. You have reached, religiously, politically, physically, and spiritually, a certain point, which will develop, as you pass beyond it, very great changes, which will reveal to you, as mortals and spirits, that which has never been revealed to you before. The earth and its products have been steadily rising in the scale of being till the present, and that present is pregnant with great changes. Marked changes are taking place amongst you to-day; those still more marked are to come. The established religions of the world are about to be swept away, and the fine gold of good that there is in them is to be revealed. Those which have enough to perpetuate themselves in the future will do so; those which have not will become extinct. At certain periods or cycles in the world's history, great changes have taken place. It always has been so; it always, doubtless, will be so. As the earth has grown older, and man has become more mature, and the spirit has gathered to itself elements through which it can more perfectly express itself, you must expect that the changes that are upon you will be greater than all those that have preceded this time in the world's history.

Q. Is there such a thing as sex of the *soul*, independent of sex of the body; and if so, does it ever happen that *male* souls are incarnated in female physical forms, and *vice versa?*

A. The positive and negative forces of life, the male and female forces of life, are everywhere distinct in themselves until they reach such a high spiritual altitude that they are merged in one. It is then that the male and female become one in spirit, acting in divine harmony with the God-spirit. They are then, to all intents and purposes, gods, male and female. In this sense, the male becomes the female, and the female the male, but in no other sense.

Q. Will the time ever come in their spirit-life when such souls shall assume a spirit-form appropriate, in outward seeming, to their true sex?

A. Yes; a law, divine and human, is constantly outworking itself through form, for the perfection of form, for the highest revealment of the God-life; and what may be expected for one, — namely, perfection, — may be expected for all.

By William E. Channing, Nov. 9, 1869.

Q. Are there persons in the world who really desire and strive to reform, and yet are unable, from circumstances and predisposition?

A. Certainly; we see such exhibitions almost every day. Circumstances over which we, as humans, have no control ofttimes environ us so that we cannot escape. We must obey their behest, whether we will or no. Certain conditions, forces ante-natal, are very rigid in their requirements. They lead us, as servants. They are our masters. And yet it is the soul's business to always war against everything that tends to retard its flight upward. No matter whether it can overcome the thing or not, it is its business to war with it, and it always will.

Q. There are two kinds of Spiritualists. The first are those considerably devoted to natural science, know something of the principles of logic, and see nothing at all inconsistent or contrary to the laws of nature in the idea of the communion of spirits in the body with those out of the body. These are constantly on the alert to have given to them some *conclusive demonstrative proof*, according to those natural laws, of their faith; but being very exacting, they seem generally to fail in obtaining that satisfaction. The other class seem to have no difficulty at all in satisfying their minds, although they have little knowledge of any kind, and no predisposition from reason in favor of spirit-communion. These last have abundant evidences, while the former find them much scarcer than "angel visits." Now, the question is, had not the former class better withdraw altogether from the search, and leave the field to the "babes and sucklings"?

A. That would be very much like mature age abandoning the field of science to youth and babies. It is this first class that does the hard work in Spiritualism; for, while they are oftener unsuccessful than they are successful, when they do chance to have success, it is generally in the right quarter. It is generally well balanced. It is generally well proven by facts in science that cannot be mistaken, while the other class, who require but little, and consequently search but little, go hardly beyond the surface. They only give you surface ideas, and only receive surface ideas; while the deep thinker, the clear reasoner, one who demands the most perfect tests in this matter, are those who do the cause the most good. Retire? No; your Spiritualism would die without them.

By Cardinal Cheverus, Nov. 23, 1869.

Q. We suffer here for the sins of our parents in the physical, mental, and spiritual parts of our nature. Do these predispositions follow us into the spiritual world, and are they there, also, a source of inharmony, annoyance, and discomfort to us?

A. It is written that the sins of the fathers are

visited upon the third and fourth generations; and we may go to still greater lengths: all physical sin, or that evil or disease which is the result of physical mistakes, does not follow the spirit past the boundaries of human life; it belongs to the body, therefore falls when the body falls. But all that which you call sin, which had its rise in the mental, will be carried by the thinking spirit to the spirit-world. It belongs to the thought-kingdom of the individual, and to the kingdom of the spirit; therefore it lives after death.

Q. Is it wrong to lie, in reply to a designing question intended to intrap us by admission, or convey the required impression or information by silence?

A. A lie is such by virtue of the motive that prompted it. It is not always the highest wisdom to speak what you consider to be absolute truth; it is sometimes wise to conceal that which is asked for. When an answer is given to any question in the negative that truth would decide should be given in the affirmative, the evil, or that which you call the lie, would consist in the motive. If that was good, then there could be no evil; and if it were not good, then it would give birth to a child or thought corresponding with itself.

By Theodore Parker, Nov. 30, 1869.

Q. There is ample scope for the exercise of all our faculties in spirit-life, so we are told; but is there scope for the exercise of the craft of the politician, the malice and control of the tyrant, and the ambition of a Xerxes or Napoleon?

A. Yes, there is liberty in all those several directions; but here, in the spirit-world, spirits are very soon educated to know that whenever they injure another, they injure themselves correspondingly. Whatever they do that is detrimental to the happiness of another, is correspondingly detrimental to their happiness. So they very soon learn to be careful in all their doings towards their fellow-creatures.

Q. Does this result immediately?

A. Very soon; for education begins at birth there, as physical education begins at physical birth here.

Q. Does the law of "might makes right" prevail to any extent in spirit-life?

A. The law of right is better understood in the spirit-world than here, and spirits are more desirous of acting under the rule of the law of right than under the rule of the law of might, for they are never safe there. It may turn and rend them at any moment.

Q. Is not the faculty of secretiveness a form of selfishness?

A. No; it may be very nearly related to selfishness, but is by no means a form of selfishness.

Q. Is life in the spirit-world a continual strife, turmoil, and self-defence, as in the earth-life?

A. For a time it is, till the spirit has outgrown earthly propensities, outlived them, gone beyond them.

Q. Shall we, who have been born into this earth-life, ever find another home than this sphere?

A. It is quite certain that your strongest attractions will be here; so you may infer that your home will be here.

Q. Where are spirits located after they have thrown off the mortal body?

A. Anywhere and everywhere. Wherever there is life, there is the spirit-world — there spirits dwell.

Q. Do we ever outgrow our attractions for this earth-home?

A. So far as this material life is concerned, you will outgrow them; but there are spiritual attractions that it is hard to go beyond.

Q. Do spirits who have passed away within a year or two have power to communicate with those who passed away thousands of years ago?

A. They have.

Q. Why is it that some can see spirits while in their mortal bodies, and others cannot?

A. Some are so chemically organized, that, under certain chemical conditions, they can see spirits, or the clothing that covers the spirit — not the spirit. It is simply a chemical difference that exists between human bodies.

Q. Is that clothing made up of chemical particles of matter?

A. Yes, it is.

Q. Is the spirit itself matter?

A. So etherealized as not to be, under any circumstances, apparent to human senses.

Q. Can this spirit-body be seen with our natural eyes, or in a different way?

A. No man, woman, or child, hath ever seen a spirit at any time, or under any circumstances. They have only seen the outer covering of the spirit?

Q. Is that seen with the natural eyes?

A. Sometimes with the natural eye, sometimes with the clairvoyant eye, or second (inner) sight.

Q. Some assume that they converse with spirits. Is that done orally?

A. Sometimes; but oftener mentally.

Q. Sacred history records the communion of Saul with the woman of Endor. Was she like the mediums of the present day?

A. Yes, precisely the same. The woman of Endor, who called up the spirit of Samuel, was a medium, such as you have amongst you at the present day.

Q. By what process does the spirit change its locality?

A. It exercises its will, which becomes the vehicle to convey it from one point to another. The spirit glides through the air as light or sound passes through the atmosphere.

Q. Does it take its spirit-body along?

A. Certainly it does; for without that it could not express itself — the spirit could give no expression without matter.

Q. Can our departed friends return and aid us in any way?

A. That is a self-evident fact — at least, a fact to myself. They can return — can aid you in all the various avocations of this life.

By Theodore Parker, Dec. 6, 1869.

Q. Does each one of us have a guardian spirit?

A. In all probability each one of you have many, since it is to be expected that you have each one, perhaps more than one, friend in the spirit-world, who is anxious for your welfare, who would be true to you, desiring to do you good.

Q. How can we know?

A. You may never know while here in the body.

Q. Do they watch over us for our good?

A. If they love you and are your friends, they certainly will watch over you for your good.

Q. Will they direct us in the right way?

A. So far as they are able to; but their power is finite, like your own.

Q. Can spirits who lived two thousand years ago come back to earth and see the advancement in science?

A. Yes; there are many who return communicating with you, who have been away thousands of years.

Q. Can they see the progress that has been made in science?

A. Sometimes they do. It depends very much upon how much they are interested in those things.

Q. Are our guardian spirits necessarily our earthly relatives?

A. O, no; any one who finds profit or pleasure in your mental or spiritual sphere may become your guardian spirit.

Q. Are they supposed to be with us continually, or only occasionally?

A. They are not always with you.

Q. How do we know when they are?

A. You may not always know, unless you are susceptible to spirit-influence. Then you will be very likely to know.

Q. Must we not be very yielding to spirit-influence in order to know?

A. Yes, you should be negative, passive, ready to receive whatever good may be ready to come to you.

Q. Are any spirits so low that they cannot communicate with their friends?

A. Yes, there are many who are so low they have no special desire to communicate with their friends, and therefore do not.

Q. What hour is best adapted to communing with unseen intelligences?

A. The hour that you are the most quiet, most free

from earthly annoyances; whether it be by day or night, it matters not.

Q. When we first become unconscious in this world, do we at that moment wake to consciousness in the spirit-world?

A. Not always. Sometimes souls remain unconscious for years, for centuries.

Q. Why is it?

A. The reasons are various. Sometimes those remedies given in sickness cast such a blight or shadow over the spirit that it cannot throw them off for a long time after entering the spirit-world. A variety of narcotics that are used will often do this.

Q. Then are not the spirit and mind two things, two beings or substances?

A. To me the spirit is the inner life. The mind may be called the glass through which the spirit reflects its deeds, its purposes. Mind is the result of physical formation, while spirit is not.

Q. Do not some spirits return very soon after death?

A. Yes, almost before you are aware that they have departed.

Q. Do our spirit-friends know what we are doing in this world?

A. They very often do know your most secret thoughts.

Q. Will they do anything we ask of them, if it is for our good?

A. Not always. That depends upon conditions, as they exist with you or with the spirit who desires to aid you; upon conditions in the atmosphere, spiritual and material, surrounding you and surrounding them.

Q. Cannot spirits read our thoughts at any time?

A. Not always, but they very often can.

Q. Is not the race of North American Indians destined to become extinct?

A. So far as earthly existence is concerned, I believe that is their destiny. But they live in the spirit-world, a nation more powerful and grand than you have any idea of.

Q. What is the condition of the Indian race in the spirit-world as compared with the white race?

A. The Indian lives nearer to Mother Nature, consequently nearer to God, than his white brothers. His white brothers have sought out many inventions, and have followed largely after them. His white brothers live more in art than in Nature, and are therefore farther from their Mother, Nature, and their Father, God. In intellectual attainments, of course the white man is far superior to the Indian, because they are based more upon art than Nature.

Q. Is the negro capable of being on the same level of intelligence as the white man?

A. In my opinion the negro has capacities which, when unfolded, would stand side by side with our own.

Q. You say the Indian lives nearer God than the white man. Is he happier in the spirit-world?

A. Generally he is.

Q. Why are they permitted to become extinct?

A. That we cannot tell, except it is their destiny — written in the book of their fate.

Q. Can that destiny be changed by the angel-world exerting an influence on the Government to protect them?

A. Large efforts have been made in that direction. If they are crowned with success, perhaps the tide will turn. If not, we may feel quite sure that the end that is coming will not turn aside for us.

Q. What is the difference of the origin of the white and the black man?

A. None whatever; at least I have been able to find no difference — to draw no line of demarcation between the essential of the white man and the essential of the black man.

Q. Which race is the oldest?

A. That is hard to determine. Some authors declare that the negro had an existence on this planet long before the white man. I should be inclined to doubt that. I think it is the reverse.

Q. Is it true, as some contend, that the older the race, the higher in intellect?

A. I do not think it is. The Chinese, as a people, are very old; but, except in certain directions, we know they are far below other races much younger than themselves.

Q. Do the spirits of our departed friends know about us at any time they wish?

A. No, they do not possess absolute power to come whenever they may wish. They are governed by law and circumstances, and these do not always favor their coming.

Q. Can all of our spirit-friends come some time or other?

A. I think so. I think there is a time for all.

By John Pierpont, Dec. 7, 1869.

Q. Suppose an individual has inherited or is possessed of a strong inclination to steal, commit suicide, or murder; is it possible to outgrow such inclinations without actual commission of the deeds, either in earth or spirit-life? If so, please point out the principles and means by which such result is reached.

A. We may have certain germs of evil implanted in us, but they may never come to maturity, or find an exhibition in the external world, unless circumstances shall be thrown around them to favor their coming forth, to foster their development. "To be forewarned is to be forearmed," said a certain writer; and I believe that is a truthful utterance. It is our duty, as immortal spirits, to make ourselves acquainted with ourselves, externally and internally, at as early a period as possible. Just as soon as we are able to receive instruction, it is our duty to seek for it. And if we find that any of these germs of evil are implanted in our natures, it is our duty to use all possible means to destroy them; and we can do it only in one way, and that is, by denying those conditions under which they can be unfolded. When you have certain organs that are poorly developed, what do you do? Why, you seek to develop them — you cultivate them. If you do right, you do this. You throw around them those conditions that are most favorable to development. If you have others over-active, you seek to take away those conditions which foster their development. If you can do this in your phrenological unfolding, you certainly can do it throughout all the different departments of your physical life. If those germs of evil are unmistakably implanted in your nature, if you are only wise enough to know of their being, you can do something towards restraining them from coming into actual life. The wise husbandman would not allow his garden to be overrun with weeds, but when he sees one coming into being he plucks it out.

Q. Is it necessary that these germs be developed in the next world?

A. No, it is not necessary. These things belong especially to this mundane life.

By Theodore Parker, Dec. 9, 1869.

Q. How do you explain the fact that a spirit will give a message through one medium, and afterwards, in controlling another, will have no recollection of having spoken through the first medium?

A. Allow me to illustrate. I am here speaking to you through a certain special organism, and if I remember what I say at all, I remember it through the power of that organism, and no other. I am dependent, so far as my thoughts and words are concerned while in control, upon that organism, but when I come forth from it I do not carry memory with me concerning that which has transpired in that organism; it remains with it, and I can only fully call up the events that have transpired through that organism, in relation to myself, by coming into *rapport* with it again. I can do it through no other, because the law opposes me. I must act upon the same ground, through the same organic life, to remember the events that transpired there.

Q. Then you will not recollect anything that occurs to-day, after leaving this medium, while you remain away?

A. I do not say that I shall not remember in my spirit, for I shall; but I cannot project that memory through another organism than the one through which the events transpired.

Q. Are there not cases where it may be projected, to some extent, through a second medium?

A. O, yes; but fragmentary, therefore in an unreliable manner.

Q. Do spirits, in passing from one plane to another, pass through anything analogous to physical death here?

A. O, yes; we part with our spiritual bodies when they can no longer be of service to us.

Q. Is it done at any particular period of time, or gradually?

A. No; decay of the spiritual body comes on gradually, and when we can no longer use it well — can no longer make it serve us — we part with it, and there is a spiritual chemical separation.

Q. Is there an organized form left?

A. There is an organized spiritual form, unseen to human eye, but it is there, nevertheless.

Q. Left behind in the progress of the spirit?

A. Yes.

Q. It is often said by those familiar with the writings of Theodore Parker, and with his utterances in this life, that there is a great falling off in what we receive from him now. Is this so? and can you explain it?

A. Well, I should not so determine, only as I look at it from an earthly stand-point. If Theodore Parker has changed his views since living apart from human life, of course, if he comes, if he returns at all, with the reflection of the change, and if that does not suit his old hearers, of course he has fallen from grace, in their opinion; in other words, is not up to the high mark, according to their judgment.

Q. Is there no other reason?

A. Yes, there is; since Theodore Parker nor any other spirit ever has been, nor, in all probability, ever will be, able to find an organism precisely like their own, of course their spirits must of necessity be measured by the organism through which they express.

By Theodore Parker, Dec. 28, 1869.

Q. Spirits generally tell us that in Summer-Land what a person wants comes *by wishing* for it. Please explain this. You say, for instance, if a spirit wants to go from one place to another, he merely wishes to go, and is there. From a material plane this is incomprehensible. Can you make it understood by any plane of thought? Do spirits never have to struggle, to bear burdens, to suffer defeat, to enjoy conquest? Do they never have to plan out their work, to contrive how to do this and that? Is spirit-life merely wishing, and no working? If so, then I think it not much of a life, after all.

A. To wish for a thing, in the spirit-world, is to act in conjunction with the law that will bring it to the soul wishing for it. In soul-life the soul never wishes for anything without putting forth all its powers to obtain it. The world of mind is the world of causes; the world of matter is the world of effects. You here see through a glass darkly; we there see face to face. The law is more clearly understood to the spirit who has passed beyond the shadow called death; he has done with using the organs physical; therefore, knowing the law better, he can make better use of it. To you, in most instances, the law is beyond your vision; you feel, you believe it exists, because you have evidence that it does; but you do not know — you cannot grasp it as you can after death. After death, should the soul wish for a certain thing, that proves that the soul has need of it. And more than that: the wish cannot be born in the soul without the soul's putting forth all its powers to obtain it. And by putting forth all its powers, I mean that it places itself in harmony with the law — acts in harmony with it; consequently the result must be favorable.

Q. In observing the phenomenon of death, generally, it is much alike in both men and animals. Now, in both cases, it is more like the extinction of life than the birth of a soul. Why, if a soul goes out at death, cannot we get at it in some tangible way, and demonstrate it not only to Spiritualists, but everybody?

A. Simply because you do not go the right way to work to do it; because, in your ignorance, you set up a way by which you desire to obtain it, and it is not the right way. Human sense cannot, by any possibility, be thoroughly cognizant of spirit. You see it in its manifestation, and in that alone; and when this ceases, you have no more proof that it exists. But there is a power outside of physical sense, which you may make use of, if you will. You have spiritual senses which even here, in this life, you can use to great advantage. These spiritual senses can follow the soul beyond death, and learn what its condition is; but you fear to exercise this spiritual sense, because your religion has taught you to do otherwise. It is high time you had a religion that belonged more especially to the soul.

By Theodore Parker, Dec. 30, 1869.

Q. Modern scientific discoveries go to prove that the imponderable agents, such as heat, light, electricity and magnetism, which were formerly considered as separate fluids, are simply modes of motion; and inasmuch as all we know of anything we know through motion, has suggested the idea that all so-called matter, all the different objects which constitute the external world, are simply so many different modes of action of one and the same all-pervading element; that all matter is so many different forces acting and reacting upon and with each other, and producing all the phenomena of the physical universe; that, these forces being spiritual or intelligent in their origin, material things are simply thought-forces becoming fixed and congealed, as it were, so as to be palpable to the external senses. What are your ideas upon this subject?

A. Precisely the same as your correspondent's.

Q. Are the white races that now occupy the territory of America in any way influenced by its previous occupants, the red Indians? Does the race of the red man, either past or existing, really affect the white man?

A. You are affected by the magnetic life that the Indian has left on the earth — largely affected by it; and in turn he, as a spirit, is largely affected by the magnetic life that he draws from you as spirits in body human.

Q. Are our friends that have passed from this life hindered by the extreme grief of their friends?

A. They are. Your grief for those who have passed beyond your sight holds them — sometimes, not always, but generally it holds them within the sphere of your own melancholy thoughts, and they cannot pass from this till you rise out of that melancholy condition.

By William E. Channing, Jan. 10, 1870.

Q. I wish to ask our spirit-friends if they cannot and will not, with other inestimable favors, give to suffering mortals a substitute for opium, or such instructions as will enable them to free themselves from its habitual use. I sincerely ask this, not only on my own behalf, but that all others who believe in spirit-guidance may share the blessed boon freely. If I have not taken a proper course to obtain such information, I beg you will pardon the error, and indicate the correct way.

A. The application of magnetism properly, not improperly, is destined to do away with all narcotics as remedial agents. They are at present an absolute necessity to human ignorance. But when ignorance shall have given place to knowledge, the veriest child will know how to use the magnetic powers with which every single human body is endowed. You all hold within your grasp all the remedial agents that you have need of, but you do not know how to use them. Disease being an imponderable, it can best be treated by the application of an imponderable. That all-powerful force which you call magnetism, holds within itself the power to harmonize all the forces of the human body — to prevent disease. When disease, or inharmony, — which is the same, — has found an abiding-place in the physical form, magnetism has the power to eradicate it, to overcome it; not only to subdue it, but to entirely overcome it; but the time for these things is not yet. You are standing, to-day, upon the threshold of this new science. It has always been with you, but because of its simplicity men and women have considered it of no account. But the time is fast speeding when you will understand what disease is, and what is its remedy. You will also know how to apply the remedy. But you grow slowly, and you can grow no faster than the earth grows. Were we to be endowed, this hour, with infinite wisdom, it would be of small account to us, because we are not ready for it. We must grow up to a condition fit to receive it, to use it well, ere it can come to us. So humanity must suffer a while longer ere the angel of healing can come perfectly to your conscious lives, and teach you what you so earnestly desire to know in the present.

By Theodore Parker, Jan 11, 1870.

Q. Why is God called Father and Mother?

A. Simply because we have found no better terms by which to convey our idea of the all-sustaining principle that cares for us throughout all eternity, has brought us into being, and protects us with the wisdom of a father and the love of a mother. They are only terms used to convey the idea to human sense.

Q. Is the resurrection of some spirits completed before that of others?

A. Yes; it is a rare circumstance that the spirit is thoroughly and absolutely free from the body and its law till the third day. It requires just about so much time to withdraw all the electric forces or the magnetic spirit-body. Sometimes it is performed quicker, but not often. So have a care how you place your bodies under the soil before the third day of what you call death.

Q. Does any of our other treatment of corpses interfere with the complete separation of the spiritual form?

A. Yes; the abandoning of the body immediately after death into the hands of strangers, — those who have no particular sympathy with the new-born spirit. It chains them more closely to the body, because the spirit has not abandoned its care of the body. It cannot so readily do it when it has been thrown into the hands of strangers. Friends, those who loved the indwelling spirit best, should perform these sacred duties always. Remember that, every one of you.

Q. Does the practice of putting dead bodies on ice have any effect on the spirit?

A. If they are placed upon ice before the third day, it certainly does have a very bad effect.

Q. What is the effect?

A. It produces positive distress to the spirit. It retards the natural process of chemical dissolution. You interfere with the operation of Nature's law, and because of that interference, inharmony ensues, which the spirit feels most acutely, I can assure you.

Q. It sometimes seems necessary to do this very soon after death.

A. I know, for the protection of physical life, it is absolutely necessary to do this. In those cases, perhaps, it would be better that the spirit suffer than that many spirits here, together with their physical bodies, should suffer. But under ordinary circumstances, this should not be.

Q. Can you retain the spirit longer in the body by freezing the body?

A. No, certainly not.

Q. Do *post mortem* examinations previous to the third day produce distress?

A. It is an interference with the natural and quiet operation of the law — not in precisely the same, but in a similar way. And again, the introduction of poisons into the venous system for the purpose of preserving the form, has a very bad effect upon the spirit, if performed before the third day, or before the spirit has entirely separated itself from that body, be it the third, fourth, or tenth day.

Q. How does the rapid decay of the body, as it takes place in warm weather, affect the release of the spiritual form?

A. It accelerates it. It is one of Nature's means,

under certain circumstances, to accelerate the resurrection of the spirit from the body.

Q. Is death by drowning, and the submerging of the body for a considerable time, a process that retards the separation of the spiritual form?

A. No.

Q. Does the separation of the spirit-body from the physical form require a longer time when the body is bruised?

A. No; it requires no longer time, but it is performed under more difficult circumstances, and if the spirit is conscious of these circumstances — and it generally is — it is painful to the spirit.

By Father Henry Fitz James, Jan. 18, 1870.

Q. Our spirit-friends inform us that the present is the most momentous and perilous period of the world's history, but leave us in the dark as to the natural forces that are producing the crisis. Can the spirit-world enlighten us upon the subject more in detail?

A. It is, indeed, the most momentous, at least since the Christian era dawned, because it holds within itself so great an influx of spiritual truth which acts in religion, in philosophy, in all the arts and sciences with which you are engaged, that it is in one sense overturning the world, mentally and socially. Now, every effect has its cause. What is the cause of this? Why, your human minds and bodies unfold in correspondence with the growth of the earth. The earth has grown into that condition materially, as to be able to sustain your connection with those great spiritual truths that are finding manifestation through human bodies all over the land. The time was, when these truths could not be uttered.

They were in the air; they were all about you, but there was nothing by which they could be expressed, because the earth, your mother, had not the power to sustain you, physically, in the expression of those truths with which the very air was filled. But in the present, your mother earth is able to sustain you, therefore you are able to give expression to those truths. And what will be the result? Why, the Christian era must die. It has lived nearly its appointed time. It has performed its mission, and even now the angels are calling it hence. Mourn not over your idol, for the Father doeth all things well; and he hath done well in this. Shall he leave you without a comforter? No; but he will give you the comforter which is found in the holy spirit of the new revelation. You have it with you the present hour. It has found a resting-place all over the earth. Wisdom never tears down till it is ready to build again. It leaves no waste, desert places. It is always ready to build more beautiful structures upon the ruins of the old. Your religion has served you well; but to-day you are living in the very vortex of change — religious change; and as you live socially, politically, mentally, and morally, by your religious beliefs, we can see at once how great an effect it must have upon you when the change takes place.

Q. In what condition does a spirit appear on entering the spirit-world, after having lived on earth to a good old age? or of one who dies in childhood? Do they appear the same externally there as here?

A. The child enters the spirit-world as a child, because its growth has not been perfected, either in stature or in mind. But the old man enters it, not as an old man, but as a fully developed spirit, corresponding to what he was at mature life here. The conditions of old age belong to earth, and not to spirit-life.

Q. Are there such conditions as heat and cold, hunger and thirst, in spirit-life?

A. There is what corresponds to those conditions that are known to you, in spirit-life, but it is not precisely that hunger, thirst, heat, and cold which the physical body recognizes. It is a spiritual something equivalent to that; a something that appeals to the spiritual senses, but does not to the physical senses.

Q. What does the spiritual sense of hunger require?

A. It would be absolutely impossible for me to clearly demonstrate it to you, because there is nothing by which I could demonstrate it. Spiritual things are to be spiritually discerned. It is a sense of want of spiritual sustenance. The spirit-body recognizes its losses, and the need to make up for them by obtaining sustenance from such food as is adapted to the spirit.

Q. I supposed that spiritual hunger was the counterpart of physical hunger, and required spiritual food.

A. So it does — so it is the counterpart of physical hunger.

Q. You speak of having trees and fruit as we have here. I supposed spirit-hunger to require such food.

A. Yes, you are right.

Q. It was hunger in that special sense that I understood the first questioner to mean, not a mere general sense of want. We have that general sense of want here, and we have also the special hunger for something to satisfy the stomach. We sometimes hear of a spirit with a great thirst for liquor, seeking for a medium by which to gratify it. Will you explain this?

A. It certainly is so. He has that thirst because he

is as yet in *rapport* with some physical form here which is addicted to the same excess. He is attracted to that form because there is a shadow upon his spirit that has been thrown there by the life he led here. He returns, and perchance comes in contact with some media who naturally have no inclination that way. But he throws his desire upon them, because as soon as he comes in contact with physical life his desire becomes intense. He psychologizes his subjects, and satisfies the desire through them. It is generally not repeated; once suffices, and he rises redeemed from that condition of earthly thraldom.

Q. Do spirits eat the fruit of their fruit trees?

A. They do.

Q. Then is not the hunger by which they crave it analogous to the hunger of our bodies here?

A. Yes, it is.

Q. Then they do have the hunger and thirst that we have here?

A. Yes.

Q. Does the denial of that desire cause discomfort to the spirit, as it does to us?

A. Yes; but fortunately for the spirit, the law of mine and thine is not in existence in the spirit-world. There is plenty for all there, as there is here. Your false customs make it right for one person to have more than enough, while his neighbor is starving. It is not so in the spirit-world, but the blessings of the Infinite Spirit are free for all, and no one can claim more as their own than they can well appropriate. There is no hoarding there; you can have all you need, but no more.

By Thomas Paine, Jan. 20, 1870.

Q. It is worthy of notice that Indian spirits, on their return, so far as we are able to judge, exhibit a greater amount of truthfulness, and express less regret of their conduct in earth-life, than spirits who have passed from what is denominated highly civilized and refined society. How is this? Are civilization, education, and so-called refinement detrimental to spiritual progress?

A. That the Indian lives nearer to Nature, and thus nearer to Nature's God, is a well-attested fact. They demonstrate this fact as they return from the other life to you, and they demonstrate it here, before they pass on to that other life. Could you live with them in their homes and become thoroughly acquainted with them, you would see that they live nearer to Nature and to Nature's God than you do. Civilization is the result of art. The more civilized you are, the farther you are from Nature. The Indians who return to you are more truthful, and for this cause: they are more simple. They tell you their story in their own simple language; they make use of no art; they do not clothe their ideas so that you cannot understand them; they have no desire to mislead you — no motive to carry you away from the truth; they intuitively, in the other life, feel your need of truth, and feel as intuitively that they are to become the agents in the hands of the Great Spirit to lead you to truth; they feel that the Great Spirit has bestowed many blessings upon you that he has withheld from them, but they are anxious to tell you what the Great Spirit has done for them — what they see — by what they are surrounded — how they live in the other life; and they tell it in such a plain, simple manner, that you cannot misunderstand them.

Q. The writer knows a lady medium in New York who has a small dog that will never rest while she is giving séances, except in her lap, or behind her, in the chair. She states that when she herself, or her son (the only other member of the family), is sick, this dog is always sick, too, and exhibits symptoms of a like malady. An Indian spirit, who sometimes controls the medium, avers that the dog is a *spirit-medium*. Will the controlling influence please throw some light on the matter, if practicable, and oblige one who has at length learned that it is not safe to deny anything outside of pure mathematics, and hardly then?

A. Everything, from the smallest atom to the largest body in life, is a medium for spirit — everything — and the higher you rise in the scale of human progress, or natural being, the larger and more perfectly defined are the mediumistic qualities of the thing, the individual, the animal, the atom, it may be. It is absolutely useless, in these days of investigation, to say that animals cannot be influenced by spirit-power. You know very well that you can influence them here by a look — by simply fixing your attention upon them. You can psychologize them; you can magnetize them; you can invest them with certain qualities of your own life. Now, if you, in the body, can do this, certainly they who are out of the body, and know more about the laws of these things, can do far more. I have no knowledge of this particular case to which you refer, but I have no doubt myself that the Indian has correctly informed the lady.

By Father Henry Fitz James, Jan. 24, 1870.

Q. Is it possible, while a medium is entranced, and the medium's spirit away from his body, for the magnetic cord uniting the medium's spirit with his body to be severed, and the spirit controlling still keep possession of the medium's body and manifest through it, and all the processes of life go on as before, for any great length of time?

A. No, it is not possible, because diametrically opposed to the laws of nature and spirit.

Q. It has been said, through Mrs. Conant, that spirits change their forms, as humans do theirs. Now, if this is so, I would inquire if, upon such change, the spirit assumes a form invisible to spirit-vision, or to the spirit-friends left behind, as is the case with us humans when we die, or change the mortal form for the spiritual? And is death, or change of form, in spirit-life, similar in its attendant circumstances to death in the earth-life?

A. Spirits are constantly changing their forms. They are constantly laying off what they have no longer need of, and gathering to themselves what they have need of. There are certain marked changes in the spirit-world that take place with reference to the spirit and its body, in that world, as there are here with you. There are changes that are equivalent to the change you call death. Spirits passing from lower to higher degrees in life, become invisible to those who remain beneath them. They take on more sublimated forms; they come out of the degree of life that belongs to those who are beneath them, and therefore those dwelling in that sphere cannot see them any more than you can see those who dwell where I do.

By Father Henry Fitz James, Jan. 25, 1870.

Q. Benjamin Franklin, the philosopher and philanthropist, has recently been seen in the city of New York.

You would have pledged your solemn oath that he was present, and yet he may have been a million leagues from the place of the chemical manifestations. Will you explain?

A. Spirits have the power to project likenesses of themselves to almost any distance from their spirits. For instance, they may wish to show you the external, the objective part of their being here in Boston, while they themselves, their thinking part, may be in London, or perhaps in the farthest distant star. By the science of chemistry, in the spirit-world, this is done. Those who have given such demonstrations tell us that it is simply and easily learned.

Q. When they show themselves to the clairvoyant, are they able to convey their thoughts in the objective form?

A. Yes, because there is a magnetic connection between the image and the spirit of their thought. They can understand your thoughts, and can answer them.

Q. And can they project these bodies to different persons at one and the same time?

A. Yes.

Q. Is it because your mode of thought is so much more rapid than ours?

A. Yes, and so much more volatile. You have well-attested accounts of the appearance of apparitions of persons who are still in the body. Spirits who have made this science a study, tell us that these apparitions are not always the result of will on the part of the spirit from whom they are projected, but they sometimes come as an electrical consequence of their mental condition.

Q. Can a spirit be seen in different localities at the same time?

A. Not the spirit, but the spirit-form can.

Q. There is a lady whom I have never seen, who testifies to my presence and power to relieve her from extreme suffering, in some manner wholly unknown to me in my external consciousness. Is such a thing possible?

A. Certainly it is.

Q. Is there a spiritual sphere surrounding each planet, separate and distinct from every other planet?

A. There is a spiritual sphere surrounding every single object of being, however small or however great; therefore there must be one surrounding every planet. In that sphere spirits of course dwell.

Q. Can they pass from one to the other?

A. Certainly they can.

Q. Will they be recognized in the other planets as spirits of human beings?

A. Yes.

Q. Can they communicate with one another?

A. Yes.

Q. Can we obtain likenesses of our spirit-friends through media?

A. Provided the medium can be used by the spirits who desire to represent themselves. Not without.

By Father Henry Fitz James, Jan. 27, 1870.

Q. Was the witch of Endor a medium?

A. In all human probability she was; but wherefore do you call her the witch of Endor?

Q. She is called so in the Bible.

A. No, you are mistaken. She is not called so in the Bible. The Bible speaks of her as the woman of Endor.

Q. Had the Salem witchcraft anything to do with Spiritualism?

A. It certainly was a phase of modern Spiritualism.

Q. Do those that have lived in mortal life carry their guidance to spirit-life? and can they control our circumstances here?

A. They are often permitted through natural and diviuc law to come and assist you to remain here. They carry their love with them, and all the purposes that fill the soul pass on to the spirit-life with the soul.

Q. Can those who have transgressed the laws of this life, by the law of progression control and guide us to purity?

A. They certainly can.

Q. What is it causes men to do wrong, the human or the spiritual?

A. That is a difficult question to answer. Since humanity, apart from spirit, could not act, we are to suppose that if the spirit does wrong or evil at all, it does so in consequence of the spiritual forces, not of the material.

Q. Has the spirit power to keep the carnal in subjection?

A. The spirit has control over all matter.

Q. Then can wrong result from it?

A. Seemingly wrong, or the lesser good.

Q. Is not humanity sometimes in the ascendant?

A. No, I do not so understand it. Matter never gains the ascendency over spirit.

By Joseph Lowenthall, Feb. 8, 1870.

Q. Does insanity affect the spirit after it leaves the body?

A. Only relatively. There is no permanent effect left upon the spirit. It is but a temporary shadow. There are no insane spirits. They sometimes make insane manifestations, in consequence of the inharmonious condition of the organism through which they must manifest; but that is all.

Q. According to that theory a spirit could not manifest its real self, except through a physical organism corresponding to its former self.

A. Yes, that is a correct inference.

Q. And the more nearly the organism corresponds to that of the spirit, the more nearly you get the conception of the spirit?

A. Yes.

Q. Does color or complexion go with the spirit to the spirit-land?

A. Yes, relatively. Since it does not proceed from the external, but comes from the internal to the external, it must of necessity be deep-seated. It is incorporated with the entire physical life of the being, and more than that, it is a part of the spirit-body — belongs to that — therefore the spirit-body is affected by it; is colored by it, if you please. In that way it is translated from the physical to the spiritual world, and affects the spirit after death. The Indian is the Indian still in color as in feature and form. The negro is the negro still.

Q. Then man must have originated in plurality, not in unity?

A. No, I do not so understand it. I believe that of

one spiritual essence God has made all nations of the earth, yea, of all universes, however far distant from this planet. I believe in one principle of life. It is the same in this table that it is in you and me. The Bushman and the Anglo-Saxon in essence are one. In expression they widely differ, but in essence they are one.

Q. Whence comes divergence of complexion?

A. Climatic influences produce this in a very large degree — outward circumstances. The conditions of a race produce its characteristics, organic and otherwise.

Q. What will be the result of the large emigration to this country, to the poorer classes, in years to come?

A. It must result in the elevation of the Anglo-Saxon. It is a well-known fact that those races that exclude, that isolate themselves from all other races, soon become extinct. They are dwarfed in intellect, and very soon are lost from the face of the earth. That is the case with the aborigines of this country. They are fading away simply for the want of amalgamation with a higher race. The inhabitants of this country are destined to take a grand place in the scale of intellect, and it is principally owing to the tide of emigration that flows from all points of the compass, bringing the physical, intellectual, moral — in fact, the wealth of all the different conditions from which this emigration flows, to this centre, sowing the intellectual soil with seeds that will spring up bearing fruit to the glory and honor of the great Guider of human events.

By William E. Channing, Feb. 10, 1870.

Q. It is a well-established fact that the spirit does communicate independent of the animal senses, which indicates two entities. The animal nature has its experience, while we are informed that the spirit is as pure as God. If the above is true, what becomes of the animal life, when it leaves the body, and what will be its future mission? As the spirit has its experience in the spiritual world, which cannot become reconciled with the external consciousness, so, also, the external faculties have their experience in the external world, which indicates two distinct natures, of which I desire an explanation from our invisible friends.

A. Round and round the circle runs. Spiritually and physically, we seem to be perpetually repeating ourselves. In other words, we move in circles, rotate forever and forever around the great central sun of all being, of life. The soul, the spirit, — to me these are terms seeking to express but one idea, — while it sojourns in the tabernacle of physical life, must express itself in accordance with the laws of this physical life. It is a power playing upon a machine. You would scarcely understand me were I to tell you that you, every one of you, as spirits, stand outside and apart from your physical bodies, and play upon them as a musician would play upon an instrument. But it is so. The animal life, or electrical vitality, that belongs to the body, does its share of the work in keeping in tune all the functions of the animal body. It does not think; it does not express itself intelligibly; it does not aspire. It can be inspired according to its own degree, but it never aspires. The spirit-body and the spirit are one. The animal body and animal life is another distinct entity, precisely as the instrument is the instrument, and the performer is distinctly separate from it. The dual nature of humanity is being slowly understood. Step by step you are coming into an understanding of what you are; but growth in this direction, as in all others, must be slow. You cannot readily understand how you, as an individual, can be in two places at one time. Many of you do not believe this, but it is a fact. The body may be here, the spirit thousands of miles away, communicating with its friends, talking through its spirit-body. The science of this world is slowly rolling away the stone, and by and by the angel will appear in fair, white robes. You will understand yourselves better, and as you understand yourselves you will understand your God. But it is not for me or any other spirit, however exalted they may be, however wise they may be, to return, giving you what knowledge I may have upon the subject. It must grow up with your consciousness slowly, in order that you may understand and appreciate it.

Q. Don't you think the artificial adornments worn by men, and especially by women, detrimental to the normal growth and development of the human spirit? Would it not be better to adorn ourselves more in harmony with Nature and physical health?

A. The human race, without exception, is endowed with the love of the beautiful, from the rudest savage to the most highly cultivated mind. The soul instinctively worships anything that is beautiful, whether it be a rose or a work of art. This love of the beautiful causes all this display of dress that we see in every age. Whatever an individual conceives to be beautiful, that they desire to appropriate to themselves. The savage thinks he looks better when he is in full paint; so he paints himself. The modern belle thinks the same; so she paints herself. The savage and the modern belle both gain their love of the beautiful from Nature and Nature's God. As yet, they do not know how to fully and perfectly express this love. When they do, they won't paint their faces. And in all probability they won't load themselves with useless articles of dress. I say, when they learn better, they won't do this. But by slow degrees, man, in the external, comes to know of the gems, and their glory and their use, that lie in the internal of his being. This love of the beautiful is one of the most beautiful of all God's gifts to man. But at present it is poorly understood, and is therefore made an idol of.

Q. It was stated last week, by the controlling influence, that punishment for wrong doing in this life was inflicted by another for the same in spirit-life. Now, if repentance has been experienced by the wrong doer here, will his punishment be permitted to extend in the other life by any revengeful spirit that might have power to inflict punishment?

A. There are ignorant spirits outside, as there are inside, of physical bodies; and so long as there are, we must expect exhibitions of ignorance. Let me illustrate: Mr. A., in this world, fancies that he has been injured — and perhaps he has — by Mr. B., and he desires to be revenged upon him. He thinks he has not been punished for his crime towards him. They both come to the spirit-world. Perhaps Mr. B. has repented of his evil, and, according to his own conscience, has paid the penalty in deep remorse. They both appear upon the stage of spirit-life. Mr. A. feels that Mr. B. has wronged him, that he has not been punished. He desires to inflict punishment upon him, and he has the power to do it. So he does it. But he would not do it if he were wise enough to see that the man had already been punished, that he had suffered, and that there was no necessity for more suffering; that he had been his own judge, and had condemned himself, had paid the uttermost farthing, and, according to his own light, had gone clear. But Mr. A. does not see this. He is ignorant, and so desires to take God's work out of his hand, as many do in this life. So he goes to work to punish him — deals out to him what he supposes to be a just punishment. Spirits have the power to do this in our life, as they have to do it in this.

Q. We see at funerals both the dead and coffin covered with flowers. We make our graveyards beautiful with them. And on all occasions, whether joyful or the reverse, we invariably have flowers, if it is possible to procure them. At your circles you request those interested to bring flowers. Now, we ask the question, what is the meaning of it? Of what use are they?

A. Flowers cannot fail to inspire the soul with a love of the Maker of the flowers, cannot fail to lift the soul, even though it be transiently, a step higher in the scale of being. You desire to be lifted beyond sorrow when your dead are before you, and so Nature instinctively calls for flowers. On your occasions of joy you desire to be still more joyful. Nature again calls for flowers. One writer has truthfully said they are the language of the angels. They talk to the soul of God. As you rise higher and higher in your love for God and the beautiful, you will love flowers more and more.

By Father Henry Fitz James, Feb. 14, 1870.

Q. How is it that questions in sealed envelopes are answered by other spirits instead of the one to whom they are addressed?

A. Allow me to explain the process. In the answering of your letters, some spirit who is best adapted to the work is selected to take control of the medium, either partial or entire, as the case may be. That spirit is then, to all intents and purposes, a dweller in physical life, here with you. At the same time he is in connection with those invisible ones who are your guests at this place. The spirit who is answering the letters cannot see beyond the external any more than your medium, any more than you could. He knows only what is upon the external, what appeals to the eye — nothing more. That is why it is necessary for some name to appear upon the envelope, either of the spirit you desire to call or your own name. Then the spirit who is answering the letters calls out — silently, to be sure, but potently to the spirit — the name that is upon the envelope. If any one is present that can respond to it, they do so; if not, the envelope is generally laid aside, they being unable to answer it. It would consume a much greater length of time and a much larger amount of magnetism in order to have each spirit who is called for come forward and control the medium, and give the answer. Perhaps seven times out of ten they would fail in the attempt; so one is selected who can serve as amanuensis for all the rest, it being easier for the medium, easier for the spirits who desire to give an answer. We have only just so much time at our command, and just so much magnetic power that we are at liberty to use up.

Q. I have been informed frequently that children, dying when quite young, progress and learn in the spirit-world the same as when living. If so, why is it, as I have noticed in several instances, children that have passed away many years come back and control the medium, and talk childishly, and indistinctly, the same as when here?

A. Such manifestations are not normal; they are abnormal, even to the spirit who produces them; they are given to appeal to your past lives. For instance, you knew your child as a little child. It has grown to maturity in the spirit-world, but it desires to appeal to your consciousness, to be remembered. Consequently it comes to you as it was when here, as nearly as it is able to. If they came to you as they are now in spirit, you would find that the same progress had been made by them as spirits that would have been made under proper circumstances in physical life here.

By Theodore Parker, Feb. 15, 1870.

Q. Have our spirits been clothed with mortality previous to the present existence?

A. Many of you. What is true in one case is not in all. Some of you have doubtless but just started on the highway of human experience; others have travelled a long distance that way.

Q. After our spirits have passed from this body, will they ever return from the spirit-land to dwell again on the earth?

A. It is my belief that they will.

Q. Can a man live so well in this life that he can overcome many of the laws of Nature, as Christ is said to have done?

A. I do not believe that Christ did overcome any natural law. I believe that he, understanding the law, acted in harmony with it — made it his servant — did not overcome it.

Q. Was it by the perfection of his nature, by a spiritual approximation to his father?

A. I believe that had a great deal to do with it.

Q. Did it not have *all?*

A. No.

Q. Is it an accident of Nature?

A. No.

Q. An incident of Nature?

A. Yes.

Q. Can one transmit this Nature?

A. Yes, I think so. The more holy you are, the more confidence you have in yourself, the more positive you are. Jesus, if he lived a blameless life, of course had confidence in himself. He felt that he should have whatever strength was necessary. To the production of any great work, whether it be of mind or matter, confidence in one's self is absolutely necessary to its performance.

Q. Did his perfect humanity enable him to be more fully connected with the law of Nature?

A. Certainly. He attracted to him those high and powerful intelligences that could best aid him in his work.

Q. The consciousness of doing right gives extraordinary powers.

A. It certainly does.

Q. Did Jesus rise from the tomb in his natural body?

A. I do not so believe.

Q. What did he mean, then, by saying, "A spirit hath not flesh and blood, as ye see me have"?

A. He meant that he had adorned himself with a physical body for the time being. He did not say he had taken the old body that had been crucified and laid in the tomb. He had gathered to himself by his knowledge of natural law those elements that would appeal to physical sense. In other words, he made himself a physical body, through which he could temporarily act. They did not see his spirit — only that body.

Q. Do prayer and fasting perfect one's nature?

A. Yes, provided you pray because you feel that you

ought to. A great many people pray because they have been taught to believe it is right. That is no kind of honest prayer — will never avail anything. But if, when you pray, you feel that prayer to come from the sacred depths of your soul, it will effect something for you.

Q. Is it the same with fasting?

A. It will amount to little or nothing, only so far as physical life is concerned. It will, for the time being, change the elements of physical life. That is all.

Q. Was there a necessity of Christ's fasting?

A. He said so.

Q. And of Elijah and John?

A. They so affirmed.

Q. And the ancient saints who made themselves conspicuous for holiness?

A. Many of them have so affirmed. We have no right to dispute them. If they believed in that rite, it was sacred to them. If they fasted because they felt they ought to from the sacred depths of their souls, it was right. It would elevate them in the spiritual scale of being.

Q. Does not fasting reduce the animal nature, while prayer brings out the spiritual? Should not both be employed?

A. There is a truth, doubtless, in this idea. But there are some persons that can be brought into spiritual relations much better by taking the opposite course. It is not a rule that can be applied successfully to all.

Q. Many affirm that Christ's natural body was raised. He said to Thomas, "Thrust your fingers in my side." How is that?

A. I know that many so believe, but I know also, it is not true. That body, as I remarked a few moments ago, that Jesus manifested through when he appeared to his disciples after his crucifixion, was a body he had manufactured, if you please, from the air. He had gathered those elements from the air, and manufactured a physical body precisely as spirits at the present time manufacture faces and hands with which to greet you through the cabinets of the Davenports and others. It is the same law.

Q. Was it flesh and blood?

A. Yes, flesh and blood to all intents and purposes.

Q. What are the equivalents of flesh and blood in the spirit-world? Are they electricity and magnetism?

A. Yes; you may as well call them by that name as any other. You would understand it just as well.

By Theodore Parker, Feb. 21, 1870.

Q. When the body suffers decapitation, does the spirit-body suffer mutilation in any sense?

A. No, it does not. You can kill, you can decapitate the physical body, but you cannot injure the spirit-body. That defies all such processes. It never suffers by accident. It is always intact in itself.

Q. It is said that the head of a decapitated person retains sensation, sometimes for three hours, and seems to exercise its brain for an hour or so. Does this interfere with the formation of the spirit-body?

A. No, for the spirit-body is already formed.

Q. Is there any difference between the effect of this and that of a natural death?

A. Yes, that difference which belongs to circumstances. The spirit leaves the body very slowly. The attraction that holds the spirit to the body physical, has been violently sundered, and the natural result is, the spirit holds its grasp upon physical life much longer than under other circumstances, because the attraction there is stronger than it would have been had the separation taken place by disease.

Q. Is there ever a consciousness left in the brain of its condition?

A. I think not. The brain may act magnetically, but not intellectually.

By Rev. Arthur Fuller, Feb. 28, 1870.

Q. At one of your circles the controlling intelligence, in answer to the question, "Why don't some of my spirit-friends communicate?" gave as a reason "that there is a law which controls the communications of spirits. When the law is favorable, then they will." We wish you would explain how and on what principle this law operates. Many are earnestly desiring more light on this subject.

A. It is a universal law of nature by which spirits return, communicating with those who remain on the earth. It is presumed that you all know that this natural law makes certain demands of every living soul, that must be complied with. For instance, if I wish to hold control of this body, I must breathe, I must make use of the atmosphere in which I find myself. I must act in conformity to the law as I find it expressed through this human organism, else I cannot remain in control. And again, if I find on approaching this, or any other foreign organism, that it is not at that time adapted to my use, — that is to say, is magnetically and electrically opposed to me, — the law of repulsion acts towards me. If it says, "You cannot approach," I cannot. But I must wait till the law of attraction, or that feature of the law called attraction, beckons me on, and invites me to use the organism. Sometimes the physical sphere of the medium may repel us, while the spiritual atmosphere may attract, and *vice versa*. We can never tell whether we are going to succeed in controlling a medium till we come within the radius of the magnetic sphere. Then we know at once. There are an infinite number of points in this great natural law, infinite even with regard to the cause of spirit-control; therefore it would be impossible for us to elaborate them all.

Q. What are some of the conditions necessary to be observed by those who are asking the spirit to control?

A. One of the conditions requisite is a passive state of mind on the part of the questioner. Be willing to receive whatever the spirit is able to give, at all times weighing whatever is given in the balance of your own reason, and accepting such as your reason sanctions, and nothing more. Again, it is necessary that you lay down all prejudice. Put all your preconceived notions under your feet, and be willing to receive whatever is true, for its own sake. Persons who seek to investigate this phenomenon should remember that it is the voice of God talking to his children. And remembering this, you will come in humility asking the Great Father Spirit to bestow upon you what you most need. And ask in all honesty of heart, equivocating not at all, either in thought or speech. Send out from the centre of your being, honest thoughts, honest purposes, and rest assured you will receive such in return.

Q. I ask of a communicating spirit concerning the condition of a certain soul in spirit-life, and am answered that the soul is suffering severely from remorse of conscience. An Indian spirit comes and testifies that he sees the same soul covered over with worms, or otherwise greatly afflicted physically. Will the intelligence present explain why the first spirit communicating does not see the same external surroundings of the soul described as the Indian does? Please explain the why and wherefore of the thing, so as to bring it level with our senses, if possible.

A. Souls are continually changing states of being—conditions of existence. Therefore it is quite possible that one intelligence might have seen a soul under certain special conditions, while another looking at it another time, might have seen it under different conditions. You are not to suppose that souls in the spirit-world are always externally the same, for they are not.

Q. In the case in question, the spirit was seen by both at the same time, and the intelligent spirit said that the Indian saw it in the manner described.

A. The Indian stands, spiritually, ever upon Nature's platform, and if any condition of mind is to be presented to him, some symbol must be shown him by which he can recognize the true condition of that mind. He learns by symbols in the spirit-world as here. He commenced his education that way, and it is generally carried on in that way in the spirit-world. Again, it may be accounted for in this way: For instance, I may see great beauty in the rose. To me it may be exceedingly beautiful. It may talk to me of heaven, while my brother may see in it no beauty at all. It is only a form of vegetable life. He does not see, does not realize the beauty. God in beauty does not talk to him from the rose. But he does to me, because we are differently constituted. We perceive things from our own particular plane of perceptions;

even here in your life you do this, and in the spirit-land it is carried to still greater perfection.

Chairman. I will read the following letter: —

FRANKFORT-ON-MAINE,
GERMANY, Jan. 23, 1870.

TO THE EDITORS OF THE BANNER OF LIGHT.

Dear Sirs: Fifteen years ago I became convinced of the truth of Spiritualism, which has ever since been my greatest comfort and consolation. I was then residing in New York. Since my arrival here, I find that our beautiful philosophy is spreading vastly in Germany; but I have been surprised to find that the spirit-guides of the societies of Vienna, Breslau, Leipsic, &c., as well as those of Paris and Bordeaux, invariably teach that we have to pass through many re-incarnations in this or other worlds; that the higher our development, and the greater the progress we make during our sojourn on earth, the fewer re-embodiments do we need. Will you kindly request the spirit-guides of your "Banner circle" to inform me whether this doctrine be correct, as I never heard it promulgated in the United States?

Yours for truth and progress,
ROSETTA KLEIN.

A. The theory of re-incarnation in America is a baby. In some portions of Europe it has attained its majority. Since we have the evidence of thousands of spirits — I say we, meaning myself and the spirit-band with whom I am associated — since we have the evidence of thousands of spirits who remember having lived through several physical existences, of course we know that the theory is correct. We do not know that we, too, shall be again and again re-incarnated in physical life, but we believe we shall. Judging from the experience of others, we believe it to be our own fate also.

By William E. Channing, March 7, 1870.

Q. How do you account for so much apathy among Spiritualists in regard to the phenomena of Spiritualism?

A. All states of being, of thought, and of feeling have their high tides and their low tides. Sometimes the believer is carried, whether he will or no, upon the heights of inspiration and aspiration. He reaches out intuitively and instinctively to those things that belong to the spirit. At other times he seems to sit in the valley and shadow of spiritual darkness, spiritual apathy. Why is it? It is because he is so constituted that he cannot always seek. He cannot always be asking. There must be a time when there is a lull in these things. A few years ago, Spiritualists were borne upon the high tide of desire for phenomenal Spiritualism. They battled with the waves for months, ay, for years, and the majority received satisfaction from the warfare. They came forth victorious, and in their ignorance they said, "Now we have enough of this. The world has no longer need of phenomenal Spiritualism, because, forsooth, we have been satisfied." I say in their ignorance they say this, forgetting that there are others, and always will be, coming up the same ladder that they have come up, who have the need of phenomenal Spiritualism. They must have it in order to satisfy the first demands of curiosity in this matter. Those who have said that the world has had enough of phenomenal Spiritualism will perceive their mistake. They will presently be called to look back, to view the scenes through which they have passed. They will pause and reflect concerning the necessity that exists for others to pass through the same, in order that they, too, may know concerning Spiritualism.

Q. Would sickness, accident, or habits of dissipation destroy the power of mediums, as the Davenports and others?

A. Sickness has been known to so entirely change the magnetic currents, or forces, of mediums, as to destroy their mediumistic power. I believe it is a law which will apply to all mediums.

Q. It does not always happen — does it?

A. Not always. Dissipation of itself rarely destroys the mesmeric power, unless it breaks down the physical constitution, and disease ensues. Then it is a secondary matter.

Q. Is this the commencement of our existence?

A. Taking the testimony of those persons who declare to us that they have lived prior to this human existence, I should say, certainly, in their case, it was not the commencement, and I should also infer from their state, that it was not the commencement, perhaps, with any of us; that we had lived ages, perhaps, and cycles of ages ago.

Q. Is there any certainty of this, excepting in their statements?

A. No, there is no certainty to us, because we cannot be certain of a thing that we have not experienced. To them it is an absolute certainty; to us it is not.

Q. Is it possible that some may have existed previous to this life, and others not?

A. Yes, that is my belief.

By Father Henry Fitz James, March 8, 1870.

Q. In communion between spirits and mortals, do they come to us, or we go to them? In other words, is locomotion required with spirits or clairvoyants?

A. Yes, it is. Though I could communicate with

you were I residing in the farthest distant star, and did not move out of my position, yet I might wish to go personally to you, and wishing, I have the power so to do. It is not an absolute necessity that a spirit should be personally with you in order to communicate, but it is generally the case.

Q. Is not omnipresence an attribute of the human soul?

A. No, I do not so understand it.

Q. Is there no possibility of development to it?

A. No; that belongs to God, and to us as parts of God; but we cannot exercise it because we are not the whole.

Q. Then we are never to become gods?

A. Not in that sense.

By Cardinal Cheverus, March 10, 1870.

Q. Having read in "Questions and Answers," in a recent issue of the "Banner," of the effect upon the spirit of the various dispositions of the body within three days after death, I would like to inquire of the controlling intelligence, if proper, what would be the effect, or advantage, if any, both upon the spirit and upon physical humanity in general, of burning the body, and the most proper time to do it?

A. That was a favorite method of destroying dead bodies with a certain class of ancients. They believed it to be most in conformity to nature and spirit. They believed that so long as the atoms composing the physical body were held together as a body, the spirit could not enjoy perfect freedom; that it was attracted so powerfully to that body, that in that sense it was a prisoner. So they took the shortest method to destroy it, to dissolve the elements, and so thoroughly change the conditions as to separate the spirit and give it its freedom. That there was a great truth, a scientific fact, underlying this belief of the ancients, we know. I say we — we who have experimented in that line, we who are free from the flesh. We can stand outside, and view the operations of law with reference to matter and spirit. And yet I believe that there is a good accruing to the spirit by the process of slow decomposition of the body. I believe that, under certain circumstances, the spirit has need of just that kind of discipline, and will enjoy its freedom all the more, when it receives it in full. I believe it can gain an experience, through its relations with that decaying body, that it could gain in no other way; an experience concerning the operations of the laws of nature, that it could obtain in no other way. Being intimately connected, spiritually, magnetically, and electrically, with the decaying body, it can view at pleasure the operations of nature upon that body, and gain great information therefrom; can, in a word, talk with Almighty God through that open book. It has been said, and with truth, that you should have a care as to how you dispose of your deserted bodies. You do not always know when they are really deserted by the spirit. Outward signs are not always sure. It is a scientific fact that the spirit rarely departs thoroughly from the physical body in less than three days after they are what you deem to be dead. So, then, whatever you do to the body, you do to the spirit also. And although it may not sense what you do externally, physically, yet spiritually it will. And we have the evidence of many who tell us that they suffered the keenest pangs in consequence of the ignorance of their friends with regard to the disposition of their bodies.

Q. What is the effect of putting the body on ice, as is frequently done immediately after death? Does the spirit feel it?

A. Certainly it does, and suffers more intensely than you in mortal have the power to conceive of; therefore have a care and not do this unless it is absolutely necessary to the preservation of the health and life of those who remain in the body.

Q. It is done, in most cases, in order to give time for friends to arrive before the body begins to decay.

A. In most cases, the same object may be reached by delaying three days before using ice.

By Theodore Parker, March 14, 1870.

Q. Of what benefit is the beard upon the face of man?

A. Medical men tell us it is given as a protection for those sensitive facial glands peculiar to man. Woman has no need, because those glands are less sensitive. Nature provides for all the necessities of her subjects, however small or however great they may be.

Q. Are sex and affections recognized in the spirit-land? If so, to what extent?

A. Yes, to be sure. There is there the male and female distinctly defined; and since affection does not belong to the body, but to the soul, of course the soul carries it with it after it leaves the body.

By Father Henry Fitz James, March 17, 1870.

Q. In the message department, some time since, referring to spirit-forms seen by mediums, the statement was made that the atmosphere of our earth contains everything belonging to this planet and much more, and all the elements necessary to the formation of everything known to our human senses; that spirit-forms, as seen by mediums, are not really the absolute and genuine forms of spirits, but those they have temporarily created out of the atmosphere, and consequently perishable. My wife sees spirits — at least the exact appearance of persons who once inhabited the mortal form; the question is, if what she sees is *not* the real form of the spirit, what kind of form *does* it have?

A. By the real form is meant the permanent spiritual body. By that which we may call the unreal we mean that which has been temporarily woven out of atmospheric elements. Such a body can be seen by the natural eye, but a spiritual body can be seen only by the spiritual eye, perceived by the spiritual senses. When spirits clothe themselves out of the atmosphere, you can all see them, handle them. They have bodies that are flesh and blood, and bones, and sinews, and nerves, all manufactured out of the atmosphere. But when media alone see them, they see them with the spiritual eye. Their spiritual perceptions are opened, while those of the masses are not, and they see the spirit-body, — that which is permanent with the spirit.

Q. In one of the prayers offered here, the petition was offered that God would bless those who pray for blessings. Will persons be any more likely to receive blessings by praying for them?

A. Prayer brings us nearer to the spirit of good, to that infinite spirit of good that exists everywhere. It changes our spiritual condition, and makes us more receptive of the blessings we ask for. This is all prayer can do for us. It cannot change the purposes of the Infinite. It cannot bring God nearer to us, only as we come nearer to God.

Q. In proportion as our desires are, shall we not be prepared to receive these blessings?

A. Yes.

Q. Is not there more benefit arising from work than from prayer?

A. To me, work is prayer, and prayer is work. By prayer, I do not mean simply mouthed utterances.

Q. Does not the moral welfare of society depend more upon work than upon prayer?

A. Yes, certainly. A man might pray to all eternity for his field to be sown with wheat, and the harvest to be gathered in, but unless he or some one else worked in that field, the wheat would not be sown, the harvest would not be gathered.

Q. Does prayer without works amount to anything?

A. No, certainly not. It is prayer without a spirit, without a soul.

Q. As Spiritualism advances, will the churches crumble, and a new organization be erected on their ruins? or will the churches be likely to adopt Spiritualism, and retain their organization?

A. The churches will be most likely to adopt it. Can you not see that it is even now being incorporated into all the churches? They are drinking it in just as fast as it is possible for them to. Their old theological darkness will quietly depart before this spiritual light. In other words, this leaven, which is in all the churches, will by and by leaven the whole lump. They will be changed unconsciously to themselves. It is the purpose of returning spirits not to tear down, but to spiritualize all the churches.

By John Pierpont, March 21, 1870.

Q. Have we any evidence in Nature of an intelligent design working in Nature to the accomplishment of specific ends, or are the perceptions of apparent adaptation and design but the necessary relation of cause and effect to the forces inherent in the primal elements of matter?

A. Those primal forces that are inherent in matter must have had a cause. There must have been a power behind them, and that power I believe to be spirit, and also intelligence.

Q. Is there any self-conscious intelligence in the universe except the organized self-conscious intelligence of the human spirit?

A. No; I know of none; consequently it is right for me to answer as I do.

Q. May we not as lawfully infer that there is a power beyond spirit as you do that spirit exceeds all the primal forces?

A. Yes, it is lawful for you to infer that, but the next thing is to demonstrate it.

Q. May we not look for some important changes soon in this general movement which we call Spiritualism?

A. Yes, and I think you will not look in vain.

Q. Will you please indicate some of those changes in general outline?

A. There will be more marked physical manifestations, as you call them, for it should be understood that you have need of them as yet. There will be more marked intellectual manifestations. Clairaudience will become more general; clairvoyance, clear seeing, will become more general. In fact, all the different phases that you have been familiar with in the past will become more exalted, and other phases will be revealed to you.

Q. What is meant by the spiritual breathing?

A. You refer to the action of the spiritual body in some persons, while the spirit is incorporated in the physical body. There are some amongst you whose spirit-bodies are as actively used, even while they are here in the physical body, as are their physical bodies. For instance, their spiritual lungs are used by the spirit; their spiritual senses are used; their spirit-bodies are just as much used as their physical bodies are, and more so. These persons you call mediums. The action of this spirit-body gives them predominance over physical life. They are able to depart from their bodies almost at will. Foreign spirits are able to control not only their spiritual bodies, but their physical bodies also, giving a variety of manifestations in Spiritualism with which you are all familiar.

As small-pox is now prevalent, we close the volume with some statements (out of chronological order) made in reference to a particular case.

By Doctor Sidney A. Doane, March, 1871.

Small-pox generally gives certain premonitory symptoms — sends forth certain couriers in advance of its coming, that cannot be mistaken, especially if one is looking for such a guest. Now, then, in case these symptoms are felt by you, which, in your case, will be severe pain at the base of the brain, coldness of the hands and feet, undue heat at the stomach, attended with nausea — these will be the first premonitions of the coming of your guest — then you will have ample time to procure for yourself a house as far in the outskirts of the city as possible; secure for yourself two attendants who have had the disease; take the largest and airiest apartment in the house for the room in which you are to be sick; and, if it is not properly ventilated, make a hole anywhere through the side of the house, if there is no chimney in the room. If there is, open an avenue into the place, and let it remain always open. Then keep one of your windows dropped at the top, not so a draft will come upon yourself; keep the room at a temperature of sixty-five degrees, not much below and not much above. And this should be done by a wood fire, nothing else. Then take plenty of warm drinks, and drink particularly free of Indian-meal porridge made of water, and very thin, and use but little salt, if any, in your food.

If the disease should be obstinate in coming to the surface, the attendants should roll you in a sheet wrung out of warm water — not cold — and pack you well in blankets till you are thoroughly steamed, giving you, the mean time, to drink, a tea of hemlock and saffron. Care always should be taken that the room is dark, so dark that you can scarcely see a hand before you. This precaution will preserve the skin, and render the disease less likely to take an inverted turn after it has been out a few hours, as is sometimes the case from the admission of too much light into the apartment.

Pursue this course, taking no solid food for fourteen days, and unless it is decreed that you shall leave the body, you will weather the disease, and come out better than you entered upon it.

Q. Do you recommend vaccination?

A. Never! never! never! It is one of the most damnable of all practices that have ever been introduced; it is a direct clog in the way of Nature's effort to do you good, and they who have suffered from the practice are legion. Your insane asylums are overflowing with its victims, and consumption, that is so prevalent in the New England States, may — ninety-nine one-hundredths of it — be traced back to vaccination; indeed, a majority of the ills that afflict humanity may be traced back to that most terrible practice; and Dr. Jenner to-day, in the spirit-land, mourns over its advent upon earth. Small-pox, to the ignorant, is a curse, but to those who understand Nature and her laws and workings, it is a blessing; therefore why should we ask to impregnate the system with the virus which will work only evil results through life, by keeping out the physician which Nature sends in with probe and scalpel to drive out disease?

INDEX.

A

Adversity, 153.
Alcohol, 66.
Andrew, John A., 73.
Animal faculties, 343.
Association, national, 227.
Astrology, 54, 313.
Atmosphere, 270.
Attraction, 40, 185.
Aura, mediumistic, 48, 178.

B

Beard, 392.
Better land, 213.
Bias, 33.
Bible, 258.
Bigotry, 41.
Body, 263.
" celestial, 117.
" burning of, 390.
Brainerd, David, 163.
Burial, 390.
Business, 282.

C

Chinese, 353.
Chrishna, 308.
Christianity, 87, 261, 394.
Clairvoyance, 122, 139, 212, 231, 297, 348.
Clergyman, a, 248.
Coffee, 295.
Communication, difficult, 37, 142.
" friendly, 219.
" laws of, 37.
Compensation, 158.
Congress, 99, 128.
Consciousness, 155, 323, 351.
" double, 267.
" God's, 189.
Cotton, 215.
Credulity, 100.
Criticism, 100.
Cures, 216.

D

Darkness, 139, 270.
Davenports, 41, 58, 204.
Day of judgment, 117.
Death, 109, 127, 169, 214, 249, 287, 358, 361.
Death scenes, 38.
" successive, 86.
Deity, 220, 223, 235, 256.
Destiny, 151.

Development, 239.
Devil, 123, 153.
Disease, 360.
Dog-medium, 368.
Dove, 35.

E

Earth changing, 96, 295.
" dying, 149.
" size of, 169.
Electricity, 113, 300.
" a motor, 173.
Elijah, 250.
Embryo soul, 210.
Endor, 348, 371.
Eternal progress, order of, 146.
Evil, 64, 153, 231.

F

Faith, 279.
Family reunions, 113, 284.
Fasting, 381.
Fate, 151.
Father, Son, and Holy Ghost, 247.
Fay, H. M., 204.
Feathers, 215.
Flowers, 121, 271.
Foreordination, 54.
Force, 110.
" ante-nature, 67.
" vital, 317.
Foreseeing, 203.
Forgiveness, 91, 93.
Franklin, Benj., 369.
Freedom, 33.

G

Gifts, 157.
God, 160, 172, 189, 194, 220, 256, 361.
" impersonal, 112.
God, where? 58.
" his impossibilities, 122.
Godliness, 206.
Gold making, 143.
Gorilla, 274.

H

Hallucination, 217.
Hands, imposition of, 216.
" spirit, 204.
Healing powers, 300.
Heaven, infants', 34.
" where? 53.
Hereditary biases, 33.
Holy Ghost, 154.
Hunting, 290.

I

Ice, 361, 392.
Idea, 318.
Identity, 46.
Idiocy, 173.
Ignorance, 232.
Immigration, 374.
Immortality, 165, 286, 322, 335.
Imponderables, 312, 358.
Impossibilities, 122.
Impression, 183.
Indian, 290, 299, 352, 367, 385.
" religion, 331.
Individual, 49.
Individuality, 134, 169, 225, 292.
Infinite spirit, 217, 287, 364.
Insanity, 113, 196, 373.
Instinct, 193.
Intermediate state, 85.

J

Jesus, 221, 262, 282, 313.
" body of, 251.

Jesus, conception of, 55.
" divinity of, 55.
" light, a, 248.
" medium, a, 35, 45, 48, 188.
" only begotten, 175.
" spiritualist, a, 308.
" sufferer, a, 305.
" resurrection of, 96, 100, 248, 381.
" second coming of, 201.
" uneducated, 83.
Judgment day, 117.
Jupiter, 182.

K

King Alcohol, 66.
Klien, Rosetta, 387.
Knowledge, 327.

L

Land, 207.
" better, 213, 222.
Landholders, 207.
Languages, 332.
Lavoisier, 143.
Law, 145.
" prohibitory, 62.
Learning, 157.
Lee, Ann, 61.
Letters, blood, 269.
" Banner circle, 124, 136, 378.
Levitation, 226.
Liberty, 346.
Lie, 346.
Life, 168, 285, 310.
" essence of, 52, 247.
" germs, 318.
" unconscious, 190.
Lightning, 194.
Liquor, 50.
" law, 62.

M

Madness, 196.
Magnetism, 114, 300, 360.
Man, 274.
" attributes of, 280.
" deterioration of, 194.
" dual, 375.
" triune, 119.
Mangum, Mr., 217.
Manifestation, 47.
" physical, 41, 43, 118, 174.
March winds, 180.
Marriage, 138, 195, 233.
Matter, 51, 95, 133, 286.
Mediums, 47, 108, 111, 131, 235.
" bad, 45, 220.
" mirrors, 39.
Mediumship, 45, 131, 175, 226, 296, 339.
Memory, 329.
" dependent on form, 77, 260, 355.
Memory, recording angel, 39.
Men, their differences, 212, 247.
" visit Spirit Land, 262.
" are living three lives, 268.
Mesmerism, 121, 178.
Millennium, 203.
Mind, 133, 192, 351.
" war of, 68.
Moon, 161.

N

Names, 337.
" difficult to give, 36.
Narcotics, 36.
Negro, 68, 299, 321, 333, 352.

O

Oblivion, 34.
Objectivities, 89, 280.
Occupations, 230, 265, 332.
Opium, 359.
Organizations, 99.
Oyster supper, 270.

P

Parker, Theodore, 105, 237, 356.
Paris, 281.
Phrenologic bias, 33.
Physicians, 60.
Planets, 79, 112, 140, 182, 207, 295.
Polar extensions, 169.
Prayer, 166, 278, 381, 393.
" through mediums, 180.
" to whom? 234, 307.
Pre-existence, 260, 264, 380, 389.
" conscious, 70, 162.
" unremembered, 77.
Progression, 70, 215, 225, 304.
Property, 206.
Prophecy, 54, 203.
Prophet, 47.
Providences, 307.

Q

Question, a proper one, 117.

R

Recognition, 65.
Records, 175.
Reformation, 344.
Reincarnation, 72, 150, 294, 387.
" not optional, 113, 242.
Religion, 154, 331, 343, 358.
Repentance, 118.
Responsibility, 54, 306.
Rest, 272.
Resurrectionists, 71.
Retrogression, 304.
Return of spirits, 109, 264.
Reunions, 76.
Revenge, 181.
Revolutions imminent, 342, 363.

S

Sabbath, 103.
Sages, 201.
Sawyer, 94.
Schawle, Professor, 161.
Science, 123.
Séances, Banner, 275.
Secretiveness, 347.
Seer, 47, 122, 201.
Shakerism, 61.
Sin, 91, 192, 284, 297, 345.
Slander, 281.
Sleep, 108.
Somnambulism, 160.
Soul, 165, 192, 209, 210, 293, 343.
Sovereignty, state, 130.
Sphere, mental, 112.
" second, 104.
Spirit, 51, 95, 133, 168, 263, 285, 293, 334, 348, 351.
" accidents, 273.
" advisers, 282.
" animals, 171, 311.
" attraction, 185.
" artists, 332.
" birth, 319.
" body, 43, 298, 305, 383, 393.
" bones, 96.
" breathing, 396.
" cold, 170, 268, 365.
" color, 236, 373.
" communication, 40.
" control, 60.
" day, 65, 205.

Spirit death, 86, 127, 356, 369.
" desires, 43.
" development, 239.
" disease, 59.
" elements, 221.
" eternal, 51.
" exchange, 277.
" faculties, 94.
" flesh, 96.
" flowers, 121, 261, 369, 378.
" food, 301, 365.
" forms, 167, 271.
" gardens, 184.
" guides, 328, 349.
" hands, 204.
" heat, 170, 268, 365.
" homes, 76, 184, 186, 333.
" hunting, 290.
" infants, 33, 287.
" influx, 150.
" knowledge, 326.
" land, 65, 222.
" language, 59, 127, 172, 355.
" lights, 206.
" likenesses, 370.
" marriage, 138, 195, 233.
" memory, 355.
" motions, 349.
" music, 59.
" names, 337.
" nationality, 127.
" night, 65, 205.
" objectivities, 89, 280.
" occupations, 230, 265, 302, 332.
" organs, 298.
" perceptions, 84.
" physicians, 59.
" property, 206.
" recognition, 65.
" records, 175.
" rest, 205, 272.
" reunions, 113, 284.
" science, 340.
Spirit senses, 319.
" sight, 48.
" sex, 343, 392.
" size, 102.
" sounds, 128, 149.
" stigmata, 269.
" sufferings, 120.
" time, 51, 205, 273.
" trance, 232.
" wishes, 357.
" world, 44.
" zones, 76.
Spirits, business, 382.
" communicate, 168.
" injure, 273.
" journey, 112.
" kill, 70, 291.
" lead men, 218, 326.
" low, 350.
" lying, 244.
" make drunk, 63.
" make sick, 63, 115.
" mediumistic, 40.
" objective, 221.
" pass through matter, 168.
" are still on earth, 274.
" testing, 197.
Spiritualism, 41, 80, 87, 100, 121, 131, 133, 146, 224, 227, 229, 261, 314, 394.
" tested, 132.
Spiritualists, 133, 227, 345, 388.
" bigoted, 41.
" malignant, 79.
Spleen, 86.
Star of Bethlehem, 55.
State, intermediate, 85.
Stigmata, 269.
Suffering, 120, 153, 159, 182, 235.
Suffrage, female, 81.
Suicide, 64, 291.
Surroundings, 283.
Swedenborg, 244.

T

Tea, 295.
Telegraphy, 193.
Testing spirits, 197.
Thought, 266.
" forms, 88, 150.
Tobacco, 338.
Trance, 139, 232.
Transmigration, 78.
Trinity, 119.

U

Unconsciousness, 156.
Uranus, 182.

W

War of mind, 68.
Warnings, 215.
Waves, 57.
Winds, 57.
Will, 151.
" power, 144.
Winds, March, 180.
Witch, 371.
Woman, 147, 348.
World, spirit, 44.

Z

Zones, spirit, 76.

Will be Issued September 2d, 1872.

A BIOGRAPHY

OF

MRS. J. H. CONANT,

The World's Medium of the Nineteenth Century.

A HISTORY OF HER MEDIUMSHIP

From Childhood to the Present Time;

BEING A NARRATIVE OF THE

Personal Experiences, Sharp Trials, and Liberalizing Victories achieved in the cause of Human Reason and Spiritual Knowledge.

Let the heart-stricken read it, and be comforted;
Let the earth-weary peruse it, and be glad;
Let the world's workers explore it, and be encouraged;
Let the doubter scan its incontrovertible testimony, and be confounded;
Let the true man and woman, wherever abiding, recognize in it the life-line of a *kindred soul.*

WILLIAM WHITE AND COMPANY,

PUBLISHERS,

158 Washington Street,

BOSTON, MASS.

www.ingramcontent.com/pod-product-compliance
Lightning Source LLC
LaVergne TN
LVHW020104110826
845151LV00001B/58

* 9 7 8 1 4 2 5 5 4 4 3 0 0 *